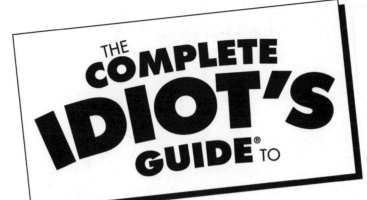

D0905154

The Gnostic Gospels

by J. Michael Matkin

ALPHA

A member of Penguin Group (USA) Inc.

For Christine, who knows.

ALPHA BOOKS

Published by the Penguin Group

Penguin Group (USA) Inc., 375 Hudson Street, New York, New York 10014, U.S.A.

Penguin Group (Canada), 10 Alcorn Avenue, Toronto, Ontario, Canada M4V 3B2 (a division of Pearson Penguin Canada Inc.)

Penguin Books Ltd, 80 Strand, London WC2R 0RL, England

Penguin Ireland, 25 St Stephen's Green, Dublin 2, Ireland (a division of Penguin Books Ltd)

Penguin Group (Australia), 250 Camberwell Road, Camberwell, Victoria 3124, Australia (a division of Pearson Australia Group Pty Ltd)

Penguin Books India Pvt Ltd, 11 Community Centre, Panchsheel Park, New Delhi—110 017, India

Penguin Group (NZ), cnr Airborne and Rosedale Roads, Albany, Auckland 1310, New Zealand (a division of Pearson New Zealand Ltd)

Penguin Books (South Africa) (Pty) Ltd, 24 Sturdee Avenue, Rosebank, Johannesburg 2196, South Africa

Penguin Books Ltd, Registered Offices: 80 Strand, London WC2R 0RL, England

International Standard Book Number: 1-59257-388-6
Library of Congress Catalog Card Number: 2005926961

07 06 05   8 7 6 5 4 3 2 1

Interpretation of the printing code: The rightmost number of the first series of numbers is the year of the book's printing; the rightmost number of the second series of numbers is the number of the book's printing. For example, a printing code of 05-1 shows that the first printing occurred in 2005.

Printed in the United States of America

Note: This publication contains the opinions and ideas of its author. It is intended to provide helpful and informative material on the subject matter covered. It is sold with the understanding that the author and publisher are not engaged in rendering professional services in the book. If the reader requires personal assistance or advice, a competent professional should be consulted.

The author and publisher specifically disclaim any responsibility for any liability, loss, or risk, personal or otherwise, which is incurred as a consequence, directly or indirectly, of the use and application of any of the contents of this book.

Most Alpha books are available at special quantity discounts for bulk purchases for sales promotions, premiums, fund-raising, or educational use. Special books, or book excerpts, can also be created to fit specific needs.

For details, write: Special Markets, Alpha Books, 375 Hudson Street, New York, NY 10014.

Publisher: *Marie Butler-Knight*
Product Manager: *Phil Kitchel*
Senior Managing Editor: *Jennifer Bowles*
Senior Acquisitions Editor: *Renee Wilmeth*
Development Editor: *Jennifer Moore*
Production Editor: *Megan Douglass*
Copy Editor: *Jan Zoya*
Cartoonist: *Richard King*
Cover/Book Designer: *Trina Wurst*
Indexer: *Brad Harriman*
Layout: *Ayanna Lacey*
Proofreading: *Mary Hunt*

Contents at a Glance

Contents

Foreword

Whether gardening or reading, whether dealing with co-workers or attending church, whether writing a check or opening a document, whether microwaving leftovers or starting a car, we depend on people in our past. We do not know who these people were. We could not know them; these people are long forgotten. Many overlooked people, however, have put an idea or a value into our lives, without our knowing how that idea or value got there.

The Gnostics are such people. That Christian community we know today as "Gnostics" represent one very rich source for our world today. Except for references to them in their ancient Christian enemies, Gnostics themselves have disappeared from history. This group remained unknown and uninteresting for more than a thousand years.

This book changes that. In an engaging way, this book presents a treasure trove of Gnosticism's lost ideas, offering us in detail the original and oddly intriguing ideas of this one lost element of Christianity. In the 1940s many of these books were uncovered by accident from where they had lain hidden underground in jars in the Egyptian desert. Digging now through these Gospels and Secrets and Letters in their raw and eccentric originality, the author here offers us a chance to view Gnostic ideas in their original form. Now we can see how they have trickled into our lives from the distant past.

Like evangelicals and Catholics today, like Quakers and Baptists, like Orthodox and Coptic Christians, Gnostics once practiced their beliefs as part of Christianity. Eventually rejected as heretical by mainstream Christianity, Gnostic ideas seemed to have died away. Then along comes a best-selling novel, like *The DaVinci Code* and its many "decoders." These modern books have stirred our curiosity and drawn us to examine some of our unknown past.

For some fifty years, scholars have been unraveling the scrolls. This book, *The Complete Idiot's Guide to Gnosticism*, updates us on the originality and importance of this lost Christian current—reminding us that in the past some things were very different. These Gnostic writings give a variant on the role of Christian women. They rejected our physical world as something sinful. Some Gnostics thought Jesus faked his death. They saw knowledge of the secrets of God as true virtue.

No matter how unorthodox, some of this Gnostic material returns us to the time of Jesus himself. *The Gospel of Thomas*, for example, probably quotes Jesus from sources before our Four Gospels. Another Gnostic writing suggests a much greater role for Mary Magdalene in Jesus' life and resurrection than the Four Gospels tell us. Still other writings emphasize lesser Biblical characters, like Simon Magus in *Acts*; characters who may have had far more importance in shaping Christianity than we suppose today.

In short, Gnostics held significant early Christian beliefs about Jesus Christ, about Biblical events and the ancient world. In examining these beliefs, this book, suggests threads leading from our time back to Jesus himself, alternate threads than the ones we grew up with. These writings from the Gnostics themselves suggest—hint—imply—that by following these threads through the maze of Christian centuries, we may discover in the recesses of history, a locked chest of ideas, values, and insights. The Gnostics have found their voice again; here are the off-center thoughts they once expressed, unearthed and explained. Not in the form of an imaginative novel, nor in a dry-as-dust scholarly tome, but with clarity and understanding, the author guides us through these writings and shares them with us.

—Joris Heise

Joris Heise is an author and former seminary professor at St. Leonard College.

Introduction

Hello and welcome. I hope you're ready, because we're setting out for unfamiliar territory. We'll be wandering through some pretty rough spots, going down trails that haven't been used in some time, and sometimes traveling in darkness. If you're up for the adventure, come on along.

Gnostics and Gnosticism

We can't very well head off into uncharted terrain without some kind of an orientation. The documents that make up the Gnostic Gospels didn't just spring up out of nowhere. An entire history lies behind the gnostic movement, filled with colorful figures and tragic conflicts. The new library of gnostic texts that are coming to light reflect a time and place very like, yet very unlike, our own. If we don't know who wrote them and why, it'll be harder to hear what they are trying to say.

The first few chapters of the book are dedicated to getting started on the right track. After a brief look at reasons to read the gnostics in the first place, you'll find a short thumbnail sketch of what the gnostics believed. Then we'll spend some time getting to know both the major gnostic teachers and some of their most dedicated opponents. Last, we'll take a stroll through the past two millennia, looking at how gnostic thinking continued to survive.

The Gnostic Gospels

They are the reason you picked up the book, aren't they? Five of the new documents discovered in the last century bear the title "Gospel": the Gospel of Thomas, the Gospel of Mary, the Gospel of Philip, the Gospel of Truth, and the Gospel of the Egyptians. We're going to look at each of them one by one. We'll explore their content and their significance for our understanding of the gnostics and of Christianity.

The Gnostic Library

I've got a bonus for you. Along with the Gnostic Gospels, over the past 100 years scholars have unearthed a treasure trove of gnostic literature. These new texts offer us an unprecedented view of the gnostics, their communities and worship practices, and what they thought about one another and their opponents.

The largest and most important collection of these gnostic documents is known as the Nag Hammadi library. We'll talk about where it came from in Chapter 5.

Throughout this book, we'll be looking at various topics central to Gnosticism. Along with each of these topics I'll introduce you to texts from the Nag Hammadi library that illuminate that subject for us. Chapter by chapter, we'll look at this new literature for clues to help us better understand who the gnostics were and what they have to say to us today. Finally, we'll end the book with a couple of chapters looking at ways that gnostic thinking continues to exist today.

How to Use This Book

A map is a wonderful thing. It can give you a bird's-eye point of view and help you locate yourself when you're lost. It can also intrigue you with the promise of new places that you've never been before. But most of all, a map is designed to get you out on the road.

This book is a map to the Gnostic Gospels and the library of literature that they come from. I'll try to give you a head start on your own exploration of the gnostic texts by giving you that bird's-eye view and, hopefully, by intriguing you with hints of what awaits. But ultimately, if you don't read the gospels for yourself, you'll never really understand them.

You won't find a lot of interpretation in this book. I'll give you as objective a perspective as possible on each of the texts, describing what it says and unpacking some of the less familiar ideas. The goal, however, is to create a safe environment for you to get familiar with the gnostics without being told how to understand them. That part is up to you.

I encourage you to get a copy of these texts and begin reading them. If you don't know where to start, check out the list of recommended reading in Appendix B. Some of the websites listed in Appendix C have free translations of most of the texts we'll be looking at.

Deeper Knowledge

Throughout this book, keep your eyes peeled for the following sidebars. In them you'll find additional information, quotations, and stories that will broaden your appreciation and deepen your grasp of the gnostics and their writings.

Word Knowledge

The Gnostic Gospels may be written in Coptic, but it's still all Greek to you? Here you'll find handy definitions for the odd jargon that you'll confront as you begin reading the gnostic documents.

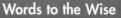 **Words to the Wise**

Scholars, thinkers, and writers have been pondering the words of the gnostics with greater intensity since the discovery of the Gnostic Gospels 50 years ago. I'll bring you some of their insights in this sidebar.

 **From the Source**

Nothing beats hearing from people in their own words. Whether it's the gnostics themselves, their opponents, or other ancient literature, check this sidebar to hear from the horse's mouth.

Did You Know?

The second century was a very different place and time. Look here for clues to better understand the gnostics and their times.

Acknowledgments

Every creative work is a personal expression that arises out of a community, and this book is no exception.

Thanks to the entire community at Hillcrest Chapel in Bellingham, Washington. I continue to have the deepest admiration and respect for senior pastor Bob Stone and the staff that he leads there. Special thanks go out to pastors Dale Pollard and Jim Murphy for their enduring friendship and gracious trust. You have been true brothers to me. Thanks to the four years' worth of Pastoral Care interns who have endured my lectures on all things theological and spiritual. Thanks to Bill Akers and Envoy Theatre Company, all the Prodigal guys, and to Gary Thomas, without whom this book would simply not exist.

When we first opened The Brendan Center, it seemed like a crazy idea. If anything, it seems even crazier today, but it's a successful insanity. I want to express my appreciation to everyone who has come along for the ride. My deepest thanks and affection go out to Dale and Diane Pollard (and their girls, of course), Caroline Smolij, Baron Miller (who never misses a single detail, thank God) and his wife Christina,

Josh Parrish ("the pancake maker") and all the gang at the House of Subdued Excitement, Pete Williamson and Oikos Fellowship, Abraham Bates and everyone who comes out to Fight Night. To all the folks who have come out to participate in our events, programs, gatherings, and insane experiments, and to anyone that I may have forgotten, my humble thanks. It has been your conversations, controversies, contributions, and even complaints that have deepened my own understanding of the spiritual state of our times.

Thanks to Scott Waxman and Farley Chase for giving me a shot. Thanks and appreciation to Renee Wilmeth and the entire editorial staff at Alpha Books for their patience with a newbie.

If any part of gnostic thought resonates with me, it is their equal appreciation for the feminine. This book is dedicated to the women in my life. For my grandmother, Jean, who refused to take "no" for an answer when I told her I wasn't interested in spiritual things. For my mother, Anita, who helped me fight for every breath. For my daughter, Emily, for the many, many nights that I couldn't play because I had to sneak off and write. Above all, for my wife Christine. More than anyone else, it is to you I owe an immeasurable debt of gratitude. Thank you.

Special Thanks to the Technical Reviewer

The Complete Idiot's Guide to the Gnostic Gospels was reviewed by an expert who double-checked the accuracy of what you'll learn here, to help us ensure that this book gives you everything you need to know about gnostic literature. Special thanks are extended to Joris Heise.

Trademarks

All terms mentioned in this book that are known to be or are suspected of being trademarks or service marks have been appropriately capitalized. Alpha Books and Penguin Group (USA) Inc. cannot attest to the accuracy of this information. Use of a term in this book should not be regarded as affecting the validity of any trademark or service mark.

Gnostics and Gnosticism

The Gnostic Gospels weren't written in a vacuum. They emerged during one of the most energetic and fertile periods of spiritual exploration in human history. The first, second, and third centuries A.D. witnessed an explosion of religious questioning. The rediscovery of the Gnostic Gospels, and the other documents that were discovered with them, have provided fresh insight into a little-understood chapter of that story.

In Part 1, we'll take a bird's-eye view of gnostics and their teachings. We'll also get down into the trenches with the gnostic teachers and their opponents in the mainstream church. Once we understand the depth of the conflict between the two, we'll be better prepared to look at the actual gnostic literature.

Why Read the Gnostic Gospels?

In This Chapter

- ◆ How the gnostics helped develop early Christian doctrine
- ◆ Finding hints of gnosticism in the New Testament
- ◆ Learning from the gnostics for dealing with today's culture clashes
- ◆ Why the world is so rotten, according to the gnostics

In her most recent book, *Beyond Belief*, Elaine Pagels describes her shock at attending graduate school at Harvard University and discovering "file cabinets filled with 'gospels' and 'apocrypha' written during the first centuries, many of them secret writings of which I'd never heard." Pagels, whose 1979 award-winning book, *The Gnostic Gospels*, largely introduced the general public to the existence and significance of the newly discovered gnostic writings, was at one time one of only a relative handful of people, nearly all of them scholars like herself, to know about and study the recently unearthed manuscripts.

Due to her own books on the subject, Pagels has a lot more company these days. The Gnostic Gospels, discovered buried in a jar in Egypt, are now fodder for pop culture. Documents that were once the exclusive province of academics are now casually referenced in knitting groups, Sunday School classes, and coffeehouses. Despite their popularity, however, few people have taken the time to actually read any of these gnostic texts. And why should they? Well, I'm glad you asked.

The Road Not Taken

As with human history in general, Christian history is littered with ideas that didn't pan out, movements that went nowhere, ways of imagining the faith that were rejected. Not all of them deserved to be. Protestants and Roman Catholics will remember that not so long ago they were divided by a no-man's-land of anathemas and burnt stakes. Western Christians and Eastern Christians are beginning even now to heal a rift more than a millennium old. Recent discoveries have kicked off a reassessment of Nestorius, long regarded in the West as a proponent of one of the most notorious divisions in the early Christian era. These are just a few examples of rifts being healed, debates being reopened, and so-called "heretics" being embraced.

There is no guarantee that a reevaluation of the gnostics will lead us to any different conclusions than those reached by the second- and third-century Christian writers who opposed them. On the other hand, taking another hard look at the gnostics can at least give us a more nuanced vision of the development of Christianity during its earliest period.

Baby Gnosticism

Gnostic ideas were already beginning to permeate the church at a very early stage. The earliest of the New Testament writings, principally the letters of Paul, already reveal a kind of incipient gnosticism. Paul, and letters that are associated with him such as Colossians and the *Pastoral epistles*, frequently confronted members of his churches who were developing ideas and practices that failed to faithfully consider the Jesus story as he had taught it to them. The Acts of the Apostles hints at such controversies within the church, and the *Johannine writings* (the Gospel of John and 1 John in particular) are almost nonsensical without a grasp of the kinds of gnostic thinking that the Christian community was confronting.

Word Knowledge

Three letters in the New Testament—1 Timothy, 2 Timothy, and Titus—differ from other works attributed to Paul in that they are written not to churches but to the leaders of churches and, as such, they are called the **Pastoral epistles**. Timothy and Titus were two of Paul's companions and coworkers, men who Paul often entrusted with sensitive missions, including the leadership of certain churches. Consequently, they focus more on church administration, leadership, and teaching than do other New Testament writings. Many biblical scholars today question the authenticity of these letters, alleging that they were not written by Paul.

The **Johannine writings** constitute five New Testament works—the Gospel of John, 1, 2, and 3 John, and the Revelation—which have all been attributed to the apostle John Zebedee. Only one of the five, the Revelation, names its author, and even then only as "your brother John". The others are anonymous, and their link with the apostle John comes from early church tradition. According to modern biblical scholars, the five texts were not all written by the same person, and many experts argue that the apostle John could not have authored any of the works now attributed to him.

A quick look at Paul's first letter to the Corinthians makes clear how a better grasp of gnostic ideas deepens our understanding of the New Testament. Paul was confronting individuals within the Corinthian church who were convinced that they were "spiritual" and "perfect." In fact, because they had received the Spirit they were now living as angels. These people, members of the Corinthian Christian church, were asserting that they all had received "knowledge" (gnosis), and Paul is forced to point out that gnosis, as opposed to love, puffs people up and makes them proud (1 Cor. 8:1–3). They were teaching that the resurrection had already occurred (1 Cor. 15:29–32) and were adopting a liberated attitude toward a variety of moral laws (1 Cor. 10:23). Although there's no reason to suspect that the Corinthian controversy is due to the same kind of fully developed gnostic thought that we see in most of the gnostic writings we'll look at in this book, the seeds are there as Greek and Roman Christians were struggling to make sense of the Jesus story in the context of their own culture.

Echoes and Ripples

It is possible, as one scholar has suggested, to say that the gnostics were Christianity's first theologians. The gnostics tried to reinterpret the Christian story into a form that was more accessible and understandable to the non-Christian population of the Roman

Empire. Early Christian writers, particularly the apostle Paul, had already made some moves in this direction by dressing up Jesus' story with words and ideas that would have been easily recognizable to Greeks and Romans. They had to in order to communicate with audiences that had grown up with the myths and philosophy of Greece and Rome rather than the story of Moses and the Jewish prophets.

Still, even in Gentile drag, the story the apostles told remained Jewish to the core. The gnostics took things a step beyond Paul. They didn't just borrow bits and pieces of Greco-Roman culture to camouflage Jesus' story. Instead, they created a new Christian story that was both myth and philosophy. With the Jesus story as their central focus, the gnostics wrestled with the same universal questions that occupied the minds of their contemporaries. They attempted to present a Christian worldview that was systematic and all-encompassing, just like any other philosophy would be. In the process, they raised the intellectual bar in the early Christian community and forced their critics in the mainstream church to respond in kind.

> ### Words to the Wise
>
> What distinguished Gnostics, in the eyes of their enemies, was their use of myth as a chosen vehicle of religious instruction. Their teaching consisted of what a modern reader would regard as mythical accounts of the origins of the material universe and of the processes by which mythical figures had found redemption.
>
> —Peter Brown, *The Body and Society* (106)

By the end of the second century, orthodox Christians were compelled to answer the gnostic teachings. To do so, they had to emulate the gnostics to some degree. So when Irenaeus (we'll meet him in Chapter 3) wrote his magisterial work *Against Heresies* to combat the spread of certain gnostic groups, he explained the orthodox viewpoint in a way that at times mirrored the techniques that the gnostics were using. Origen (also in Chapter 3) was motivated to write his *Commentary on the Gospel of John* in order to answer a previous work by the gnostic teacher Heracleon (more about him in Chapter 9), yet in the process he ended up adopting Heracleon's method of interpretation. As conflicts arise later over the nature of Jesus Christ, the relationship between the persons of the Trinity, and the question of free will and predestination, echoes of the dispute with the gnostics can still be heard. Over and over again, we see that, while the gnostics didn't necessarily win the debate about how to understand the Jesus story, they often set the terms for that debate in ways that profoundly impacted the shape of orthodox Christianity.

Equally important, clashes with the gnostics as well as several other groups that also were later excluded by the mainstream Christian community, pushed the church toward defining not only the content of the Christian faith but also the manner in which one goes about defining the faith. These conflicts motivated orthodox Christians to gather more intentionally around what they considered to be centers of authority. For example, greater care was taken in selecting what should be considered Scripture as the New Testament canon began to take shape. Summary statements of the core teachings of the church, examples of which can already be found in the earliest Christian documents, became lengthier and more specific. Finally, increasing emphasis was placed on the role of the bishops as the authorized interpreters of Scripture and tradition. These trends were already at work in the Christian communities before the conflict with the gnostics got serious, but the need to clarify teachings and traditions accelerated the process.

Strange New Christians

An examination of the debate between gnostic and orthodox Christians might help us to better evaluate our own controversies and the manner in which we deal with one another in our disagreements. Around the world, Christianity is growing by leaps and bounds in regions where the Christian faith has not been strong before and in many cases where it has never existed at all. The center of gravity for the Christian faith has been steadily shifting from the Northern hemisphere to the Southern, as Christianity spreads like wildfire in Latin America, Asia, and Africa even as it is dissolving in Western Europe and, to a lesser degree, the United States. A century ago, for example, there were roughly 10 million Christians in Africa. Today, that number is closer to 360 million. The growth of Christianity in Asia and the shift from Catholicism to evangelical Christianity in Latin America have been equally as spectacular. And,

in nearly every case, this explosive growth has taken place not through Western missionary endeavors but through the efforts of indigenous Christians who have retold the Jesus story through the lens of their own culture and history. These new "local theologies" often appear disturbingly alien to the modern-day heirs of European Christianity, who are often uncertain about how to identify with the rising dominance of non-Western churches and non-Western ways of understanding Jesus.

Gnostic Christianity was, in part, a byproduct of the first such shift in Christian history, when Christianity emerged from its Palestinian Jewish background to move out into the

> ### Words to the Wise
>
> Today it is possible to outline the Gnostic planet with more precision and accuracy … In addition to a Gnosis that arises and has established itself upon the very framework of Christianity and draws sustenance from it, there is clearly another, non-Christian Gnosis. The boundary line between the two is still disputed territory.
>
> —Giovanni Filoramo, *A History of Gnosticism*

Mediterranean world of the Roman Empire, eastward into Persia and India, and westward into Egypt and Ethiopia. As the Christian faith was reinterpreted to speak to new cultures, there was always an uncomfortable question of how far to go. At what point did the gospel of Jesus Christ cease to be the gospel and simply become a Christian variant of whatever any given culture already believed? The conflict between gnostic and orthodox Christians in the second and third centuries, from the perspective of orthodox Christians both then and now, revolved around precisely this question. As a test case in how or how not to craft a local theology, the debate between gnostic and orthodox Christians may provide wisdom for navigating the question of what it means to be Christian as we move into the twenty-first century.

Chesterton's Cat

The twentieth century writer G. K. Chesterton asked a blunt and visceral question about the nature of evil in the world and in the human heart. What do you do, he asked, with the fact "that a man can feel exquisite happiness in skinning a cat"? For Chesterton, a convert to Roman Catholicism, there were only two reasonable answers. You "must deny the existence of God" or "deny the present union between God and man."

From the Source

The same subject matter is discussed over and over again by the heretics and the philosophers; the same arguments are involved. Whence comes evil? Why is it permitted? What is the origin of man? And in what way does he come?

—Tertullian, *The Prescription Against Heretics*

The gnostics offered a different answer to this question. They denied any connection between the true God and the Creator of this universe. Since God is not the maker of the world, God is not responsible for the many troubles, tragedies, and evils of human existence. For that matter, neither are we. Our gut level feeling that things are wrong, the gnostics argued, is absolutely right. The fundamental human problem, however, is not sin but ignorance. What is wrong in the world *is* the world, not us.

Regardless of what you think of the gnostic prescription for our ills, the rediscovery of the Nag Hammadi documents provides us the opportunity to engage with their arguments and weigh them in the light of our own time and place in history.

The question becomes all the more pertinent if author and Presbyterian pastor Philip J. Lee is accurate when he argues that gnostic movements in history emerge during moments of cultural despair in a society. These moments come, Lee asserts, not when the culture is young, full of "rising hopes, ambitious political, and social expectations." Rather, it is societies that perceive themselves as in decline that are susceptible to "ennui, cynicism, inwardness, and, finally, despondency." Whether you view it as something to be embraced or feared, the current cultural mood in the West seems open to precisely that kind of despair. If that is so, and if Lee is accurate, we may begin to see a revival of gnosticism in one form or another as those ideas begin to resonate within our communities.

A Note About Terms

Throughout this book, I'll be using the terms "gnostic" and "grthodox" when referring to different ideas and writers. However, Christians in the first and second centuries would not have distinguished themselves so easily. Controversies and arguments have been part of the Christian experience from the beginning. Christians in the earliest centuries struggled to define themselves and their beliefs, and not all views prevailed. We use the terms "gnostic" and "grthodox," but we could as easily have called them "Those Who Lost" and "Those Who Won."

For the purposes of this book, I define "gnostic" and "orthodox" in the following way:

"Gnostic" refers to those authors and writings that, by and large, hold the following views:

- The God and Father of Jesus Christ is not the same being as the Creator-God of the Jewish faith, but exists prior to and "above" the Creator-God.

- This physical universe is a mistake, a corrupt and meaningless deception that needs to be done away with.

- True salvation is found not in freedom from the guilt of sin but in freedom from ignorance through an intimate experience of the Divine, which is intensely personal and subjective.

Other items could be added to that list, but these will serve as a bare-minimum definition. These were the points most in contention in the late second century.

"Orthodox" (or "mainstream") will refer to those authors and writings whose views eventually won the day. What they fought for was less a matter of specific beliefs, though they certainly disagreed with the gnostics on many issues. Rather, they argued that there was a right way that you should go about deciding what beliefs were true and what weren't. These include …

- A Biblical canon that used only a limited selection of early Christian writings (which we now call the New Testament) and included the Hebrew Scriptures (what Christians call the Old Testament) as authoritative Scripture.

- Adherence to the "Rule of Faith" as a trustworthy summary of the larger story that the New Testament teaches (see Chapter 3 for details).

- A church community led by a hierarchical clergy who safeguard the true teachings of Jesus and his apostles.

Nearly all modern Christians—Protestants, Roman Catholics, and the various Eastern Christian churches—adhere to this latter definition in some way.

It should be clear that neither term is used to imply that one group was right or wrong in their beliefs. The goal is not to judge but to describe, making a very complex situation simple enough to understand without (hopefully) oversimplifying it.

Additionally, you will notice that throughout the book the words 'gnostic' and 'orthodox' are not capitalized. This is to prevent us from simply seeing these two sides as two distinct camps in the early Christian community. Few people in the second or third centuries perfectly embodied either the gnostic or the orthodox viewpoint. As we'll see in later chapters, there were degrees of gnosticism just as there were degrees of orthodoxy. There were some orthodox Christians who felt more comfortable with gnostics than they did with others in the mainstream of the church. To extent, then, that we use these two labels let's be clear that they refer to the character of a person or group's beliefs rather than to black-and-white categories.

The Least You Need to Know

- Yesterday's so-called heresy may hold the key to today's insight.

- Elements of gnosticism appear as early as the New Testament writings.

- Fighting the gnostics helped shape the earliest forms of what became the standard form of Christianity.

- The gnostics have a diagnosis for the problems of the world and a prescription for dealing with it.

Are You in the Know?

In This Chapter

- ◆ Gnosticism emerges at a time of religious ferment
- ◆ The gnostic diagnosis of human problems
- ◆ How Christ figures into the gnostic philosophy
- ◆ The pedigree of gnostic teaching

Are you still with me? Good. Before we go any further, it's important to get at least a brief idea of who the gnostics were and what they believed. We'll delve a lot deeper into many of these ideas later in the book, but for now, let's learn a few helpful terms and get a snapshot of the gnostics.

Life in the Old Country

Step on board the time machine as we shoot back nearly 2,000 years into the past to a time and place very different from our own. We're going back to the Mediterranean world at the end of the second century A.D., at a time of great prosperity and even greater innovation. The Roman Empire, fresh from a string of capable emperors, was at its height. It was a time of peace, brought about by Roman might.

It was also a time of spiritual anxiety. Disease could strike without warning and without cure. Natural disasters were seen as the acts of gods or demons. Evil spirits and hobgoblins were very real. Magic could affect life, dreams could cause suffering, and nearly all who could afford to had their horoscope read to find out the day they would die. People longed for safety from other worldly powers.

Into the midst of these conditions, spiritual seekers began to find a number of alternatives to the age-old worship of the gods. Some discovered mystery cults like Mithraism. Others found solace in philosophical schools of thought like Stoicism or Epicurianism. Many people, especially women, found solace in the Jewish faith. Still others turned to a somewhat obscure but growing branch of Judaism that had emerged from the southeastern corner of the Empire. This Christian religion offered a unique take on the world and its ills.

Christianity, however, was still forming. Although they had a shared story in the life of Jesus, a smattering of sayings associated with him, and some common practices, Christian communities had a welter of differing beliefs about what those practices signified, which of those sayings were authentic, and how to interpret that story. We see those conflicts even in the New Testament, which offers up evidence of sometimes-vicious debates and disagreements between followers of different disciples of Jesus.

That's not to say that no core set of Christian beliefs existed. In fact, all early Christians agreed upon some very significant realities. Yet even those could become sources of disagreement as the Christian community began to expand outside the boundaries of its Jewish birthplace and into a world dominated by Greek ideas and Roman politics. Obeying the mandate from Jesus to transmit his teachings to all nations, early followers of Jesus found it necessary first to translate his teachings into a cultural idiom that their hearers could understand.

Will the Real Gnostics Please Stand Up?

In the middle decades of the second century, the cutting edge of this Christian missionary attempt was rooted in Alexandria. It was in Alexandria that a series of teachers experimented with ways of communicating the Jesus story in a manner that was more relevant to the beliefs and questions that prevailed in their culture at that time. Drawing from a broad range of religious and philosophical sources, they crafted a new philosophical version of Christianity. Going beyond the earthy parables of Jesus, the gnostics asked big, abstract questions like "where do we come from?", "what is the true nature of evil?" and "what does salvation look like?" Not only did they take on these difficult pursuits, but they tried to do so systematically and were unafraid to speculate about the answers.

Life's big questions require big answers—and the Alexandrian teachers and their followers thought they had figured out how to get those answers: through the acquisition of something they called *gnosis* or intimate knowledge. In this case, gnosis referred to a personal knowledge of the Divine, the experience of a direct encounter with God. These gnostics, "ones who know," sought out a kind of instantaneous spiritual illumination that would enable them to penetrate the mysteries of the existence and nature of God.

Word Knowledge

Gnosis means "knowledge" in Greek, but it's not simply head knowledge. Instead, gnosis refers to intimate knowledge, being in relationship or having acquaintance with something or someone else. For gnostics, gnosis is an experience of divine self-knowledge that catapults the knower into a new and higher realm of being.

Ghost in the (Broken Down) Machine

The gnostics were in many ways motivated by a desire to understand the meaning and nature of the human experience. Specifically, they wanted to know why the world and human existence was so full of pain, suffering, and death. Drawing on the various sources available to them, the gnostics came up with an answer: life is painful and futile because this physical, material existence itself is inherently bad. This world is, literally, rotten to the core.

It didn't start out that way, of course. For the gnostics, God is the source of all life and goodness. The gnostics created an entire myth to explain the nature of the world and the reason why things were so screwed up. This perfect, Divine Parent had surrounded itself with a series of other beings, or *aeons*, through a process of *emanation*. These beings together constitute something called the *Pleroma*. Don't let all the terminology throw you. Basically, the gnostics saw the "real world" as a spiritual realm filled with light and peace and populated by glorious beings unencumbered by suffering and pain. This was the perfect universe that existed before the creation of our own physical world.

Word Knowledge

In gnostic thought, **aeons** are emanations of the Divine. As such, they are both creations of and expressions of the Divine. While they are characterized as individual beings, they also seem to represent impersonal cosmic or psychological forces.

Emanations are the various aeons that emerged out of the unknown God or original Divine Being.

Pleroma in Greek is "that which fills." It is usually translated as "fullness," and in gnostic teaching refers to the real, spiritual world as opposed to this corrupt physical world.

We'll take a closer look at this mythology in later chapters (particularly in Chapter 13). For the moment, it's enough to say that at some point something went terribly wrong with this perfect world. Parts of the divine essence became separated from the Pleroma and trapped in a newly fashioned physical world. The divine essence is present in at least some human beings, and these are the ones who have the capacity to receive gnosis.

This world, the product of a lesser being called the *Demiurge*, now acts as a prison for these sparks of divinity. In most gnostic thinking, the Demiurge and his fellow *archons*, or rulers, are committed to keeping things that way. Worse yet, the Demiurge is synonymous with what the gnostics saw as the false God of the Jews—the same false God worshipped by the orthodox Christians. Gnostics taught that Jesus Christ came to Earth to destroy the power and works of this false God and to liberate those divine sparks.

Word Knowledge

The **Demiurge,** which can mean craftsman or maker, first appears in Platonic philosophy as a kind of middleman between the unknowable God and the physical world. For gnostics, the Demiurge tends to be a much more sinister character.

Archon, which is Greek for "ruler," was used by the gnostics to refer to those spiritual beings—usually demonic in nature—who hold sway over the material world and consequently prevent human spirits from returning to the Pleroma.

Here I Come to Save the Day!

For orthodox Christians, the key to salvation was found in the crucifixion and bodily resurrection of Jesus. Whether it was triumphing over evil powers or atoning for sins, the death of Christ on the cross was a redemptive act. Like a slave purchased and then set free, salvation was something done *on behalf of* helpless human beings. Guilty of sin, people need some means of pardon. Jesus Christ's death on the cross provides that release from judgment.

The gnostics had a completely different understanding of Christ's role. Their idea of a savior didn't depend on a physical death or suffering. In fact, they reveled in the idea that the spiritual Christ had avoided the cross, either by separating itself from the human Jesus at the crucifixion or by substituting someone else in his place. According to the gnostics, human beings aren't guilty of sin. "Sin" to them was an illusion born of our blindness to the real nature of this dead-end existence. They didn't believe they needed a pardon for crimes committed; instead, they thought it was necessary for people to realize that we are not bound to the rules of religion that we call "sin". We need someone to open our eyes.

For the gnostics, Christ was on a stealth mission. Some of the texts that we'll be seeing in later chapters rhapsodize about how he descended to the material world secretly, sliding past the gatekeepers, the rulers who hold the world in bondage. His task, gnostics argued, was not to create an objective redemption but to impart gnosis. Jesus came to tell us who we really are, that we are not beholden to this physical world and its death and suffering. We can escape this prison-house and return to the place that we truly belong. Christ parachuted behind enemy lines to deliver a message and then successfully, and this time openly, returned to the Divine. In doing so, according to the gnostics, he blazed a trail for all those who would follow him.

Gnosticism's Spiritual Pedigree

These days, if you get 10 scholars together and ask them to define gnosticism, you are bound to get 10 different opinions and no conclusions. Gnostic scholarship has evolved tremendously over the past 50 years as new documents and new approaches have created fascinating insights and raised equally disturbing questions about the nature and boundaries of gnosticism, the groups that held gnostic beliefs, and their relationship to the blossoming Christian faith in the second century.

Scholars have developed a variety of theories explaining what gnosticism is and where it comes from. From the fourth century or so, historians and religious experts had accepted the notion advanced by the orthodox Christian opponents of the gnostics, namely that gnostics were an aberrant offshoot of Christian faith and that it was too deeply influenced by outside philosophies. In recent years, however, this view has ceased to be persuasive. Let's take a look at what has taken its place.

Gnosticism's Roots in Judaism

More recent theories have suggested that Christian gnosticism was an outgrowth of Judaism. Those who made this argument pointed to the gnostic preoccupation with hierarchies of angels, with magical incantations, and the secret meanings of names (we'll see examples of these in Chapters 8, 13, and 16 especially). All these were characteristic of nearly all forms of Judaism in the first and second centuries. Jewish scholars like Philo of Alexandria had already laid a foundation for reimagining the Hebrew Scriptures in terms compatible with the kinds of Greek philosophy that were popular at the time. And certainly, as new gnostic documents came to light in the middle of the twentieth century, many of them appeared to be Christianized forms of originally Jewish documents.

A Little of This and a Little of That

Gnosticism couldn't have developed out of Judaism alone, however. Other philosophies and faiths were asking similar kinds of questions about the nature of God and humankind in a world of pain and suffering. The gnostic teachers in Alexandria (located in Egypt) were particularly familiar with the works of Plato, who suggested that God is entirely good and therefore not at fault for the conditions of humanity. *Hermetic* texts, Egyptian writings that focused on rising above passions to embrace a vision of the Divine that transcends the temporary physical world, also had an impact on gnostic philosophy. New ideas from Persia and India were filtering into the Western religious consciousness. It's clear that the gnostics operated in a time of fertile spiritual thinking. Given the importance of both Alexandria and the Hermetic writings to the development of

> **Word Knowledge**
>
> **Hermetic** writings are those that stem from the practice of an occult form of magic and philosophy associated with Hermes Trismegistus, a legendary deity in Egypt formed by a combination of the Egyptian god Thoth and the Greek god Hermes. The Codex Hermetica preserves a number of Hermetic works.

gnostic beliefs, it should come as no surprise that the gnostic documents that we'll be exploring in this book were also discovered in Egypt.

What About Christianity?

The important question, however, is whether gnosticism would have existed without Christianity. Was the story of Jesus the necessary ingredient to a gnostic understanding of the world and of God? Given our new understanding, the answer is probably not. A great deal depends on whether the actual teachings of Jesus were in any way gnostic. And that will depend on how we approach the Gnostic Gospels that we'll be looking at. Are they an accurate reflection of Jesus' teachings, or are they the product of the later gnostic community reading its own ideas back into the Jesus story? Orthodox Christians opposed gnostic Christians on precisely these points. Several early orthodox writers weighed in to question gnostic claims about Jesus. With this brief orientation in mind, then, let's start by looking at those very opponents of gnostic teaching, the orthodox Christian writers of the second and third centuries.

The Least You Need to Know

- Gnosticism showed up at a spiritually tumultuous time.
- According to gnostic philosophy, the present world is a prison designed to entrap those who have an element of the divine nature within them.
- For gnostics, Jesus is more a teacher and a revealer than someone who died and was resurrected as a sacrifice for sin.
- While Christian gnosticism is uniquely related to the Jesus story, its roots can be found in a variety of faiths and philosophies.

Fighting for the Right

In This Chapter

- ◆ Early orthodox Christians begin to sniff trouble in the wind
- ◆ A landmark book puts the gnostics on the defensive
- ◆ Not everyone is excited about a philosophical Christianity
- ◆ A different kind of Christianity flourishes in the gnostic's hometown

I'll pause for a moment, before going on to look at the men who developed gnostic philosophies, and take a look at those who opposed the emerging gnostic beliefs. These opponents of gnostic beliefs are important first of all because their arguments became the dominant view of the church through most of its history. At the same time, and largely because of their success, they are our primary source for information about the gnostic teachers and their ideas. Like it or not, even with the discovery of new gnostic documents, we are still dependent on these orthodox Christian authors for insight into how to read the gnostics. Still, it's important to be aware of their biases.

Earliest Voices

There are some indications in New Testament writings that elements of later gnostic thinking were already percolating up into the church. That tendency became more pronounced in the early second century. Although certain teachers were beginning to feel their way toward a set of ideas that we now call gnosticism, early orthodox Christians were swift to oppose them.

Ignatius of Antioch

Among the first of these early opponents was Ignatius, the bishop of the city of Antioch in Syria. Antioch was a significant city during the earliest years of the development of Christianity. It was the site of the first church that included large numbers of non-Jews. According to the Bible, it was also where followers of Jesus of Nazareth were first called "Christians," and it was the original base of operations for the Apostle Paul's missionary journeys. There is pretty good evidence that the Apostle Peter was active in Antioch, and some scholars have suggested that the Gospel of Matthew was written there as well. All in all, the church in Antioch rated high on anyone's list of important Christian communities. As its leader, Ignatius represented a Christian community intimately connected with the teaching and tradition of the apostles.

Born somewhere around A.D. 50, almost nothing is known of Ignatius's early life. Some evidence suggests that he was a student of the Apostle John along with Polycarp of Smyrna, who we'll look at next. Church tradition says that the Apostle Peter personally selected Ignatius as bishop of Antioch, though that seems unlikely given that Ignatius would have been only a teenager when Peter was executed in Rome somewhere around A.D. 65.

We don't know much about Ignatius's beginnings, but we certainly get a front-row seat for his end. The church in Antioch faced some sort of opposition during the reign of the emperor Trajan (A.D. 98–117). As a consequence, Ignatius was arrested and sentenced to die in the Ampitheatre in Rome. Sometime around A.D. 110—we don't know for sure the precise year—Ignatius died at the hands, or teeth, of the lions. But, as you might have guessed, Ignatius did not go quietly. Escorted by a unit of Roman guards who he called "ten leopards … whose treatment of me grows harsher the kinder I am to them," Ignatius's final journey from Antioch to Rome turned into a triumphal procession. Christians from around the Roman Empire, hearing of his sentence, flocked to see him. In city after city, he was greeted like a hero.

Encouraged by this response, Ignatius wrote a series of seven letters to various churches that had sent representatives to see him. In the letters he shared his thoughts about the well-being of the churches as they faced both external opposition and internal divisions.

In his correspondence, Ignatius was quick to strengthen the positions of the bishops and the elders of the churches. He called on the Christians in Smyrna to "Follow the bishop as Jesus Christ followed the Father." "It is right for you to set your minds in harmony with the bishop," he encouraged the well-known church in the city of Ephesus. One of Ignatius's key concerns was that Christians should unite around the teaching and authority of the bishops.

Unity in the churches had practical benefits given the state persecution under which Ignatius was suffering. Still, Ignatius expressed greater concern for the way that heeding the bishop's authority preserved the integrity of the church's teachings. He was sensitive to certain ideas making the rounds in Christian communities, which he compared to wine that has been poisoned. These teachings, later called *docetism*, alleged that Jesus Christ did not have an actual body. Instead, he was a spiritual being.

Consequently, he was not born in any real sense and he did not suffer crucifixion. We don't know if Ignatius had any gnostic groups in mind when he criticized docetism, but those teachings he railed against certainly fit well within what we know about gnostic beliefs. Ignatius was quick to attack these ideas, which were apparently prevalent in his own church in Antioch. He warned other churches against them while at the same time offering brief but powerful refutations.

Word Knowledge

Docetism (from a Greek word that means "to appear" or "to seem") is the belief that Jesus of Nazareth had no physical body and therefore could neither suffer nor die.

Though his letters predate the emergence of a recognizable kind of gnosticism, Ignatius's one-two punch of strengthening the hierarchical church leadership and attacking the docetists established a pattern that would be expanded and perfected by later orthodox Christian writers. The docetist ideas that he argued against eventually helped to form part of the larger gnostic outlook. Ignatius would not be the last orthodox Christian to wrestle with them.

Polycarp of Smyrna

During his long journey to his death in Rome, Ignatius stayed for a while as a guest with his younger contemporary, Polycarp the bishop of Smyrna. Later, Ignatius would write a letter to Polycarp, addressing his fellow bishop as both a friend and confidante.

Very little is known about Polycarp, but it is clear that he carried a great deal of moral authority in the churches in Asia Minor. Later writers said that he was a disciple of the Apostle John. He was certainly on good terms with Ignatius. In A.D. 154, Polycarp traveled to Rome to meet with Pope Anicetus. Roman Christians and Christians in Asia Minor celebrated Easter on different dates, and the dispute over this practice was causing some friction. The two failed to come to a compromise, though, and shortly after his return to Smyrna, Polycarp was arrested and executed for being a Christian. He was 86 years old.

The only writing that we have from Polycarp is his Letter to the Philippians, where he expressed many of the same concerns as Ignatius, both for the unity of the Christian community around the bishop and for combating the docetic teaching. His principle importance is his influence on later writers, particularly Irenaeus, who we'll meet in a moment.

Word Knowledge

The **apologists** (from the word *apologia*, which means "defense") were Christian writers primarily in the second and third centuries who presented the Christian message to nonbelievers and defended the Christian faith against rumors and misunderstandings. After Christianity became a legal religion in the fourth century, the apologists became less significant.

Justin Martyr

Whereas Ignatius and Polycarp seem to have been life-long Christians, Justin was a convert to the faith. A philosopher and a seeker, he tells us that he had examined all sorts of different ways of living until finally, around A.D. 132, he met an old man who persuaded him to consider Christianity. He did, and ended up becoming one of the first *apologists* for the Christian faith.

After wandering around for a while, Justin set up shop in Rome, where he gathered a group of students and began writing. Two of his Apologies still exist. The first, the longer of the two, gives us an important look at the early orthodox Christian community in Rome. Unfortunately, Justin's most important works for our interest were an apology referred to as "Against Marcion" and a text called "Refutation of All Heresies," both of which are lost. Justin's career ended when a jealous rival outed him to the local authorities. He was tried before the magistrate and condemned to death in A.D. 165.

Justin is our source for the earliest knowledge about several of the gnostic teachers we'll meet in Chapter 4, some of whom were near contemporaries of his. His lost works on non-orthodox teachings were known to later writers and certainly influenced them. As we'll see later in this chapter, other writers would expand on Justin's attempt to integrate some aspects of Greek philosophy into his defense of Christian faith.

Irenaeus

Irenaeus was the most important and influential of the orthodox Christian writers in the second century. His monumental work, *Against Heresies*, almost single-handedly defined the shape of orthodox Christian faith and remains today the most important source of information about Christian gnosticism.

Word Knowledge _____

Heresy (from the word *haeresis*, which means "choosing") originally referred to the act of choosing between several opinions. As such, it was a fairly neutral term. It was the Apostle Paul in Galatians 5:20 who gives "heresy" a negative meaning, calling it one of the "works of the flesh" and listing it in between "seditions" and "envy." Following Paul, the mainstream church used the word to indicate a person or group that was deviating from the publicly received Christian story in order to pursue an alternative private belief or practice. The key distinction between a heresy and a schism is that schismatics break away from the church in order to pursue their own views, while heretics follow their own visions while remaining within the church.

Irenaeus was born in Asia Minor sometime around A.D. 140. He tells us that as a young man he was a student of Polycarp of Smyrna. This fact, when combined with the possibility that Polycarp sat at the feet of the Apostle John, means that there may have been a direct line of witness and tradition stretching from Jesus, through John and Polycarp, to Irenaeus in the late second century. Irenaeus used this spiritual lineage as a weapon against his gnostic opponents, arguing against their claims to possess a secret tradition passed down from the apostles.

Close Encounters of the Gnostic Kind

Irenaeus had an early career as an envoy and mediator, helping to resolve disputes between churches. While working with a church in southern France, in what is today the city of Lyon, Irenaeus had occasion to travel to Rome. In Rome he gained first-hand knowledge of some of the gnostic groups and their teachings.

While Irenaeus was in Rome, the bishop back in Lyon was persecuted and murdered. Irenaeus was quickly elected to take the dead bishop's place, and so became the leading church official in Lyon. When he returned to take his new position, however, Irenaeus was dismayed to find that some of the gnostic teachings he had encountered in Rome had found their way to Lyon. Out of concern for the well-being of the church, he began to investigate.

Against Heresies

Irenaeus's principal work came out of his investigation into the gnostic teachings. Although the official title of the five-book series is *The Refutation and Overthrow of Knowledge Falsely So-Called*, it is generally known simply as *Against Heresies*. The text was completed in Greek in A.D. 185, but the earliest existing copy of it is a Latin translation.

The publication of *Against Heresies* became a watershed moment in the relationship between the orthodox and gnostic Christians. Although there was no immediate impact, over time the momentum and initiative shifted away from the gnostics. Irenaeus wasn't solely responsible for that turning of the tide, but he was an important part of it.

The special focus of *Against Heresies* was to describe and attack what Irenaeus saw as heretical teachings. His immediate concern was the school of the Valentinians in Rome (we'll meet Valentinus in the next chapter), but he ranged widely in his attacks on gnostic teaching. The picture that emerges is one of many groups, some more popular and powerful than others, who are united by certain tendencies and beliefs.

In addition to refuting gnostic doctrines, Irenaeus laid out several important and far-reaching arguments in favor of the orthodox position. He reminded his readers of what he called the "Rule of Faith." He championed the authority of the bishops, and he insisted on the unity of the Old and New Testaments.

The church is everywhere united behind a basic set of truths, Irenaeus claimed. Whether in Syria or in Spain, the Christian churches hold to what he termed "the Rule of Faith." The "rule" was a sort of cheat sheet for reading and understanding the message of Scripture. It gave readers the gist of the story, the bird's-eye view of what God was up to. According to Irenaeus, the Scriptures weren't open to any kind of interpretation. Instead, he said, they have a story to tell, and the "rule" is an authoritative summary of that story.

From the Source

Compare this description of the "Rule of Faith" from Irenaeus' *Against Heresies* with the later Apostle's Creed, a universally recognized statement of orthodox Christian beliefs:

The Church, though dispersed throughout the whole world, even to the ends of the earth, has received from the apostles and their disciples this faith: In one God, the Father Almighty, Maker of heaven, and Earth, and the sea, and all things that are in them; and in one Christ Jesus, the Son of God, who became incarnate for our salvation; and in the Holy Spirit, who proclaimed through the prophets the dispensations of God, and the advents, and the birth from a virgin, and the passion, and the resurrection from the dead, and the ascension into heaven in the flesh of the beloved Christ Jesus, our Lord, and His manifestation from heaven in the glory of the Father "to gather all things in one," and to raise up anew all flesh of the whole human race, in order that to Christ Jesus, our Lord, and God, and Savior, and King, according to the will of the invisible Father, "every knee should bow, of things in heaven, and things in earth, and things under the earth, and that every tongue should confess" to Him, and that He should execute just judgment towards all; that He may send "spiritual wickednesses," and the angels who transgressed and became apostates, together with the ungodly, and unrighteous, and wicked, and profane among men, into everlasting fire; but may, in the exercise of His grace, confer immortality on the righteous, and holy, and those who have kept His commandments, and have persevered in His love, some from the beginning, and others from their repentance, and may surround them with everlasting glory. (Irenaeus, *Against Heresies* [1,10])

Apostle's Creed:

We believe in God, the Father Almighty, Maker of heaven and earth.

And in Jesus Christ, his only Son, our Lord. Who was conceived of the Holy Spirit and born of the Virgin Mary. He suffered under Pontius Pilate, was crucified, died, and was buried. He descended into hell. On the third day he rose again from the dead. He ascended into heaven, and is seated at the right hand of God the Father Almighty. From there He will come to judge the living and the dead.

We believe in the Holy Spirit, the holy catholic church, the communion of saints, the forgiveness of sins, the resurrection of the body, and the life everlasting.

For Irenaeus, the continuity of the traditions of the church was proof against any kind of secret tradition or hidden teachings. Irenaeus offered the church in Rome as an example of the connection, from one bishop to another, of the essential orthodox teachings. He gave a list of Roman bishops, beginning with the Apostle Peter and continuing to his own time.

Surely, Irenaeus argued, if there were any secret teachings, the apostles would have passed it on to those who they appointed as bishops over the churches. And, he continued, surely the bishops would have passed it on to their successors. With this argument, Irenaeus fleshed out Ignatius's insistence on standing in unity with the bishops. They were the guarantors of genuine Christian faith because they alone possessed a tradition handed down from the apostles. Every other teacher, he insisted, is a fraud and an imposter.

Irenaeus's defense of the Old Testament was critical not only in his fight with the gnostics but as part of the process for deciding which texts should be considered Scripture. Irenaeus rejected the gnostic notion that the Old Testament had little or no connection to Jesus of Nazareth or the God that Jesus represented. He insisted on the unity between the Old and New Testaments.

At the same time, Irenaeus was the first orthodox Christian to advocate the four gospels that are now included in the New Testament: Matthew, Mark, Luke, and John. Although earlier writers had quoted from them, Irenaeus was the first to define these four as the only valid expressions of the story of Jesus Christ.

From the Source

It is not possible that the Gospels can be either more or fewer in number than they are. For, since there are four zones of the world in which we live, and four principal winds, while the Church is scattered throughout all the world, and the "pillar and ground" of the Church is the Gospel and the spirit of life, it is fitting that she should have four pillars, breathing out immortality on every side, and vivifying men afresh. From which fact, it is evident that the Word, the Artificer of all, He that sits upon the cherubim, and contains all things, He who was manifested to men, has given us the Gospel under four aspects, but bound together by one Spirit.

—Irenaeus, *Against Heresies* (3,11,8)

Jerusalem and Athens

Whether we're talking about the gnostic groups excoriated by Irenaeus or someone as mainstream as Justin Martyr, philosophically minded seekers were beginning to notice Christianity, and Christian teachers were beginning to present Christ as the answer to the philosphers' questions. Irenaeus was not the only orthodox writer who objected to this Christian engagement with Greek philosophy, gnostic or otherwise. In fact, from the perspective of our next two gentlemen, the gnostic heresies were a perfect example of what happens when you mess with things best left alone.

Tertullian

His full name was Quintus Septimus Florens Tertullianus, and he lived up to every syllable of it. One of the most colorful, enjoyable, and exasperating of the orthodox Christian writers, Tertullian stood out as both incisive and passionate. The first of the orthodox Christians to write in Latin, he stretched the language as far as it would go, and then invented several new words to communicate Christian ideas. Impatient with abstract and academic questions, he was drawn to controversy like a moth to a flame. In the process, he created a body of writings that addressed the whole spectrum of the Christian life.

From the Source

What indeed has Athens to do with Jerusalem? What agreement is there between the Academy and the Church? What between heretics and Christians? Our instruction comes from "the porch of Solomon," who had himself taught that "the Lord should be sought in simplicity of heart." Away with all attempts to produce a mottled Christianity of Stoic, Platonic, and dialectic composition! We want no curious disputation after possessing Christ Jesus, no inquisition after enjoying the gospel! With our faith, we desire no further belief. For this is our palmary faith, that there is nothing which we ought to believe besides.

—Tertullian, *The Prescription Against Heretics* (ch. vii)

Tertullian was born sometime around A.D. 160 to non-Christian parents. It is possible that his father was a Roman soldier. His family lived in Carthage. Once Rome's greatest rival, the city had been destroyed in 146 B.C. at the end of the Punic Wars. Carthage has been resurrected by Julius Caesar, however, and in Tertullian's day it was one of the most important cultural centers in the Roman Empire.

A Fierce Convert

After a brief stint in Rome, where he studied law, Tertullian returned to Carthage in the throes of a spiritual crisis. Like Justin before him, he was looking for something to believe in. Christianity had put down strong roots in North Africa and was quickly becoming a force to be reckoned with in Carthage. Somewhere around A.D. 194, Tertullian converted to the Christian faith. Nowhere does he tell us why, but his writings reveal that he was impressed with the rigorously moral lives Christians lived and the ferocious courage that they exhibited during their executions.

He quickly became a leading member of the church, becoming a priest (though he was married) and using his pen in the defense of his new faith. Of particular interest to us are two works written specifically to combat gnostic teachers: "Against Marcion" and "Against Valentinus" (for more on these texts, see Chapter 4). He wrote a more general book, *Concerning the Prescription of Heretics*, dealing with a broader group of heretical teachings.

The Montanist Phase

At some point prior to A.D. 210, Tertullian finally got fed up with the laxity he perceived in the mainstream church and joined a morally stringent new movement called *Montanism*. As a Montanist, he vigorously defended the new sect, which was under pressure from the orthodox community.

Word Knowledge

Montanism is a second-century prophetic movement that began in modern day Turkey. The leader, Montanus, claimed that the Holy Spirit promised in the Gospel of John was now beginning to speak through him. The group was strictly moralistic and expected an imminent Second Coming of Jesus Christ. After a period of tolerance, the mainstream Christian community felt compelled to identify the movement as a heresy. The Montanists continued to exist until the sixth century.

Tertullian eventually broke with the Montanists to create his own group, and he continued to write until at least A.D. 220, when he disappears from the scene. Some evidence suggests that he may have lived until as late as A.D. 240.

Hippolytus

In contrast to the mercurial but fascinating Tertullian, who was his contemporary, Hippolytus was a slow and plodding thinker. Not given to much originality, he was best at piecing together bits and pieces of other writers' thoughts. As much a moralist as Tertullian, his manner was more bitter and angry.

Hippolytus was a leader in the Roman church and an opponent of Pope Zephyrinus (A.D. 199–217). Their theological disagreement about the Trinity spilled over into political discontent. That discontent turned to outright dissent when Zephyrinus died and his assistant Calixtus was elected to take his place. Hippolytus broke with the Roman church and had himself elected bishop by his own group of followers. He continued to run his dissident church until he and one of Calixtus' successors, Pope Pontian, were both exiled to the mines on the island of Sardinia in A.D. 235, part of the emperor Maximinus's persecution of the church. While there, the two were finally reconciled. Both men resigned their offices in favor of a third man, Anterus, ending the feud between the two sides. Hippolytus died immediately afterward.

Hippolytus authored several important works. The most important with regards to the gnostics was his humbly titled *The Refutation of All Heresies*, also known as the *Philosophumena* (Philosophical Teachings). In its 10 chapters, 2 of which have been lost, Hippolytus attempted to show that gnostic teachings were nothing more than extensions Greek philosophy (we'll see how this works when we actually look at gnostic writings like the Gospel of Truth in Chapter 9).

The True Gnostics

On the other end of the spectrum from men like Tertullian and Hippolytus, Christians in the Egyptian city of Alexandria lived in an environment drenched in the language and practice of Greek philosophy. These Christians approached the allegedly aberrant teaching of the gnostics by fighting fire with fire. They vigorously engaged both non-Christians and gnostic Christians by utilizing the same philosophical and mythological sources. They were as comfortable drawing on the writings of Aristotle and the stories of Homer as they were the letters of the Apostle Paul. Taking a page from their opponents' playbook, they described themselves as the "true gnostics," the ones who *really* know.

Christians in Alexandria

Alexander the Great built Alexandria in Egypt in 332 B.C. and, in a characteristic display of self-exaltation, named the city after himself. Beginning with Alexander's patronage, Alexandria became a mecca for philosophers, scholars, and religious followers of every sort. For centuries, its famous library hosted some of the greatest minds in Mediterranean world.

A powerful Jewish community existed in Alexandria as well. It was there, around 200 B.C., that the Hebrew Bible was translated into Greek for the first time. One of the leading members of the Jewish community in Alexandria, a man named Philo, reworked Jewish faith together with Greek philosophy to create a powerful and persuasive synthesis of the two. On many levels, the Jewish experience in Alexandria paved the way for the later growth of the Christian church. As large numbers of Greek intellectuals began to convert to Christianity in the second century, they were eager to discover links between their Hellenistic (Greek) cultural background and their newfound faith. Alexandria was the perfect place to begin that exploration.

To meet this interest, the Christian community in Alexandria founded a school for *catechesis* as a way of instructing new believers in the ways of the faith. The school also became a public forum for offering more mature Christians a curriculum couched in philosophical concepts. The school was ostensibly under the control of the bishop of Alexandria, but it operated with a certain degree of independence. Founded sometime around A.D. 185, the same year that Irenaeus published *Against Heresies*, the School of Alexandria launched the careers of two of the most significant early Christian theologians, Clement of Alexandria and Origen.

Word Knowledge

Catechesis is oral instruction given to new Christians as preparation for baptism. The earliest Christians, all of them Jews or converts to Judaism before they became Christians, required little in-depth instruction on such issues as the authority of Scripture and biblically-based ethics. As the numbers of non-Jews entering the church increased, it became clear that these new believers would require a deliberate reorientation. Early in the history of the church, catechesis (from the Greek "katecheo," meaning "to echo the sound") came about through a one-on-one relationship with a teacher. Later, schools for catechesis like the one in Alexandria were founded to work in cooperation with the church in preparing new believers to take their place in the Christian community. As infant baptism became more and more the norm in the church, the process of adult catechesis gradually faded away.

Clement of Alexandria

Clement of Alexandria was the gentleman-scholar of the early church. He was born to a family of Athenian non-Christians in A.D. 150. He spent time traveling around meeting Christian teachers. His wanderings finally brought him to Alexandria around A.D. 180, where he sat under the teaching of Pantaenus, the founder and first head of the Christian school in Alexandria, and converted to the Christian faith. Clement quickly became Pantaenus's protégé and a leader in the Alexandrian church. When Pantaenus left the school around A.D. 190, Clement was the logical choice to take over.

Clement taught at the School of Alexandria until the reign of the emperor Septimius Severus in A.D. 201. During that time he expanded the school's influence and mentored a number of excellent students, many of whom became leaders in the Alexandrian church and elsewhere. When Severus began persecuting the church, Clement's visible role made it necessary for him to flee. He took refuge with a former student in Cappadocia (eastern Turkey) and passed away sometime between A.D. 210 and 215.

A Middle Way

In Clement's day, Alexandria's Christian community was divided between two groups. On the one hand, the majority of Christians were native Egyptians, more inclined to strict morality with little use for the intellectualizing of the philosophers. On the other hand, the better educated minority of Christians were fully at home in Greek culture and philosophy. They were more comfortable with the speculative theories and complex mythologies of the gnostics.

Clement tried to create a middle way between these two extremes, hoping to keep them united. He advocated a pattern of moderate Christian living that, he argued, characterized the "true gnostic." He accepted the basic notion, championed by the gnostics, that there are differences between the average believer and the more mature, advanced "gnostic" Christian. The difference, he suggested, was due not to a sudden burst of enlightened insight or a deep personal experience as the gnostics claimed. Rather, it was the growing ethical maturity of the Christian whose faith led him or her to greater and greater knowledge. For Clement, true gnosis was the product of a lifetime of refined morality and methodical advancement into deeper knowledge of God.

Clement wrote several important works that bear on gnostic teachings:

- *Protrepticus* (Exhortation to the Greeks): Writings intended to persuade non-Christian Greeks to convert to Christianity.

- *Paedagogus* (The Teacher): A work of moral theology in which Clement presents his picture of the perfect Christian as the "true gnostic." This work begins with a refutation of gnostic teachings.

- *Stromata* (The Miscellanies): Clement's attempt to delve more deeply into speculative theology. Only seven chapters remain, of which chapters four and seven are of particular interest regarding Clement's view of the gnostics.

- *Excerpts from Theodotus:* A compiled collection of quotations from one of the most important gnostic schools of Clement's day. The *Excerpts* are contained in the *Stromata*, but they are significant enough to be mentioned separately.

Origen

Clement's brightest student and his successor as head of the School of Alexandria, Origen was arguably the single-most brilliant and original thinker of the early Christian period. Born to Christian parents in Alexandria, Origen's father suffered martyrdom in A.D. 202, in the same persecution that forced Origen's mentor Clement to flee.

Did You Know? _____

When his father was being led away to die, the teenage Origen wanted to follow and suffer martyrdom with him. He was unable to, however, because his mother hid his clothes. Apparently, going off to die courageously is one thing, but going off naked is another thing entirely.

This double loss thrust Origen into the dual role of head teacher of the Alexandrian church's theological training center and breadwinner for his mother and six siblings. He taught on the side to make ends meet, and lived a very austere life. Eventually he was able to bring on a junior partner at the school, which freed him up to focus on teaching the more advanced subjects.

A Growing Reputation

Origen converted a man named Ambrose away from a form of gnosticism to orthodox Christianity. The wealthy Ambrose responded by providing Origen with a virtual army of shorthand copywriters. In an age where everything was written by hand,

Ambrose's patronage was the equivalent of a having your own printing press. Origen was able to mass-produce his writings and distribute them more widely. His already considerable reputation took off, and he began to travel around the empire as a lecturer and preacher.

Origen's success caused friction with Demetrius, the bishop of Alexandria. Demetrius wanted to keep a tighter leash on his star prodigy. Their relationship had already deteriorated from bad to worse when, in A.D. 229, Origen was ordained as a priest by a church in Palestine. Demetrius viewed this as a direct affront to his authority as Origen's spiritual head. Origen had visited Palestine while on his way to debate a gnostic Christian named Candidus. During the debate, Origen suggested that it might be possible for even Satan to repent and be restored to a relationship with God. That was the final straw for Demetrius. He organized a condemnation of Origen, though it had little if any effect outside of Egypt. The relationship between Demetrius and Origen was completely broken, and Origen remained in Palestine, where he opened a new school dedicated to making orthodox Christianity accessible.

Origen continued to travel and write. He escaped the persecution of the church under the emperor Maximinus in A.D. 235, but when the emperor Decius attacked the Christian community in A.D. 250, Origen was arrested and tortured. He survived, though physically broken, for a few more years. The date of his death is unknown.

Origen's Legacy

Origen was incredibly well educated in the various forms of Greek philosophy drifting around in his day. He turned that knowledge toward constructing a version of orthodox Christian beliefs couched entirely in philosophical terms and concepts. He wanted to meet the non-Christian philosophers and the gnostic Christians on their own ground and beat them at their own game. Unfortunately, as the example of the debate with Candidus demonstrates, Origen's well-intentioned efforts could get him into trouble with his fellow orthodox Christians. Within a couple of centuries after his death, other orthodox writers were attacking Origen's reputation and viewing his writings with deep suspicion.

Debating gnostic Christians was a significant part of Origen's activity, especially later in life. A large number of the works that he wrote dealt with gnostic thinking. Of particular significance is his enormous *Commentary on John*, in which he interacted with the gnostic teacher Heracleon. Also helpful are the *Dialogue with Candidus*, a record of the debate that got Origen in such hot water with Demetrius, and *The Dialogue with Heraclides*, another gnostic with whom Origen debated.

The Orthodox Attack

It would be nice if we could simply approach the gnostic teachers directly, without the help of their opponents. Unfortunately, the success of the orthodox Christians makes that nearly impossible. Even if we had all of the facts—which we don't—and all of the gnostic writings completely intact, we would still need the fellows we've met in this chapter. They were the contemporaries of the gnostics. They all were asking many of the same questions as the gnostics and wrestling with many of the same issues.

It's certainly helpful to cull the orthodox writers for information about their opponents, especially if we are careful to recognize that they were not merely objective observers. But beyond that, they give us a living window into a time that we no longer have access to.

The Least You Need to Know

- Gnostic ideas and orthodox concern about them began to emerge very early in the Christian era.

- Irenaeus' *Against Heresies* became a critical tool in the success of orthodox Christianity.

- Tertullian demonstrated that the orthodox can be creative and energetic in living out the Christian faith.

- In the Egyptian city of Alexandria, a hotbed of Greek philosophy, Christians struggled to find acceptable ways to reconcile the orthodox interpretation of Scripture with gnostic beliefs, but the gap between gnostic and orthodox theologies proved too difficult to bridge.

Chapter 4

The Gnostic Lineup

In This Chapter

- ◆ A flamboyant Biblical character becomes an apostle of evil
- ◆ One of the world's great cities becomes a laboratory for the first gnostic thinker
- ◆ The "golden boy" of gnosticism makes it big in Rome
- ◆ A wealthy businessman starts his own church

We have reached a point where we can look at those who developed and championed the Christian forms of gnosticism. It is important to remember that nearly everything we know about these religious innovators comes through the writings of their opponents. Orthodox Christian writers had their own perspectives on the lives and teachings of the gnostics, so we will have to keep that in mind even while we remain dependent on them for insight into the origins and activities of those they classed as heretics.

In this chapter, you'll learn about four leading gnostics. These figures' activities, their teachings, and their struggles are the key to understanding gnosticism in the second century. More important, their stories offer clues to understanding the various documents that they left behind.

Simon the Magician

Although it is difficult to pin down the precise beginnings of the Christian gnostic movement, all of the orthodox writers fingered the same culprit: Simon the Magician. Simon makes a dramatic debut early in the Biblical text The Acts of the Apostles, attempting to purchase from the Apostle Peter the power to confer the Holy Spirit on those who believe. Peter tears into Simon, and Simon appears to repent. That's pretty much where the Bible leaves it, but it's definitely not the end of Simon's story.

From the Source

Now for some time a man named Simon had practiced sorcery in the city and amazed all the people of Samaria. He boasted that he was someone great, and all the people, both high and low, gave him their attention and exclaimed, "This man is the divine power known as the Great Power." They followed him because he had amazed them for a long time with his magic.

—The Acts of the Apostles 8:9–11 (New International Version)

Did You Know?

Simon's famous attempt to buy the power of the Holy Spirit is the origin of the word *simony*, which means the buying and selling of sacred things. During the Middle Ages, simony referred to the purchase of ecclesiastical offices and privileges.

Within a couple of generations, Simon's reputation took a nosedive. Orthodox writers like Justin Martyr and Irenaeus (whom we met in Chapter 3) began to paint Simon as the quintessential apostle of heresy. According to them, he was responsible for planting the seeds for every major doctrinal error. The orthodox writers found it helpful to have a single target for their criticism of later gnostic teachings. Their somewhat hazy knowledge of Simon's actual activities made it that much easier to make him bear the brunt of all kinds of attacks.

That's *Mister* Great Power to You

In the passage from the Bible where we are introduced to Simon we find a curious phrase: "This man is the divine power known as the Great Power." The Great Power, as you might guess, is God. So it appears that Simon claimed to be God in the flesh.

Simon's ideas about the Great Power were pretty unique. For instance, he believed that this perfect being existed as both male and female. The female part, called *Ennoia*, had created a bunch of angels and spirit beings who were unaware of the existence of their Father. Their job was the creation of the physical world but, jealous of their Mother, these angels overpowered her. They locked her away in the physical world, where she was condemned to be reincarnated over and over again.

Here's where it gets fun. Simon claimed to be the male part of the Great Power. He had come into the world to search for, and liberate, his Ennoia. After years of searching, Simon claimed to have found her in a brothel in the coastal city of Tyre. Soon he was parading around with a prostitute named Helen. She was, he claimed, the latest incarnation of Ennoia.

> **Word Knowledge**
>
> *Ennoia*, meaning "thought," in Greek suggests a hinting thought, a suggestive one. In gnosticism, the word refers to the female being who is brought forth by the Great Power. Her name implies that she/it is a pregnant, suggestive, forward-looking "thought." The Ennoia becomes responsible, then, for the creation of the physical world.

Take a Flying Leap

Simon's eventual fate is a matter of legend and conjecture. Later writers tell stories of renewed confrontations between Simon the Magician and the Apostle Peter in Rome (you can find this tale in the *apocryphal* Acts of Peter, of which The Act of Peter discussed in Chapter 12 may have been a part). The two engaged in a contest of signs and wonders, wowing their audience with one miracle after another. This sorcerous showdown ended with Simon's death when he plummeted to the floor of the Roman Forum in an unsuccessful attempt to fly. Whatever else can be said about Simon, he sure knew how to make an impression.

The evidence makes it pretty clear that these stories are speculation, though they are certainly entertaining. We really don't have any idea how the much-maligned magician from Samaria eventually met his end. In any case, the legend has become more important than the man. Simon the Magician provided the champions of orthodoxy with a convenient boogey man ready to jump out of the dark and snatch careless souls into hell. When battling the later gnostics, orthodox writers would argue a kind of guilt by association. Don't mess around with these ideas, they said. After all, look at where they come from.

> **Word Knowledge** _____
>
> A story or document that is of questionable authenticity is considered to be **apocryphal**. In talking about Christianity, apocryphal works would not be considered a legitimate part of the Bible. What's considered apocryphal depends on whom you're talking to. Roman Catholics and Eastern Orthodox Christians say that several Old Testament documents, such as 1 and 2 Maccabees, are inspired by God and part of the Bible. Protestants consider them "Apocrypha," saying that they are not inspired and are not part of their canon of Scripture. Catholics, as well as Protestants, call the gnostic works discussed in this book "apocryphal." No one includes them in the Bible, and few believe that they were written by the people whose name appears as their author.

And the Beat Goes On ...

Simon's influence outlived his death. He had at least one student, named Menander, who basically followed in Simon's footsteps. Menander was succeeded by Saturninus, who was active in Antioch and may have been one of those docetist teachers attacked by Ignatius (see Chapter 3). With Saturninus, the development of gnosticism kicked into high gear. It also shifted locations away from Palestine and Syria to Alexandria, and began to flourish in one of the most vibrant cities in the Mediterranean world.

Basilides

As we saw in the previous chapter, the city of Alexandria was strategically positioned in the second century to act as a kind of laboratory for Christians experimenting with the commonalities between Christian faith and Greek philosophy. Long before any of the "true gnostics" (who were orthodox Christians) that we looked at in Chapter 3, the first man to work at combining these two different outlooks, faith and philosophy, was a fellow whom most people today have never heard of.

A native of the city of Alexandria, Basilides was active in the early part of the second century (roughly A.D. 120–140). It was in the midst of that philosophical hotbed that Basilides began to piece together the different elements of gnosticism for the first time.

It is difficult to define precisely what Basilides taught. With the exception of some fragments preserved in orthodox writings, everything that he wrote has disappeared. And he wrote quite a lot. In addition to a 24-book commentary on the gospels, it seems that Basilides wrote a gospel of his own, more than likely a version of the existing gospels condensed and edited to fit his own system of thinking. There's also reason to believe that he wrote a number of songs. Remember that this was a time when everything was written by hand. Basilides was obviously a busy fellow.

A Brilliant Hodgepodge

Basilides strung together parts of Greek philosophy, Jewish beliefs in one God, and Persian mythology about angels and demons. He believed that the physical and the spiritual were at odds with each other. Sin was a matter of being too concerned with physical existence. For Basilides, real salvation meant being disentangled from our material concerns. He also acknowledged that not everyone is capable of doing this, though. Some people are perfectly happy in the physical world. Others have a sense that there is something more, though only one of a thousand people might have this sensitivity. He viewed these "spiritual" people as the ones who are being saved from this life.

Did You Know? _____

Early Christians began to set aside days to commemorate events in Jesus' life, particularly his birth. Some groups, in fact, celebrated Christ's birth on January 6. Clement of Alexandria tells us that Basilides and his followers celebrated January 6th as the date of Jesus' baptism, probably because they viewed the coming of the Spirit on Jesus at his baptism as the true coming of the Christ to Earth. The celebration included an all-night vigil with readings from Scripture. In the Western Church, January 6th is known today as Epiphany, and commemorates the coming of the Wise Men to see Jesus. In the Eastern Church, January 6th is the celebration of Christ's birth.

In Chapter 2, we saw how gnostics anticipated the arrival of a Cosmic Redeemer who would show them the way to escape physical existence. For Basilides, Jesus was that Redeemer. However, Jesus didn't save us by dying on a cross. In fact, Basilides didn't believe that Jesus had been crucified. He thought that Simon of Cyrene, the fellow in the Bible who was forced to help Jesus carry his cross, had been executed in Jesus' place. Instead, according to Basilides, Jesus escaped from this world unharmed. By doing so, he showed humanity how to break out of the prison of the physical world and the malicious spirits that rule it. By following in his footsteps, those who are "spiritual" can also escape from this world and enter the heavens.

From the Source

Wherefore he [Jesus] did not himself suffer death, but Simon, a certain man of Cyrene, being compelled, bore the cross in his stead; so that this latter being transfigured by him, that he might be thought to be Jesus, was crucified, through ignorance and error, while Jesus himself received the form of Simon, and, standing by, laughed at them.

—Irenaeus, in *Against Heresies*, depicting Basilides' account of the crucifixion

All of these beliefs and ideas were floating around in the second century, especially in places like Alexandria. By centering his whole system on Jesus of Nazareth, however, Basilides created something unique. For the first time, we get a distinctly Christian form of gnosticism.

Declining Interest

Although he seems to have enjoyed a certain popularity while he was alive, Basilides' system never really spread beyond Egypt. After his death, Isidore, who was either his son or his disciple (we're not sure which), succeeded him. Despite both their efforts, however, Basilides' version of gnostic teaching never really caught on. Nonetheless, Basilides laid the groundwork for a far more popular approach championed by a fellow Alexandrian.

Valentinus

A younger contemporary of Basilides and a native of Egypt, Valentinus was educated in Alexandria's hotbed of philosophical speculation during the early years of the second century. He almost certainly knew the works of the Jewish philosopher Philo, and it is likely that he was exposed to Basilides' teaching. Like many of the philosophically minded seekers of his day, Valentinus converted to the Christian faith. He claimed that he had received instruction from a man named Theudas, who was allegedly a disciple of the Apostle Paul. It is from Theudas that Valentinus acquired secret knowledge supposedly passed on by Paul to a select handful of the apostle's followers. Valentinus had it all. He was a powerful writer, a great speaker, and a highly intelligent thinker (check out Chapter 9 for a look at the Valentinian Gospel of Truth). Diplomatic and charismatic, he managed to create a movement within the larger Christian Church that extended to the boundaries of the Roman Empire in his own day and that continues to influence people today.

After some initial success in Egypt, Valentinus relocated to Rome sometime before A.D. 140. He became so popular there that when elections were held after the death of Pope Hyginus (in A.D. 143) to decide who would be the next bishop of Rome, Valentinus was nominated and lost by just a few votes. He subsequently broke with the Roman Church and pressed ahead with his school. According to Tertullian, the Roman Church finally *excommunicated* Valentinus.

Word Knowledge

Excommunication is a formal act of excluding someone from participation in the life of the Christian community. The exclusion is an extreme act intended as discipline rather than punishment.

Still, it seems that he stayed in Rome for several years afterward and remained an influential and controversial figure. Only in the fourth century, when the first Christian emperor Constantine began to take a hand in church matters, did excommunications begin to carry the force of law. In the second century, still early in the Christian period, an excommunication from one Christian community carried little weight unless other churches recognized it as valid. It is evident that Valentinus had enough support within the Roman Christian community to continue teaching there well into the time of Pope Anicetus (the same Anicetus who met with Polycarp about the Easter controversy; see Chapter 3), who led the Roman Church from A.D. 155 to 166. Some evidence suggests that he later left for Cyprus and possibly even moved back to Alexandria, and died around A.D. 160.

Beating the System

To the uninitiated, Valentinus's mythology was not very different from the one taught by Basilides. In Chapter 9, we'll look more closely at the system that Valentinus created. For the Valentinians, God was absolutely unknowable and inaccessible by any ordinary means. God is the source of all things. Everything that exists comes from this Divine origin. As with Basilides' teachings, God is surrounded by a series of lesser beings. In Valentinus' system, the last of these beings to come into existence was a feminine spirit named Sophia.

It is Sophia who accidentally caused the creation of the physical world. In doing so, she became trapped and was unable to return to the heavens. God launched a kind of rescue operation. He sent Christ to liberate Sophia. In the process of her own redemption, Sophia planted seeds of wisdom in the hearts of human beings. These "sparks of the divine" only need to be awakened in order to lead people out of this world and into the heavens.

From the Source

Summer Harvest

I see in spirit that all are hung
I know in spirit that all are borne
Flesh hanging from soul
Soul clinging to air
Air hanging from upper atmosphere

Crops rushing forth from the deep
A babe rushing forth from the womb.
—Valentinus, from Hippolytus, *Refutation of All Heresies*

Undercover Christians

A unique aspect of Valentinus's teaching is that he held out hope that ordinary Christians might attain to some kind of gnosis, or secret knowledge. So when he taught, he used those Scriptures that were accepted by the orthodox Christians as authentic. He recognized and offered the same sacraments as the larger Christian community. And as we've seen, he continued to be involved in the leadership of the churches. More than anyone else, Valentinus made it possible for gnostic Christians to remain part of the larger church as long as they did.

Still, secrecy was an important hallmark of Valentinian gnosticism. Valentinus' followers met separately from the rest of the church for instruction. This state of affairs was certainly uncomfortable for orthodox Christians. It took centuries to completely root out all of the Valentinian gnostics in the church.

He and his followers distinguished three classes of people:

♦ **Pneumatic** (spiritual): These are folks who have an innate openness to gnosis. The gnostics saw themselves as part of this group.

- **Psychic** (rational): This group is capable of receiving truth if it is mediated through symbols, doctrines, and good works. Ordinary, orthodox Christians fall into this group.

- **Choic** (fleshly): Those who simply have no interest in spiritual matters, but are completely captive to their passions and appetites. Nearly everyone else ends up in this category.

Marcion

The last person in our gnostic lineup wasn't, strictly speaking, a gnostic. However, Marcion and the controversy he caused are best understood in light of the conflict over gnostic teaching.

Sailor Man

Marcion was born in A.D. 85 with a silver spoon in his mouth. His parents were wealthy citizens of Sinope, a bustling seaport on the coast of the Black Sea. His father may also have been the bishop of the church there. Marcion followed in his father's footsteps and built a large fortune in shipping. That may have been the only thing he had in common with his father. It's possible that his own father threw Marcion out of the church in Sinope. For whatever reason, Marcion moved to Rome in A.D. 140.

Marcion definitely knew how to make a splash. Upon his arrival in Rome, he gave the church a gift of 200,000 *sesterces*. It was a huge sum of money. He may have expected more in return than simple gratitude, however. Rumors began circulating about some of the things that Marcion was teaching. The church investigated and, in A.D. 144, Marcion was expelled from the church. Interestingly, the church returned all 200,000 sesterces.

Word Knowledge

A **sesterce** is one fourth of a denarius, which was a typical day's pay for a laborer in the Roman Empire.

Out with the Old and in with the New

Marcion had one great passion. He simply could not reconcile the God he saw in the Old Testament with the Father of Jesus in the New Testament. The God of Moses was just and orderly, but he was also irritable and violent. He made mistakes and changed his mind. The Father of Jesus, on the other hand, was peaceful and forgiving. He was all-knowing. Marcion concluded that the God of the Jews could not possibly be the same God as the God of Jesus.

Of course, if the God of the Jews didn't send Jesus, Marcion argued, then Jesus could not be the Jewish Messiah. There might very well be a Messiah coming, but that was for the Jews to worry about. It had nothing to do with Jesus.

If the Jewish God created the world, then the world must be corrupt. Marcion picked up on the docetic ideas (see Chapter 2) that were so common where he came from. He argued that Jesus had not been born. Instead, he had appeared fully grown at the age of 30. Since he only *appeared* to have a body, he could not have been crucified. Since Jesus had no body, Marcion and his followers reasoned, the body must be of little spiritual value. In fact, physical matters were an obstruction to genuine spiritual maturity. As a result, Marcion advocated celibacy, an ascetic lifestyle, and a willingness to embrace martyrdom.

The First Church of Marcion

Marcion was deeply angered by the church's ruling against him. He was certain that his teachings reflected genuine Christian truth. So he did what many people with wealth do when they have been turned down by an organization: he started his own. He copied all the structures of Christian worship—the sacraments, clothes, music, and officers—to create his own rival church.

Marcion also set about scrubbing the New Testament of any Jewish elements. He eliminated the Old Testament, of course. He also got rid of all of the gospels except the Gospel of Luke, which he edited rather heavily. That, plus the letters of Paul, also screened for anything Jewish, formed the Bible for Marcion and his followers.

Marcion and the Gnostics

It's hard to overestimate the impact Marcion's split with the Orthodox Church had. To his opponents, Marcion's cut-and-paste work with holy texts was a serious crime, but it spurred the orthodox to create their own canon. The formulation of the

New Testament as we know it today was driven in no small part in response to Marcion. Equally as important, Marcion's rejection of the Jewish roots of Christianity sparked a vigorous defense from the orthodox community. The church would continue to insist on its link with Judaism, and on Jesus' role as the Jewish Messiah. History has to be taken seriously, they said, and this defense served equally well against the gnostic teachers.

Despite the fairly specific nature of Marcion's break with the Orthodox Church, his followers had a tendency to run to gnostic thinking for further inspiration. Eventually, Marcion ceased to be a significant threat in the West. Gnostic thought was too strong, and Marcion's thinking ran too closely beside it to remain distinct for long.

Why the Early Gnostics Matter

Okay, you picked up this book to find out about the Gnostic Gospels. So what's the point to this stroll through history? Well, each of the four men we've discussed in this chapter figure prominently in our understanding of what the Gnostic Gospels say and who they represent.

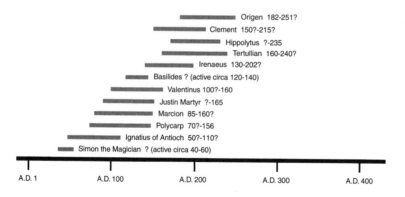

A timeline showing the relationship between the orthodox and gnostic writers in the early church.

Simon the Magician reminds us that the development of Christian gnosticism had its roots firmly planted in first-century Judaism. Gnostic teaching, as it evolved in the second century, continued to carry with it both an *apocalyptic* and *ascetic* character that fit well in Palestine and Syria. Many of the texts that we will examine later in this book are probably of Jewish origin, and were either adapted by gnostic Christians for their own use or adopted without any changes at all.

Word Knowledge

Apocalyptic is derived from the word "apocalypse," which literally means "revelation." It is often used to describe literature that is highly symbolic in character, and that describes spiritual experiences and encounters with angelic and demonic beings.

An **ascetic** lifestyle is characterized by self-denial, especially in regards to sex, and self-control, especially in regard to food and money. Ascetics also sometimes inflict pain on themselves.

If Judaism gave gnosticism its edge, Greek philosophy gave it a center. Basilides keeps us conscious that it was in Alexandria, the home of Hellenistic culture, that gnosticism came into its own. It was from the Greek philosophers that gnostics learned their dualism, the elevation of spirit above matter.

Valentinus is perhaps the most important of this bunch, largely because his system of teaching appears in several of the gnostic documents we'll be looking at in later chapters. More than just his direct influence on works like the Gospel of Truth (see Chapter 9), however, his success at remaining within the local Christian communities is a helpful perspective to keep in mind when we look at the ways that gnostics worshipped (see Chapter 13) and the conversation that took place between orthodox and gnostic Christians (see Chapter 18).

Valentinus and Marcion represent the two directions that gnostics went institutionally. Some remained within the larger Christian community, finding ways to accommodate themselves to its worship and teachings. Others stepped outside altogether, creating their own rival organizations. Although Marcion's church was by far the most successful of these, there were countless handfuls of gnostic Christians who retreated into their own enclaves.

Should I Stay or Should I Go?

The question of whether to leave the church or to remain in the fold was not just an academic question. A glance at Appendix C will show you several organizations of modern-day gnostics who were attempting to build worship communities outside of the mainstream Christian tradition. Meanwhile, large numbers of Christians were grappling with what to do about the new insights that were emerging from the Gnostic Gospels. Depending on your perspective, Marcion is either an inspiring example or a cautionary tale for modern Christians.

Gnosticism itself was beginning to face difficulties of its own. As the third century opened, gnostic groups continued to flourish both inside and outside the dominant church, but the fear that gnostic thinking would completely take over the Christian community was exaggerated. For a variety of reasons the time of the gnostics was coming to a close.

In the next chapter, we'll see how gnosticism melted away—with a little help from the authorities—as the Roman Empire converted to Christianity. In addition, we'll learn the many ways that gnostic thinking continued to survive on the fringes of Western culture, and witness a shocking discovery that completely rewrites the history of gnosticism.

The Least You Need to Know

- Orthodox writers blamed Simon the Magician with the creation of nearly all the gnostic heresies.

- Basilides championed a synthesis of all human knowledge around Jesus Christ as the focal point.

- The Valentinian system was the pinnacle of gnostic thinking in the second century and continues to find resonances today.

- The controversy sparked by Marcion forced the church to reaffirm its historical roots in the Jewish experience and Scriptures.

5

Death and Resurrection

In This Chapter

- ◆ The gnostic creative spark burns out
- ◆ An attempt to revive a gnostic church in medieval Europe meets with violent opposition
- ◆ Slowly, gnostic voices are recovered
- ◆ A pair of Egyptian farmers makes a startling discovery

This chapter will not be exhaustive by any means. It's merely a thumbnail sketch of gnostic thinking from its peak in the second century, through its most famous resurgence in Western culture, and then a leap ahead to the rediscovery of gnostic texts in Egypt in 1945.

As a movement, gnosticism reached its peak in the mid- to late-second century. After that, resistance from the larger Christian community and changes in the development of philosophy robbed the gnostics of much of their innovative energy. Still, the history and development of Christianity was indelibly marked by the gnostic controversy. And gnostic tendencies didn't disappear completely.

The End of the Beginning

The increasing pressure from orthodox writers following Irenaeus' lead in *Against Heresies* began to make life difficult for the small groups of gnostic Christians still trying to stick it out in the churches. With the conversion of Constantine to Christianity, imperial power was brought to bear on independent groups and dissidents within the church. It became harder and harder for gnostics to stay in the mainstream church.

> **Did You Know?** _____
>
> The Mandaeans are the only original gnostic community still in existence. A pre-Christian baptizing sect, they are found today almost exclusively in Iraq (a handful live in Iran) where they number around 15,000 members. During the nineteenth and twentieth centuries, Western scholars began translating Mandaean literature. This treasure trove of Scriptures, prayers, and ritual handbooks has given historians and theologians a fascinating insight into non-Christian forms of gnosticism.

As for the orthodox Christians, although they rejected the essential beliefs of gnosticism, the debate had shaped the kinds of questions that they were asking. Mainstream Christian theology is marked on every level by its encounter with gnosticism. The gnostics forced the orthodox to face issues and extend their thinking into areas that they probably would not have gone otherwise. Many of the major theological controversies in the third, fourth, and fifth centuries can be traced to the ways that orthodox Christians responded to gnostic teachings.

Manichaeism

Before the schools of Valentinus and the churches of Marcion began to fade away, a new player arrived on the scene. Late in the third century, a Persian (Iraqi) named Mani began to attract a large group of followers. He saw himself as the latest in a long line of prophets, which included Jesus, the Buddha, and Zoroaster. Unlike these previous teachers, however, Mani asserted that he had been given a mandate to spread his doctrine everywhere. His was, he claimed, a truly universal faith. The Persians later executed Mani, but his followers continued his work and the Manichean church grew quickly.

Manichaeism embodied the gnostic dualism that regarded the physical world as evil and corrupt. They believed that salvation was a matter not of repentance for sin but of gaining special knowledge. That knowledge is the realization that you are a part of the very nature of God, a fallen piece of divinity entangled in flesh. Those who die without this self-realization are reincarnated. Those who do have it follow a lifestyle of rigorous asceticism in order to let go of anything having to do with the physical world so that they may ascend to the heavens after death.

Mani's teachings spread both to the East and the West. By the ninth century, it had spread as far as China, where Turkic peoples like the Uigher living near the Takli-makan Desert embraced it. It established a tenacious hold in the region, and only the Mongols in the thirteenth century were finally able to overwhelm it. By that time, Mani's claim to be the last and greatest of the prophets had been challenged by the rise and spread of Islam.

In the West, Manichaeism had a more difficult time, though it had some successes. Augustine, the bishop of Hippo and perhaps the single-most influential Christian thinker in the West after Paul, was for a time a Manichee. Though he later rejected that faith, its influence can be seen in his writings and in the theology that he developed. Manichaeism was outlawed in the Roman Empire by the emperor Theodosius I (A.D. 375–395), which tended to curtail interest in it. Still, the presence of the Manichaeans offered a successful and attractive alternative to gnostics who were being systematically driven out of their local churches and defined out of the Christian faith.

Not Your Daddy's Plato

Gnostic Christianity emerged largely as an attempt to make sense of the Jesus story from within the cultural and intellectual assumptions of the Greek and Roman world. Uninformed by the Jewish context within which Jesus of Nazareth had operated and from which his original followers had emerged, Gentile converts to Christianity used the teachings of the Greek philosophers, especially Plato, to flesh out their understanding of Jesus' mission and message. To men like Irenaeus, Tertullian, and Hippolytus, this was the theological equivalent of putting Jesus' head on Plato's body, and they roundly condemned it. Clement and Origen, while far more sympathetic to the attempt, nevertheless argued against the gnostics by using the same philosophical language and ideas that the gnostics used.

The orthodox Christians weren't the only ones who objected to the gnostics' use of Plato to understand Jesus. Plotinus, the creator of Neoplatonism, emerged to champion what he considered to be the pure teachings of Plato, and argued against the Valentinians in particular in a portion of his *Six Enneads*. Plotinus found the gnostics pretentious in their complex mythologies and disagreed with their dualism.

> **Did You Know?**
>
> Both Origen and Plotinus learned Plato's teachings from the same teacher, a fellow named Ammonius Saccas.

The immediate significance of Plotinus's Neoplatonic philosophy was the cover it gave to philosophically inclined Christians. Plotinus reestablished the potential for Christian engagement with Platonic thought without having to buy into the gnostic conviction that the creator of this world was evil.

Medieval Eruptions

Partly through Manichaeism and partly through the continuing influence of Neoplatonism, certain gnostic tendencies continued to crop up from time to time in Europe. Some were more successful than others, but they all threatened the apparent unity of the medieval hierarchical church as both a religious and a political institution. Ultimately, both church and state felt it necessary to eradicate the more successful of these groups through military force and religious courts.

Paulicians

The Paulicians were a sect that sprung up in Armenia in the seventh century. Combining aspects of Manichaeism and Marcionism (see Chapter 4), the Paulicians believed in a pair of Gods, one good and one evil, who were at odds with one another. Because the evil God is the creator of the physical world, the Paulicans believed, any unnecessary involvement with this world is unhealthy.

Late in the seventh century, the Paulicians were involved in a military uprising that was suppressed with some difficulty. They emerged again in the ninth century, managing to survive several attempts to destroy them. Their beliefs spread into the Balkans, where they may have encouraged the rise of the Bogomils.

Bogomils

Named after the priest who founded the movement, the Bogomils emerged in the middle of the tenth century. Their central doctrine was based on the belief that the physical world was the creation of an evil being. They rejected anything having to do with the material world, maintaining a strictly ascetic life. In terms of religious belief, they denied the *Incarnation* and refused use of the *sacraments*.

Word Knowledge

The **Incarnation** is the belief that Jesus Christ was God "in the flesh." The Incarnation asserts the full humanity of Christ as well as his full divinity.

Sacraments are rites believed to be a means of or visible form of grace. The two generally accepted sacraments are the Eucharist and baptism.

The Bogomils came under suspicion in the twelfth century and were systematically suppressed by both church and state. They also spread their teachings during the eleventh and twelfth centuries and were able to link up with similar groups in France.

Cathars

The Cathars, also known as the Albigenses because of the city of Albi where some of them were located, held beliefs similar to what we've already seen in the Paulicians and the Bogomils. They saw the world in dualist terms and rejected any attachment to the material side of things. According to the Cathars, the world was an evil place designed to distract the believer from attending to the life of the spirit.

The Good Men

The Cathars organized themselves sometime around the 1140s, creating an administrative hierarchy, a liturgy, and a system of doctrine. About 1149 the first Cathar bishop established himself in the north of France; a few years later they spread to Albi and into Lombardy. Although they differed on certain points of doctrine, they all agreed that matter was evil. Humanity was not native to this physical existence and must seek to free itself by coming into a renewed connection with God. The Cathars were vegetarians and had strict rules for fasting. Sex was off limits. Theirs was a lifestyle of complete renunciation.

This extreme asceticism tended to restrict the Cathar movement to a handful of particularly committed individuals known as the perfecti or the perfect, who were set apart by a ritual laying on of hands called the consolamentum. It would seem that these kinds of restrictions would have made the Cathars unpopular, or at least kept their numbers down.

Certainly the number of perfecti was never huge. The spread of Cathar teaching and influence, however, came about when the movement created a sort of second-tier member, the credentes, or believers. While the perfecti were to devote themselves to peaceful contemplation and a moral lifestyle, the credentes were less restricted.

A French Renaissance

What kind of conditions existed to allow for a revival of gnosticism? The rise of the Cathars can't be separated from the region in which they flourished. Southern France was blossoming economically and culturally. Several major trade routes ran through the region, bringing both new money and new ideas, but also drawing the greedy eyes of outsiders.

Petty bickering and endless feuds over lands and properties tore the region apart. These conflicts tended to distract the local nobility from policing religious beliefs. Catholic faith had sunk to extraordinary lows, with clergy who were woefully inadequate to the task and a populace that had little if any real knowledge of the gospel message. Neither peasant nor noble thought too highly of the church. The people were ready for an alternative spiritual vision.

The status of women in the Languedoc was high, partly due to the emergence of the troubadours. These romantic poets extolled the virtue of love in a way that created the chivalric adoration of women that we associate now with knights in shining armor. Women could participate in nearly all forms of public life, including owning property and engaging in commerce. Along with these economic benefits came a deeper spiritual autonomy. Ladies in southern France had more freedom to pursue the kind of spirituality championed by the Cathars.

Along with the new poetic sensibility came a linguistic freedom from Latin. The Cathars were able to provide their neighbors with the Scriptures in Occitan, in the local language of the region. Latin was still the official language of faith in the Catholic Church, but the Cathars presented their ideas in the everyday language of the people. Control over language is control over thought. A new language made room for new religious ideas.

A Crusade ... Against Christians?

The emergence of the Cathars constituted the most significant threat to the unity of the church in the Western world between the gnostic controversy and the Protestant reformation. In the twelfth century, life in southern France had reached new heights. The growth of a new movement in that region, as economically and culturally important as it was, was a direct challenge to the Roman Catholic hierarchy.

The Catholic Church tried several means to bring about an end to the Cathar movement. However, the lives of the perfecti were so consistently persuasive, and the lives of the Catholic clergy by and large so scandalous and hypocritical, that support for the Cathars continued. A variety of economic and political factors also combined to make the Cathar more attractive to the local nobility. The Cathars were, if nothing else, cheaper to maintain than the land-hungry Catholic Church.

It was Pope Innocent III, with one of the more ironic names in Western history, who eventually launched a crusade against the south of France and the Cathars. When he came to the papal throne in A.D. 1198, it seemed that Innocent wanted a peaceful resolution. He sent Dominic, the founder of the Dominican Order, into the region to preach and confront the Cathars. Despite Dominic's best efforts, there was simply little reason for anyone to change. Local nobles shielded the Cathars and the bishops resented the pope's meddling in their affairs.

Ratcheting up the fight, Innocent began excommunicating nobles who refused to help. In 1207, he excommunicated the powerful Raymond VI of Toulouse. After a heated meeting with Raymond in 1208, the papal representative Pierre de Castelnau was murdered. Innocent was at the end of his rope. He issued a *papal bull* declaring a crusade in Languedoc, and promising the lands of the "heretics" to those who would fight. Nobles from all over France, eager to expand their holdings into the rich southern region, flooded the place.

Word Knowledge

A **papal bull** is a church pronouncement signed by the Pope himself. The name comes from a ball of lead, called a "bulla," which hung from document by a cord and bore the papal seal. The seal was a sign that the Pope was taking personal responsibility for the contents. Papal bulls were solemn and weighty documents reserved for serious matters.

An army of 10,000 marched on the city of Beziers in the opening months of the war. Under the control of Simon of Montfort, the army was accompanied and spurred on by the Arnaud-Amaury, the head of the Cistercian Order. The city of perhaps 20,000 was virtually depopulated in a savage and merciless massacre, all to root out a few hundred Cathars, but the message was loud and clear. Cities and towns all over the south capitulated rather than face the same fate.

After initial successes, the crusade became a back and forth struggle between papal forces and resistors. The names and faces changed, but the conflict ground on until 1229, when Raymond VII, the son of the first guy, agreed to a deal where he would root out the Cathars in exchange for the lifting of his excommunication. The military conflict gave way to the Inquisition, which appeared for the first time in Western history in the form that most people recognize.

> ### Did You Know? _____
>
> At the siege of Beziers, Simon of Montfort asked the papal legate, the Cistercian abbot Arnold, what to do with the inhabitants of the town when it became apparent that it would be difficult to distinguish faithful Catholics from the Cathar.
>
> In response, Arnold uttered his infamous judgment, "Kill them all. God will know his own." The town's residents, perhaps 20,000 in all, were slaughtered.
>
> This line still exists in our language today as the recognizable "Kill 'em all. Let God sort 'em out."

Moving from town to town, the inquisitors burned hundreds at the stake who refused to rejoin the Catholic Church. Thousands more suffered less severe punishments. The remaining Cathars retreated to their diminishing number of strongholds. Montsegur, the Cathar headquarters and site of their treasure house, fell to the crusaders in 1244, and the Cathars were virtually destroyed. The last execution for Catharism in southern France took place in 1321. Some of the Cathars made it into northern Italy and survived there until the fifteenth century.

A Newer, Friendlier Church

You don't have to be a critic of the Catholic Church to admit that this wasn't Christianity's finest hour. Even Innocent was horrified at the holocaust he had unleashed on Languedoc, and tried to limit the use of the death penalty for heretics, but to no avail. Tens of thousands were slaughtered and hundreds of towns and villages were shattered. One of the most vibrant economies in Europe had been severely damaged, though it would recover. More significantly, one of the truly brilliant cultures of medieval Europe was lost forever.

One of the longest lasting of the responses to the Cathar movement was the creation of the Inquisition. This gnostic-like heresy gave rise to a reaction that lasted far beyond the original problem. Just as the arguments between gnostic and orthodox in the early church had shaped canon and creed, the battle against Catharism put a new tool in the hands of the religious authorities to compel obedience and stifle dissent. It's no accident that the Inquisition was a factor in the eventual split between Protestants and Catholics. The use of force to command religious obedience became a pernicious habit that eventually served as one argument in favor of the separation of church and state.

As for the Cathar movement, it never recovered. Innocent, whose personal life was more akin to the perfecti than not, authorized several new Orders, including the Humiliati and the Dominicans, but especially the Franciscans. These groups of *mendicant* friars were more rigorous and exhibited greater personal integrity than had the regular clergy in Languedoc prior to the crusade. The Cathar's morally upright lives had been a point in their favor with the public, particularly when compared to the lives of the regular clergy. The mendicants met the challenge of restoring the church's reputation head on by adopting lives at least as scrupulous as the perfecti.

Word Knowledge

A **mendicant** is a beggar (from the Latin for "to beg"). The word is used most commonly to refer to mendicant friars, members of certain Roman Catholic religious orders who take vows of poverty and support themselves by work and the generosity of others. Perhaps the best known of these orders are the Franciscans and the Dominicans.

While they no longer exist as a viable movement, the Cathari themselves have gone down into legend. They have starred in numerous conspiracy theories, even figuring in the bestselling *The Da Vinci Code*. Some scholars have argued that Cathar thinking even influenced certain Protestant ideas—Calvinistic beliefs about predestination, for example, or the ascetic outlook of groups like the Shakers and even the Puritans.

New Discoveries

The destruction of the Cathar movement ended the possibility of a revival of gnosticism in Europe as an independent movement. Although gnostic ideas would continue to crop up again and again, provoking mystics and philosophers (and even psychoanalysts like Carl Jung), no actual gnostic movement ever again challenged the ascendancy of orthodox Christianity in the Western world.

Almost 18 centuries from its height, gnostic Christianity appeared to be one of history's dead ends. Apart from the Mandaeans, no living gnostic community was known to exist. Almost no literature penned by gnostics was available to scholars, and nearly all the writings that did exist were written from a Mandaean or Manichaean viewpoint. Works penned by gnostic Christians were all but nonexistent. It seemed that historians would forever be dependent on the writings of people who opposed gnosticism—men like Irenaeus and Clement—for what little they would know about gnostic Christians. Slowly, however, new documents began to come to light. These texts offered new perspectives on the ways that gnostics saw themselves. At first only a few were found, but as the twentieth century dawned, unexpected discoveries awaited.

The Library Grows

A pair of Coptic manuscripts were discovered and brought to England in the eighteenth century. They contained the Pistis Sophia (or "Faith and Wisdom"), the Two Books of Jeu, and some other incomplete texts. These documents gave the first fresh look at gnosticism that scholars had ever possessed.

The Pistis Sophia is a collection of revelation discourses between the resurrected Jesus and several of his male and female disciples. The Books of Jeu also record certain revelations of Jesus. Both works date from the third century. Compared to later discoveries, both books seem derivative and inferior. Still, for a long time they were the best insight into gnosticism that scholars had. But that was soon to change.

> **Word Knowledge**
>
> A **codex** is the first form of the modern book, which superceded the scroll. Essentially an assembly of pages stacked and bound at one end, the codex (the plural is codices) was the preferred form for documents used by Christians, since you can get a whole lot more into a codex than you can on one roll of a scroll, and they are easier to manage.

In 1896, Dr. Carl Reinhardt was browsing through an antiquities shop in Cairo. The shop owner, his name unknown to history, approached Reinhardt with a new acquisition. It was a *codex*, bound in leather, containing a set of manuscripts that proved to be from the fifth century. It had been discovered hidden in a wall, the owner assured Reinhardt. That was an obvious lie. The pages were too well preserved to have been anywhere else but buried in the sand. Reinhardt knew he was onto something unexpected, but how important the find might be he still did not know.

> **Did You Know?**
>
> Around the end of the nineteenth century, a treasure trove of manuscripts and codices was found. The huge cache of abandoned Hebrew Scriptures came to be known as the Cairo Geniza. A geniza is a repository for used manuscripts. This particular geniza was a small room in the wall of a synagogue in Cairo. Reinhardt almost certainly knew about the Cairo discovery, and knew that the manuscript in his hand, in Coptic, could not possibly have come from the "geniza" source. This is one of the reasons Reinhardt knew that he had found something new.

Reinhardt purchased the codex, now known as the Berlin Codex or the Berlin Papyrus. Upon further inspection, he discovered that it contained copies of four previously unknown documents; the Gospel of Mary (which we'll look at in Chapter 7), The Secret Book of John (check out Chapter 13), The Wisdom of Jesus Christ (look to Chapter 18 for that one), and The Act of Peter (which you'll find in Chapter 12).

A burst water pipe at the printers destroyed the first attempt at publishing the find. Two world wars and the death of the scholar responsible for shepherding the project delayed it even further. Finally, in 1955 the first translation was set to print. But before the initial printing of the Berlin Codex saw the light of day, a new discovery was made that would almost completely overshadow it.

Did You Know?

Coptic is the final development of the ancient Egyptian language. Egyptians had three different writing systems. The first, called *hieroglyphics*, was a form of picture writing. You're probably already familiar with it from pictures of the walls of tombs in Egypt. This was a very time-consuming way of writing and one that was difficult to reproduce on papyrus. It was almost entirely used on stone or other permanent mediums.

For writing on papyrus, Egyptians developed another form of writing called *hieratic*. This was a form of cursive writing that was easier to write with a reed pen and ink. It was mostly used for sacred literature. A third writing system, an even more simplified form of hieratic called *demotic*, was developed just for everyday writing. The problem with all of these systems was that they were difficult to learn and awkward to write.

Sometime around the second century A.D., Egyptians began using the Greek alphabet, with some additions from the demotic script, to write out their language. This new form of writing, which came in several dialects, was used primarily by Egyptian Christians and is still the language used by the Coptic Church today.

Nag Hammadi

It reads like something out of the Arabian Nights. In December of 1945, two brothers named Khalifah and Muhammed Ali were traveling along the Nile to a place near the modern city of Nag Hammadi. In the shadow of a jutting cliff, Jabal al-Tarif, they stopped and tethered their camels. Taking shovels, they began probing around the bases of several large boulders, looking for a highly enriched form of soil called sabakh that was commonly used as a kind of fertilizer.

Suddenly, Muhammed's shovel hit something hard with a hollow-sounding thunk. Digging a bit further, he discovered an old clay jar, its lid sealed tight. Muhammad was initially afraid to open the jar, for fear that a jinn, or evil spirit, might be locked up inside. But the possibility that the jar contained gold rather than demons overcame his trepidation, and with one swing of the shovel he shattered the lid.

Gold particles swirled out of the jar, glistening in the sunlight. If Muhammed had a heart-stopping moment of joy, imagining himself to be rich, he was quickly brought up short. The fragments floating in the light were bits of papyrus. The jar contained not gold and jewels but something far more precious. From it, Muhammed pulled several leather-bound books. He took them home and stashed them in his house, where it seems that his mother used some of them to kindle her cooking fire. Historians still cringe at the thought.

A map of Egypt showing the location of Nag Hammadi.

The story of how the library finally made it into the hands of scholars is a long and winding journey. Even more torturous was the path to the publication of the documents themselves, and there's no point in recounting that story here. Certain texts, including the Gospel of Thomas, were published in the 1950s and 1960s. Beginning in 1972, a facsimile edition of the library began to be published, a process that took 12 years to complete. In 1977, the first edition of the Nag Hammadi library in English was published, and the complete library became available to the general public.

Lost Voices

The entire Nag Hammadi library consists of 12 codices, papyrus pages bound together with a leather cover. In addition, eight pages remain from a missing thir-teenth volume. They contain a total of 52 separate documents. Five of those are represented more than once. Six others were already known to scholars. That leaves 40 brand-new works that had never been known before. It was an immense find, on par with the discovery of the Dead Sea Scrolls.

Did You Know? _____

The discovery of the Dead Sea Scrolls in the caves of Qumran by the Dead Sea in Israel is one of the most significant archaeological discoveries of the twentieth cen-tury. The find—more than 800 documents—includes copies of every book in the Hebrew Scriptures except Esther, apocryphal texts, commentaries, and other texts related to the community of Essenes that most scholars believe was responsible for hiding most of the texts.

The story of the discovery has become legend. In 1947, a young Bedouin shepherd boy was searching for one of his lost goats on the northwestern shore of the Dead Sea. He began throwing rocks into nearby caves, hoping to flush out the missing beast. Instead of a dull thud, however, he heard the sound of breaking pottery. When he explored the cave, he found a collection of clay jars filled with ancient scrolls.

Over the next two years, the scrolls gradually made there way into the hands of schol-ars. Eventually, scholars discovered the source of these amazing new texts and the recovery began in earnest. A search of nearby caves yielded even more scrolls.

The biblical texts discovered among the Dead Sea Scrolls are 1,000 years older than any we had possessed before.

All of the works included in the Nag Hammadi library had originally been written in Greek and were then translated into Coptic. The translations vary in their skill and readability, and in their accuracy at reproducing the meaning of the original work.

As we review some of the less readable translations, we'll see just how this can complicate the task of interpreting what they are saying.

Inside, the leather covers were stiffened by the use of old pieces of papyrus—letters, receipts, and things like that—in order to get a kind of hardback feel to the book. When these bits of writing were examined, some of them contained dates that help to determine when the books were put together. Some of the dates discovered indicated that at least some of the books could not have been assembled prior to A.D. 340.

Very near to the site where the buried library was discovered lie the remains of Chenoboskia, which was one of the monasteries founded by Pachomius and may be the place where at least some of the books were compiled. In A.D. 367, the Bishop of Alexandria, a very formidable man named Athanasius, wrote an Easter letter to the various monasteries under his jurisdiction that included a command to rid themselves of certain heretical texts. The fact that the Nag Hammadi library was sealed into a jar and buried indicates that the owners probably wanted to preserve the texts, perhaps until things eased up a bit and they could return to collect the books. Obviously, they never did.

Did You Know?

Pachomius (A.D. 290–346) was an Egyptian soldier who retired from military life and retreated into the deserts of Egypt to live out a monastic existence. His military background enabled him to organize other monks, who were used to living pretty much on their own, into a kind of loose, communal structure. While another famous Egyptian monk, Antony, is credited for making monastic life popular, it was Pachomius who created the first forms of what we today call monasteries. By the time he died, he had established 11 such monasteries, with more than 7,000 monks and nuns.

The Least You Need to Know

♦ The original burst of gnostic creativity eventually dissolved away, but not before leaving its mark on orthodox Christianity.

♦ In the Middle Ages the Cathar movement attracted a large following in southern France with revived gnostic ideas, but the Roman Catholic Church crushed it.

◆ Manuscripts slowly brought to light over the past two centuries have kept gnostic ideas from disappearing completely.

◆ Discoveries of significant ancient gnostic manuscripts at Nag Hammadi, in Egypt, have led to a fuller understanding of the whole Christian tradition.

Part 2

The Gnostic Gospels

The Nag Hammadi find, combined with the other texts discovered in the past century, has been a treasure trove of heretofore unknown gnostic literature. The lion's share of the attention, however, has focused on only a handful of these documents. Five in particular—the Gospels of Thomas, of Mary, of Philip, of Truth, and of the Egyptians—have fascinated both scholars and the general public.

In Part 2, we'll examine each of these so-called Gnostic Gospels in turn. We'll look at the backgrounds and traditions that produced them and what, if anything, they have to tell us about the earliest days of the Christian religion and the agonizing process that defined its core convictions. So without further ado, we give you the Gnostic Gospels.

Chapter 6

The Gospel of Thomas

In This Chapter

- ◆ A new gospel is discovered
- ◆ Identifying Thomas
- ◆ Thomas's teachings
- ◆ The not-so-gnostic nature of Thomas

Of all the documents to come out the Nag Hammadi discovery, no other has caused the kind of controversy, or provoked the kind of questions, that the Gospel of Thomas has. This text has become a battleground in the war over how to define the teachings of Jesus and the history of the early church, not to mention theories about the development of the New Testament. It is unquestionably the most important find in the entire Nag Hammadi library.

The Sayings of Jesus

There's almost nothing about the Gospel of Thomas that hasn't been hotly, even bitterly, contested. To explain why this newly discovered document has generated such fierce passions, we have to talk a little bit about how specialists explain the process by which we got the New Testament gospels.

Have you ever wondered why Matthew, Mark, and Luke have so much in common (especially when compared to John)? Generally speaking, New Testament scholars have argued that the gospels according to Matthew and Luke were dependent to some extent on Mark. Fully 94 percent of Mark's gospel finds a parallel in Matthew, while Luke uses 88 percent of Mark. Although it is no longer as dominant as just a few decades ago, this *two-source hypothesis* continues to be the most widely held explanation for how we get the so-called *Synoptic* gospels—Matthew, Mark, and Luke. It explains not only the parallels in the wording of many of the stories but also the similarity in the sequence of events described by each gospel.

Word Knowledge

The **two-source hypothesis** is the theory that the Gospels of Matthew and Luke depend for most of their content on two sources, the Gospel of Mark and another, unknown source that is usually referred to as Q.

The **Synoptic** gospels are Matthew, Mark, and Luke, so named because they can be viewed side-by-side (from the Greek words syn, "together" and opsis, "view"). These three gospel accounts are very similar, and thus offer parallel views of Jesus' ministry, literally giving a synopsis of his life.

That doesn't explain everything, though. There are still points where Matthew and Luke both have a saying or story that doesn't appear in Mark. Somehow, Matthew and Luke are drawing on a source other than Mark for this other material that they have in common. Scholars refer to this other source (or sources) as Q, coming from the German word "quelle" meaning "source." Although Q could be one of several possible combinations of written and oral sources, it is typically portrayed as a single written source.

Q Who?

Efforts have been made to isolate this alleged Q material from Matthew and Luke. What we're left with is a collection primarily of sayings along with a handful of stories. Endless books have been written about Q, some scholarly but many filled with wild speculations. Whatever the circumstantial evidence for the existence of Q, it is still just a supposition. No such document has ever been found. With the exception of an early Christian writer named Papias (on which few modern scholars would depend), no reference to a "sayings" document exists in early Christian literature. If a collection of Jesus' sayings like Q was such an important part of the earliest Christian body of literature, it does seem odd that it is never mentioned. We have to be careful about arguing from silence, of course. As the Nag Hammadi find demonstrated, one turn of the shovel can produce evidence that totally explodes our current understanding of history.

The argument put forth by some biblical experts is that the gospel literature evolved from a collection of oral stories into written collections of sayings and stories, then into dialogues incorporating the sayings material, and, finally, into full fledged gospels that include a storyline or narrative. At each stage of this evolution, the newly developed form supercedes the previous one. You don't still need a collection of sayings if you have a dialogue, and a dialogue isn't nearly as good as an engaging story. So if you were to find a copy of a sayings collection, you could be pretty sure that it is much older, and therefore potentially more accurate, than a dialogue or a gospel.

Say It Ain't So

Now you can start to see the excitement caused by the Gospel of Thomas. Here, for the first time, is what might be a sayings collection. It's like finding a crucial missing link in a fossil record. Since Thomas was first published, a new generation of scholars like Elaine Pagels, Marvin Meyer, and Stephen Patterson have championed it as a very early source for the teachings of Jesus, one that is independent of the Synoptic gospels. Because of where they think it fits in the evolutionary process we just described, they have consistently maintained a very early date for Thomas, certainly before the end of the first century.

Critics, who constitute the majority of specialists in this field, don't find the idea convincing that sayings collections are necessarily earlier than narrative-style gospels. They point to Paul's letters in the New Testament, all of which are earlier than the gospel accounts, which routinely focus not on the teachings or sayings of Jesus but on his death and resurrection. In other words, at least in the Pauline camp of the early church, there was a focus right from the start on a story rather than on sayings.

There is evidence, these scholars say, that Thomas is dependent not only on the Synoptics but on other New Testament documents such as the letters of Paul and the Gospel of John. They suggest that it is far easier to believe that Thomas had access to and drew on all of these different sources rather than supposing that they all drew on Thomas. Consequently, most scholars are more comfortable dating Thomas sometime early in the second century, perhaps around A.D. 140. The question of a date for

Thomas is very complex. Many scholars who argue for a late date will concede that parts of Thomas may be early enough to predate the New Testament gospels, while those who argue for an early date accept the notion that several different editors have reshaped, added to, and taken away from the original text of the Gospel of Thomas. At this point in time, there simply isn't enough evidence to settle the case one way or another.

The Text

The Gospel of Thomas appears in *Codex II,2* and, like all of the other Nag Hammadi texts, is written in Coptic. Also, like all the other texts, this Coptic version is a translation from a Greek original. Thomas consists of a short preamble followed by a series of sayings, most of which begin with the simple phrase, "Jesus said …" Scholars have routinely divided Thomas up into 114 separate sayings.

Word Knowledge

Throughout this book, we tell you where in the Nag Hammadi library you can find the texts we discuss. Each text is listed by the number of the codex (numbers are in Roman numerals) that it comes from, and its place within that codex. So, for example, the Gospel of Thomas is found in **Codex II,2,** which means that it is the second document in the second codex.

Prior to the discovery at Nag Hammadi, three fragments of Thomas had been discovered in Egypt, but they couldn't be identified until the entire text turned up in 1945. Although the Coptic version probably comes from the fourth century, the earliest of the fragments has been tentatively dated to sometime no later than the end of the second century.

There are some interesting differences between the Greek passages that appear in the fragments and the Coptic version, which suggest that Thomas was a pretty fluid text. That raises a lot of questions about the development of Thomas. Just how distinct is this one version that we now possess? What did other versions of Thomas look like, and how much closer are they to the original?

Most scholars tend to place the origins of the Gospel of Thomas in eastern Syria, largely because it was only in Syria that the apostle Thomas was known by the name

"Judas Thomas," the name that appears in the opening line. The Gospel also has elements that fit well in early Syrian Christianity.

Thomas the Twin

The Gospel of Thomas begins with the opening sentence: "These are the secret sayings that the living Jesus spoke and Didymos Judas Thomas recorded." Who is this Didymos Judas Thomas, and what connection did he have with Jesus?

The Gospels of Matthew, Mark, and Luke all mention a Thomas, who is listed as one of the 12 apostles. In each of their lists, he appears in the middle, which may indicate that to them he didn't have a great deal of priority. Other than his name, little else is known of Thomas from the first three gospels.

Did You Know?

Rather than an administrative team, the Twelve represent a core of authorized witnesses to the Jesus message. In the predominantly oral culture of the Mediterranean world, the importance of accurate storytelling was key. The criteria that Peter lays out in the opening chapter of the Acts of the Apostles, as the followers of Jesus gather together to find a replacement for Judas, is instructive. The new apostle must be someone who has been a hearer and follower of Jesus from the time that he worked with John the Baptist until his death and resurrection. In other words, to be an authorized witness, a person has to have been there for the whole show. As the Twelve spread out from Jerusalem to take the "good news," or gospel of Jesus, to other regions, their hearers could be assured that they were getting the real deal.

Consequently, it made sense for later writers to pen their works under the name of one of these original hearers of Christ. The name would lend authority to the work as the product of an eyewitness account.

It is from the Gospel of John that we gain the best New Testament picture of the man called Thomas. In Aramaic, the day-by-day language spoken by Jesus and his followers in Palestine, "Thomas" means "the twin." In John, Thomas is frequently referred to as "Thomas, also called 'Didymos,'" a funny little phrase since Didymos means the same in Greek as Thomas means in Aramaic, namely, "the twin." So we get this odd effect where John essentially calls him "The Twin, also called 'The Twin.'" One thing you have to say about Jesus' followers, they were consistent.

Did You Know?

A lot of speculation has surrounded Thomas's name. Whose twin was he? Was he anybody's twin, or was this just another silly nickname, like calling a tall man "Shorty" or a large man "Tiny"? A close reading of the gospels reveals that Jesus was fond of giving out nicknames to his followers. Simon got the name Peter (which means "Stone," kind of like calling a guy "Rocky"). James and John Zebedee got tagged with the name "Boanerges," meaning "Sons of Thunder." (Poor Mrs. Zebedee. Can you imagine what those two were like as little boys if they're still that feisty as adults?) So "The Twin" could just have been another of Jesus' pet names for a member of his entourage.

Some have suggested that there's more to it than that. A third-century book called The Acts of Thomas, which we'll look at more closely in just a moment, contains a tradition that Thomas's actual name was Jude or Judas, and that he was one of the brothers of Jesus listed in Matthew 13:55. Furthermore, this Jude was actually the twin brother of Jesus himself! Scholars are divided on whether this "twinness" is intended to speak of a spiritual resemblance or a physical similarity, but in either case, on account of his closeness to Jesus, certain groups in the early church viewed Thomas as a significant authority.

Doubting Thomas

John's gospel relates three stories about Thomas. The first occurred in John 11. Jesus had been informed that his good friend Lazarus was deathly ill. The young man's sisters, Martha and Mary, had sent word to Jesus in hopes that he would come to Bethany and heal Lazarus. Bethany, however, was very near to Jerusalem, where Jesus' enemies were waiting for any excuse to pounce. Jesus waited for two days, and then told his apostles that it was time to go, but given the dangerous climate, it must have seemed like a suicide mission. It was Thomas, John tells us, who turned to the others and (somewhat glumly, it sounds) said to them, "Let's go with him, so that we can die with him." In this first encounter, Thomas appeared fiercely loyal but with not the sunniest disposition.

We see Thomas a second time in John's gospel at the Last Supper. Jesus was engaged in a last dialogue with his closest followers before the events of his coming execution began to unfold. In one exchange, Thomas elicited one of the most well-known of all the passages in John's gospel. Jesus told them, "You know the place where I am going." Thomas asked in response, "Lord, we don't know where you are going, so how can we know the way?" Jesus' famous reply was this: "I am the way and the truth and the life. No one comes to the Father except through me." (This whole exchange takes place in John 14:4–6).

Still, it is the third appearance of Thomas in the Gospel of John that gave him the title by which most folks know him: Doubting Thomas. Jesus had risen from the dead and had appeared to several of his followers. However, John tells us, Thomas was not with them when that happened. When the others told him that they had seen Jesus alive and well, Thomas was (understandably) skeptical. He insisted that he would not believe until he touched the scars of the nails on Jesus' body. A few days later, Thomas got his chance. Jesus appeared to his disciples, including Thomas this time, and exposed his wounds for Thomas to see and feel. Thomas, overcome by the moment, exclaimed, "My Lord and my God!"

John's gospel is the source of almost all of our knowledge about Thomas in the New Testament. His final appearance is found in the Acts of the Apostles, where he is listed among those who were in the upper room in Jerusalem. Presumably he was present on the feast of Pentecost and was therefore a recipient of the Holy Spirit, for the Acts speaks of Peter standing up "with the Eleven" (Acts 2:14). After that, like almost all of the apostles, he fades into history.

Go East, Young Man!

That's all we get from the New Testament, but it isn't the end of Thomas's story. For the rest, we have to sort through the tangled but insistent traditions in the early church, which speak of Thomas as a missionary to the Eastern part of the world. When we travel east of Palestine, into Syria and Persia (modern-day Iraq) and even India, we do indeed find claims to the effect that Thomas brought Christianity to these regions. Let's see if we can follow the tracks of Thomas's journey, at least as later Christians imagined it.

The Christian faith made its way into western Syria very early in the church's history. According to the Bible, there was a Christian presence in Damascus, which prompted the famous visit by the apostle Paul that resulted in his conversion from a persecutor of the Christians to one of their greatest spokesmen. It was in the Syrian city of Antioch where followers of Jesus "were first called Christians" (Acts 11:26). Antioch continued to serve as a base of operations for both Peter and Paul throughout most of their lives. Some scholars have suggested that Matthew's gospel was composed in Antioch, as well. We can see the strength of Antioch's Christian community reflected in its third bishop, Ignatius (see Chapter 3).

Edessa and Nisibis.

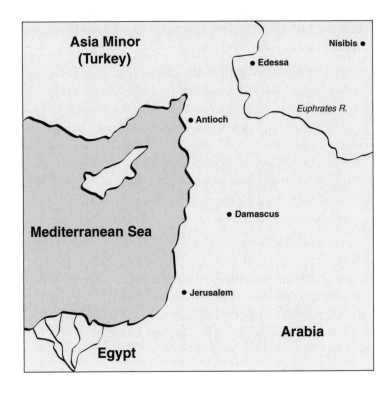

However, no New Testament figure is associated in the Bible with the spread of Christianity to eastern Syria. Acts 2:9 lists "Parthians and Medes and Elamites, and residents of Mesopotamia" as being among those who heard the apostolic message at Pentecost, but if these original hearers were the ones to carry Christianity to eastern Syria, nothing further is known of them. Certainly the Apostle Paul, a student of the Rabbi Gamaliel, would have been aware of the Jewish presence in Persia. If he was, however, he seems not to have considered it a priority to extend his evangelistic efforts in that direction.

As recently as the beginning of the twentieth century, the discovery of the Odes of Solomon, probably the oldest Christian hymnal in existence, gave new evidence of the presence of a form of Christianity in eastern Syria possibly as early as the end of the first century but certainly no later than the middle of the second century. There is nothing distinctly gnostic about the Odes.

One of the earliest-known references to Christianity in eastern Syria exists in the form of an inscription. A bishop named Abercius Marcellus composed his own epitaph, which is thought to date about A.D. 192. In it he describes his travels through eastern Syria, explicitly mentioning the city of Nisibis, and commenting on the fact that "everywhere I had brethren." Nisibis came under the protection of Rome after a war with Parthia lasting from A.D. 162 to 167; thus the window of Marcellus's travels, and the time frame for this first mention of the existence of Christian communities in eastern Syria, lay somewhere between 167 and 192.

Another early reference to Christianity in eastern Syria may be found in the Chronicle of Edessa, an anonymous work dating to around A.D. 540, which records that in A.D. 201 a serious flood inundated the city. The Chronicle mentions in passing that the flood destroyed "the Christian Church." So Christians had arrived in Edessa prior to A.D. 201 and were successful enough to have a specific meeting place that bore mentioning in a register of local events.

Tracking Thomas

The written tradition of Thomas's travels through the region begins with a third-century work called The Acts of Thomas. The Acts demonstrate that in Syria, Thomas was known as "Judas Thomas the Twin," and that he was thought to be the twin brother of Jesus. At one point in The Acts, a married couple actually mistook Jesus for Thomas because they looked alike.

In The Acts, Thomas was commissioned by Christ to go to India with the gospel. Jesus actually approached an envoy of King Gundaphar (ruler of a part of India in the first century) and arranged for the reluctant Thomas to be sold into slavery in order to get him on the boat. Thomas got the hint and headed east to fulfill his mission.

Along the way, Thomas stopped in Andropolis where the king was celebrating his daughter's marriage. The erstwhile apostle found himself attending the wedding, where he ended up causing quite a scene. Thomas arranged for the bride and the bridegroom to meet Jesus, who persuaded the two of them to forego having sexual relations. Instead, they committed to remain celibate. The king, who must really have wanted to be a granddad in the worst way, ordered Thomas arrested. But by that time, Thomas had already sailed on toward his final destination. This event established an oft-repeated theme in The Acts of Thomas: the superiority of celibacy as a spiritual state.

The story follows Thomas back to Gundaphar's kingdom, where the apostle continued to make a nuisance of himself by promising to build the king a wonderful palace and then spending all of the construction funds on the poor. When called to task, Thomas claimed that he used the money to build the king a palace in heaven built out of good works. That wasn't very convincing to Gundaphar until his own very skeptical brother had a vision in which he saw the palace that was awaiting the king in heaven.

The Acts continue to chronicle Thomas's miracles and his teachings. He traveled into eastern India, according to the tradition, where he began convincing some prominent women, including the queen, to give up their husbands and convert to Christianity. The king was a bit put out by it all, and had Thomas arrested and executed. Thomas's remains were later transferred from India to Edessa in eastern Syria, where fourth-century pilgrims described seeing them.

From the Source

Selections from the Hymn of the Pearl in The Acts of Thomas

The Acts of Thomas are filled with gnostic thinking. One of the most-famous passages is the very lengthy Hymn of the Pearl, which Thomas sang while in jail at one point. In it, a young man, a son of the king, left his home on a journey to find and acquire a pearl guarded by a fierce dragon. He was promised that he would rule beside his parents and his elder brother when he returned. Unfortunately, while on his trip, he got in with the wrong crowd and forgot who he was and what he was doing. A letter sent from his parents finally woke him up. He got the pearl and made his way home, where he was greeted with great joy. The hymn is a gnostic account of the state of humanity, that we are forgetful and far from our true home. One memorable passage relates well to the gnostic experience of awakening to a new relationship with God:

> But all this things that befell me
> my parents perceived, and were grieved for me …
> And they wove a plan on my behalf,
> that I might not be left in Egypt;
> and they wrote to me a letter,
> and every noble signed his name to it:
> "From thy father, the king of kings,
> and thy mother, the mistress of the East,
> and from thy brother, our second (in authority),
> to thee our son, who art in Egypt, greeting!
> Call to mind that thou art a son of kings!
> See the slavery,—whom thou servest!
> Remember the pearl,
> for which thou was sent to Egypt!
> Think of thy robe,
> and remember thy splendid toga, …

It (the letter) flew in the likeness of an eagle,
the king of all birds;
it flew and alight beside me,
and became all speech.
At its voice and the sound of its rustling,
I started and arose from my sleep.
I took it up and kissed it,
and I began, read it;
and according to what was traced on my heart
were the words of my letter.
I remembered that I was a son of royal parents, and my noble birth asserted itself ...
and I wrapped myself wholly in my toga
of brilliant hues.
I clothed myself with it, and went up to the
gate of salutation and prostration;
I bowed my head and worshipped the majesty
of my father who sent me,—
for I had done his commandments,
and he, too, had done what he promised ...
The hymn of Judas Thomas the Apostle, which he
spoke in prison, is ended.

We end our attempt to sleuth out Thomas by looking at the story of Addai. It's found in a book known as *The Doctrine of Addai* (the story is also found in Eusebius' fourth-century work *Ecclesiastical History*, where Addai is named Thaddeus). Prior to his crucifixion, the story tells us, Jesus received a letter from King Abgar of Edessa, the capital of the kingdom of Oshroene in eastern Syria, who invited Jesus to come to Edessa and share Abgar's kingdom. Jesus politely refused, but promised to send one of his disciples at a later date. According to both sources, Addai was sent by Thomas to keep this promise. After demonstrating healing powers, Addai was able to convert the king and numbers of people in Edessa to the new faith.

For a variety of reasons, it seems unlikely that Addai, if he actually existed, was a contemporary of Christ. Those scholars who do see a germ of truth beneath the obvious forgeries and difficulties in dating events tend to place Addai's arrival sometime in the late second century. It is intriguing, however, that the church in Edessa was willing to look to a lesser figure like Addai as its founder when it could have claimed Thomas instead. That they did suggests that the tradition of Thomas's travels to India were very strong in Edessa.

Eastern Syria played host to a number of early Christian movements and ideas that were rejected in the Western church. Toward the end of the second century, the teachings of Marcion became very popular in the region, so much so that Syrian writers would continue to combat its effects well into the fourth century (see Chapter 4). Another popular figure in eastern Syria, Bar-Daisan, is known to have been a Valentinian at one point. He wrote songs to communicate his thinking to the masses, and they were so effective that the orthodox Ephrem the Syrian later followed in his footsteps as a songwriter in part to combat Bar-Daisan's influence. What is clear is that, from a very early date, gnostic thinking had a strong presence in eastern Syria, right about the time that the current version of the Gospel of Thomas was being produced.

The Living Jesus

While determining a date for the Gospel of Thomas is very important, that doesn't alter the fact that we've got a text to look at. Whether it genuinely reflects an early tradition about the teachings of Jesus or was put together later to back up gnostic thinking, the Gospel of Thomas is trying to say something. What is its message?

As we've already seen, the Gospel of Thomas claims to be "the secret words of the living Jesus." Immediately following these words in the gospel is a promise: "And he said, 'Whoever discovers the interpretation of these sayings will not taste death.'" Jesus is presented as a teacher, one who initiates his follower into a new and higher realm of experience. Understanding and incorporating the teacher's words at the deepest level of a person's being is what brings spiritual perfection.

Now we may see why the Gospel of Thomas continued to be valuable to some gnostic Christians despite its lack of narrative. What's the point of telling a story about Jesus when Jesus himself isn't really the point? What matters are not Jesus' actions (his death on the cross, for example, which never appears in Thomas) or even the context of any particular saying. The sayings themselves are the point.

From the Source

Jesus said, "Whoever drinks from my mouth will become like me; I myself shall become that person, and the hidden things will be revealed to that person."
—The Gospel of Thomas, Saying 108

It's interesting that this sayings collection should be named for "The Twin," since becoming like Jesus is in a sense the goal behind the teaching. The teacher seeks to reproduce himself in the follower. In a way, the Gospel of Thomas sets out to make a "Thomas" out of each of its readers. The living Jesus, accessible to the follower through his sayings, becomes the model for the follower's own self-understanding.

Saying 2 is often read as a summation of the process by which this transformation takes place. "Jesus said, 'Let one who seeks not stop seeking until one finds. When one finds, one will be troubled. When one is troubled, one will marvel and will rule over all.'" The saying presents a kind of a trajectory for spiritual maturity that follows this path: seeking, finding, being troubled, marveling, and ruling. One of the Greek fragments of the Gospel of Thomas adds "resting" as the final stage.

This pattern presents a picture of a follower of Jesus as someone for whom the quest for self-identity becomes a full-time occupation. Courage is necessary to take this path, because what is discovered is often painful and usually disturbing, but for those who stick to it and refuse to back off, the end result is a self-mastery that leads to interior peace.

Back to the Garden

There are a lot of ways of oversimplifying the differences between gnostic and orthodox Christian views of the world. Here's one more: generally speaking, mainstream Christians look forward; gnostics look back. Orthodox Christians see the world moving toward a new goal. Our original state of being is no longer satisfactory. We're not just trying to get back to the Garden of Eden, so to speak. Sin has entered the human experience, bringing death with it. Christ has come and been crucified. From now on, and into eternity, at the heart of the Divine is a human being. And that human being will forever bear scars. There is no going back. The only way is the way forward, toward a new existence that is more glorious than the beginning.

From the Source

The followers said to Jesus, "Tell us how our end will be."

Jesus said, "Have you discovered the beginning, then so that you are seeking the end? For where the beginning is, the end will be. Fortunate is one who stands at the beginning: That one will know the end and will not taste death."

—The Gospel of Thomas, Saying 18

Gnostics, on the other hand, are eager to get back to the Garden at all costs. That is, if by Garden we mean our original state of perfect rest in the Pleroma. Our physical existence is essentially meaningless in the eternal state of things. Nothing that happens to our fleshly bodies is going to be a part of our beings when we finally return home to the presence of the Divine.

Yes, there are exceptions to these descriptions of the orthodox and gnostic worldviews. The goal here is not to lay down a permanent and detailed way of categorizing the differences between Christians in the second century. There were certainly gnostics who took the body seriously in some respects, and there were (and are) orthodox Christians whose idea of the future life looks remarkably like a gnostic's dream world.

Split Personalities

Several of the sayings in Thomas seem to reflect the gnostic desire to return to the beginning, and to end the current separation that dogs humankind. This separation, and the desire for its end, is sometimes expressed in gendered language. "Jesus said to them, 'When you make the two into one, and when you make the inner like the outer and the outer like the inner, and the upper like the lower, and when you make male and female into a single one, so that the male will not be male nor the female be female … then you will enter the kingdom.'" (Saying 22). Gnostics, because of their ideas about how the physical world came to exist, felt the need to transcend divisions, particularly the division between the sexes, and return to a more primitive and simple state of being.

Sexual Healing

Part of this desire to transcend our gendered identities may rest on the common belief that Adam, the first human being, was originally androgynous. In other words, he was a unified being, neither male nor female. The creation of Eve, then, involved the separating of the first human being into two sexes, male and female. This belief was held not only by most gnostics, but also by many of the early orthodox Christian writers, as well.

For the gnostics, however, the solution wasn't just a physical reunion. Spiritual healing needed to take place, and the body needed to be transcended. The gnostics weren't concerned about physical gender but about the restoration of the spirit. This appears in what to some is a disturbing saying at the end of Thomas:

> Simon Peter said to them, "Mary should leave us, for females are not worthy of life."

Jesus said, "Look, I shall guide her to make her male, so that she too may become a living spirit resembling you males. For every female who makes herself male will enter heaven's kingdom." (Saying 114)

(If you read much gnostic literature, you will quickly get used to seeing Peter and Mary Magdalene at odds. We'll definitely see that in the next chapter when we look at the Gospel of Mary.)

Ancient writers and thinkers were fascinated by the idea of women becoming men. Men didn't understand women any better back then than they do now, apparently. Explaining the gender differences could be a tricky matter, given the near-universal assumption that being male was superior. The differences between males and females lay in large part behind the idea that males gave form and shape to, for instance, a child. Without the male, the result is weak and easily dominated.

The idea that Mary must become male to enter the kingdom of heaven implies that the male has a spiritual edge, a strength and power that the female lacks. A literal reading is obviously difficult to swallow, so there have been attempts to soften it by seeing Mary in this saying as a model for all human beings. In other words, being feminine spiritually is not tied to a person's gender. Men can be feminine in spirit, too. In fact, we'll see that this concern for making the female male crops up all over the place in gnostic writings. Sometimes, as here in Thomas, it sounds very literal. In other cases, it's pretty obvious that its meant to be understood figuratively. Whether we have to take Thomas literally here or not is still a matter of debate.

The Already Kingdom

New Testament scholars will sometimes refer to the "already but not yet" nature of the kingdom of God. In other words, primarily in the Apostle Paul's writings, the fulfillment of God's purposes in and for the world are yet to take full effect, but certain aspects of that fulfillment can already be seen at work in the present moment. The reality of God's presence is here now, yet not fully.

From that perspective, Thomas is definitely an "already" kingdom document. If there is anything that the Jesus in the Gospel of Thomas

> **From the Source**
>
> His followers said to him, "When will the rest for the dead take place, and when will the new world come?"
>
> He said to them, "What you look for has come, but you do not know it."
>
> —The Gospel of Thomas, Saying 51

has no patience for, it's the idea that we should all be waiting around for his return from heaven. There is no Second Coming in Thomas, no anticipated return, no final judgment or lake of fire, and the only ones who will be left behind are those who don't know themselves.

Instead, the sayings in Thomas paint a picture of a Divine presence fully engaged in the world. Nothing is left to accomplish. The new world is already here. Resurrection is already taking place. You just have to open your eyes and see it.

But Is It Gnostic?

The funniest thing about the Gospel of Thomas is that when we really look at what it contains, it's hard to call it "gnostic" without redefining what we mean by that word. It certainly bears little immediate resemblance to the kinds of gnostic texts we'll be looking at in the rest of this book. There are no aeons, pleromas, or demiurges. The mythology that we will see in other Nag Hammadi documents just isn't there.

Of course, gnostic thinking evolved just like orthodox thinking. They each grew and were clarified by time, experience, and conflict. So we can't rule out the possibility that Thomas embodied very early, incipient forms of ideas that later influenced what we would more comfortably refer to as gnosticism. That the New Testament writers were already encountering something not unlike gnostic thinking in the first century should keep us from being too certain.

On the other hand, there are several sayings that look like they have been edited to accentuate their gnostic leanings. And it's possible that gnostic editors at some point in Thomas's history have added additional sayings that reflect their concerns. We won't really be able to determine that until and unless somebody finds another copy of the Gospel of Thomas. We should be so lucky.

The Least You Need to Know

- ◆ The Gospel of Thomas is one of most significant discoveries in the twentieth century.

- ◆ Thomas is both a biblical and a legendary figure, but his history has some value, too.

- True self-knowledge is about transcending the divisions in our own human nature.

- According to the Gospel of Thomas, the kingdom isn't coming. Instead, it's already here.

- The version of Thomas that we possess shows some gnostic concerns but probably isn't gnostic in origin.

Chapter 7

The Gospel of Mary

In This Chapter

- ◆ Looking for the real Mary Magdalene
- ◆ Making sense of an incomplete document
- ◆ Listening to Mary's vision
- ◆ What the Gospel of Mary has to say about the role of women in the church

Though not a part of the Nag Hammadi library, the Gospel of Mary has ignited almost as much attention and speculation as has the Gospel of Thomas. The publication of this relatively short text has single-handedly sparked a reevaluation of a woman whose importance has rested in large measure on how she has been used as a symbol by both the winners and the losers in the struggle to define Christianity.

Preacher or Prostitute?

The renewed interest in Mary Magdalene has ignited the imagination of Christians and non-Christians alike in recent years. While she figures prominently in at least one of the gospels in the New Testament and has appeared repeatedly in Christian art and teaching, our perception of Mary has largely been one-dimensional.

To understand the book written under her name, we're going to have to peel back the layers that time and tradition have painted over Mary's image. Once we get a better look at her and at what she came to represent, we'll be in a better position to evaluate her gospel.

A Sista' from Galilee

The earliest documents in the New Testament, namely the letters of the Apostle Paul, contain no reference to Mary Magdalene. In fact, Paul's list of those who had been witnesses to the resurrection given in 1 Corinthians 15 made no mention whatsoever of any of the women who went to the tomb that Easter morning. Paul mentioned that he was passing on the tradition that he received, which is a reference to the core story or "Passion narrative" that the early Christians told as the central focus on their evangelistic activities. Evidently, the stories about the women at the tomb were not part of that narrative, and that may explain why the gospels are not in agreement over precisely which women were present that day (though the differences are more apparent than real).

From the Source

For what I received I passed on to you as of first importance: that Christ died for our sins according to the Scriptures, that he was buried, that he was raised on the third day according to the Scriptures, and that he appeared to Peter, and then to the Twelve. After that, he appeared to more than 500 of the brothers at the same time, most of whom are still living, though some have fallen asleep. Then he appeared to James, then to all the apostles, and last of all he appeared to me also, as to one abnormally born.

—1 Corinthians 15:2–8

It isn't until we get to the gospels themselves that we finally get a mention of Mary Magdalene. Both Matthew (27:55–56) and Mark (15:40–41) mention Mary among a group of other women present at the crucifixion. Both writers also tell us that these women were from Galilee, Jesus' home region, where they had served him in some capacity and had traveled to Jerusalem as part of his entourage. Both writers take pains to mention (Matt. 27:61 and Mk. 15:47) that Mary Magdalene was one of at least two women present when Jesus was laid in the tomb, an important factor because it showed that they knew where he was buried.

All three of the Synoptic gospels (the Gospels of Matthew, Mark, and Luke; see Chapter 6) relate that on Sunday morning following the crucifixion, a group of women went to the tomb. The composition of the group differs slightly from one gospel to another, but always includes Mary Magdalene. Mark and Luke tell us that it was to anoint Jesus' body with certain spices for burial. Matthew simply says that they came to look at the tomb. In any event, in all three gospels the women encountered angelic beings that announced to them that Jesus has risen.

Although the Synoptics portray Mary as one of at least two women who were witnesses to the empty tomb, they are divided on what happened afterward. Originally, the Gospel of Mark closed with the women running away from the tomb in distress, confused by their encounter with an angel. At some point early on, several sentences were added to the end of Mark (16:9–20) which mention that Jesus appeared to Mary Magdalene but neglect to mention any appearance to Peter. The Gospel of Matthew has the women encountering Jesus on their way to tell the other disciples what they had found. They worshipped him in a manner reminiscent of John's description of Mary's encounter with Jesus. Finally, the Gospel of Luke gives pride of place to Peter and to a pair of disciples (one named Cleopas) who were on their way home.

> ### Words to the Wise
>
> Mark's description of the women rising "very early in the morning the first day of the week," to reach the sepulcher "at the rising of the sun," became from the earliest centuries of Christianity a focal point for artists and sculptors who sought to represent the drama of the resurrection.
>
> —Susan Haskins, *Mary Magdalene: Myth and Metaphor* (6)

From the Source

Early Christians faced an uphill fight when they put forward women as witnesses to the resurrection. One of Christianity's earliest and most serious critics, a second-century philosopher named Celsus, went so far as to question Mary's sanity:

But who saw [the resurrected Jesus]? A hysterical woman, as you say, and perhaps some other one of those who were deluded by the same sorcery ...

—quoted in Origen's *Against Celsus* (Bk II, 55)

Apostle to the Apostles

Mary has a special place in the Gospel of John. Although the Synoptics allude to Mary's importance within that original group of Christ's followers, John gives us a much more intimate portrait of the relationship that Jesus had with Mary.

As with Matthew and Mark, we don't meet Mary in John's gospel until the crucifixion. Even there, she is not listed first among the women present as she is in the Synoptics (in John's case, that honor goes to Jesus' mother). The visit to the tomb in John 20 takes place before sunrise, also just as the Synoptics describe. But John has Mary going alone, or at least he doesn't mention any other women with her (although her statement to Peter and the Beloved Disciple, "… we don't know where they have laid him" suggests more than one person). This sets up one of the most moving moments in the New Testament.

Did You Know?

The Gospel of John, like all of the New Testament gospels, is anonymous. The only hints as to the identity of its author are cryptic references to "the disciple whom Jesus loved," who is claimed as the source for the gospel's story. The Beloved Disciple appears in the text for the first time next to Jesus at the Last Supper (John 13), and then again at the foot of the cross, where Jesus places his mother in the Beloved Disciple's care (John 19). He is there again when Mary Magdalene comes running in to describe her meeting with the resurrected Jesus (John 20), and again when Jesus meets his disciples at the Sea of Galilee (John 21). "This is the disciple who testifies to these things and who wrote them down," the Gospel of John concludes. "We know that his testimony is true" (John 21:24)

Traditionally, the Beloved Disciple has been identified as John Zebedee, one of the twelve apostles. Many bible scholars now challenge that identification, but there is no consensus as to the Beloved Disciple's actual identity. Some have even suggested Mary Magdalene, but Mary and the Beloved Disciple appear in the same scene in John 20, so this is very unlikely.

Having summoned Peter and the Beloved Disciple to the tomb, Mary now stands by weeping. The disciples have left, bemused by the empty burial chamber and the missing body. A man, the gardener she thinks, asks Mary why she is crying. She begs him, if he knows, to tell her where her Lord is. At that moment, Christ reveals himself to her with a single word: "Mary."

Mary cries out, "Rabboni," a title of respect for a teacher. She tries to embrace him, but he won't let her cling to him (the actual wording is not "Don't touch me" as has often been translated, but rather, "Don't cling to me"). He must still return to the Father. Instead, he gives her a commission to go and tell his disciples that he is ascending "to My Father and your Father, and My God and your God." This assignment, to be the first witness to the resurrection, earned Mary the title "apostle to the apostles" among early church writers.

The Painted Lady

So how did this forceful woman, highly regarded by the gospel writers and revered by the early church in its stories and art, end up as the church's poster child for reformed prostitutes? The answer to that question is long and complex, and weaves together strands from the conflict between different groups about how to interpret the Jesus story, cultural expectations about what makes for a genuinely holy person, and of course attitudes toward women in general and within the Christian community.

There isn't any real smoking gun that we can point to as the moment when a hierarchical, paternalistic church decided to systematically suppress women. More than likely, churches developed along different lines depending on the region where they were located and the openness toward women within the larger culture. Apostles and church leaders obviously differed on the issue of women in leadership. Paul seemed to have no problems working alongside women in a variety of contexts, referring to one woman as a deacon (Romans 16:1) and to another as an apostle (Romans 16:7).

On the other hand, Pauline letters like 1 Corinthians, 1 Timothy, and Titus contain passages that are obviously intended to limit the participation of women in the churches and especially in leadership. To be fair to Paul, most scholars regard the two letters to Timothy and the letter to Titus, collectively known as the Pastoral Epistles, as having been written not by Paul but perhaps by one of his followers. As for the passage in 1 Corinthians ordering women to keep silent in church, at least one specialist in Pauline studies (Gordon Fee) has argued that it is a later addition to the text and not original to Paul. Of greater importance than defending Paul from the charge of misogyny, however, is the recognition that at least some folks in the early church were willing to curtail the activities of women, and that this approach became more and more common as time passed.

Still, that process took a while, and in the meantime there were certainly groups where women remained integrally involved in the ministries and leadership of the church. Tertullian attacked several of these in a famous passage from his work *Prescription against Heresies*, "The very women of these heretics, how wanton they are! For they are bold enough to teach, to dispute, to enact exorcisms, to undertake cures—it may be even to baptize." This from a man who later became a member of the Montanist movement, itself founded in part by two female prophets, and who once spoke highly of a female prophet who was a member of his church. Attitudes toward women's activities in the church were complex and were far from consistent.

Documents like the Gospel of Mary are evidence of the fact that there were groups who not only regarded women as potential leaders, but who actually looked to the authority of one woman in particular as an apostolic messenger. It's dangerous to assume too much about the community or communities that might have held Mary in such high esteem, but other texts, like the Pistis Sophia and passages in the Gospel of Thomas and the Gospel of Philip, report greater activity on the part of Mary than is found in the New Testament. They also echo the note of conflict between Mary and Peter that we will see at the end of Mary's gospel.

There evidently was a tradition in the early church that associated Mary Magdalene with the viability of women serving in leadership. Those who rejected or sought to limit the role of women would have found themselves in conflict with this tradition. Mary Magdalene, a hero of the earliest Christian community, became the embodiment of a practice that was at odds with powerful forces in the early Christian community. One doesn't have to buy into the teachings found in the Gospel of Mary to agree that, as Mary was adopted as a symbol and spokesperson by those who found their views marginalized in the Christian movement, leaders in the dominant Christian communities would have been under pressure to tame her image.

That evolution reached its peak in a brief sermon given by Gregory I, the most influential of the early popes. In this speech, presented sometime near the end of the sixth century, Gregory stitches together three different women from the New Testament who had interactions with Jesus. The first, from seventh chapter of Luke's gospel, was a woman described by Luke as "a sinner" who anointed Jesus' feet with perfume and, weeping over them, dried her tears away with her hair. The second is Mary of Bethany, the sister of Lazarus and Martha, who, in the twelfth chapter of the Gospel of John, anointed Jesus feet with perfume and wiped them dry with her hair. Obviously these two stories have some similarities that might be confusing. It is the third woman in Gregory's pastiche, though, that causes some real problems.

From the Source

We believe that this woman is Luke's female sinner, the woman John calls Mary, and that Mary from whom Mark says seven demons were cast out.

—Pope Gregory I (A.D. 540–604), in his famous Homily 33, grouping together Mary Magdalene, Mary of Bethany, and the "sinful woman" from Luke's Gospel into a single identity.

Mary Magdalene is mentioned for the first time in the Gospel of Luke shortly after he recounts the story of the sinful woman. In his introduction, Luke mentions that Mary had been delivered from seven demons. Gregory essentially collapsed the two accounts into one, assuming that the unnamed sinful woman in the previous chapter was Mary Magdalene. On top of that, he makes another assumption about the nature of the unnamed woman's sin, associating her with illicit sexuality. Thus Mary the "apostle to the apostles" became Mary the repentant prostitute.

In the role of prostitute, Mary Magdalene has historically served as the opposite for that other famous Mary, the Virgin Mary. Although the Virgin quickly became an object of veneration for her purity, both physically and spiritually, Mary Magdalene became associated with the penitence of those who had not kept themselves free from sexual taint. They became, in some ways, two sides of the same coin representing early Christian attitudes toward sexuality, particularly in women.

Words to the Wise

MAGDALENE, n. An inhabitant of Magdala. Popularly, a woman found out. This definition of the word has the authority of ignorance, Mary of Magdala being another person than the penitent woman mentioned by St. Luke. It has also the official sanction of the governments of Great Britain and the United States. In England the word is pronounced Maudlin, whence maudlin, adjective, unpleasantly sentimental. With their Maudlin for Magdalene, and their Bedlam for Bethlehem, the English may justly boast themselves the greatest of revisers.

—Ambrose Bierce, *Devil's Dictionary*

The Gospel of Mary

The Gospel of Mary was completely unknown until it was discovered as part of the Berlin Codex in 1896 (see Chapter 5 for a fuller account). The text is severely damaged, missing the first six pages as well as four pages from the middle. Consequently, more than half of the gospel is missing. That obviously affects how we read the remaining half, since it is very difficult now to say with any certainty what the Gospel of Mary does or does not teach.

Between the time that the Berlin Codex was discovered and the time that it was first published in 1955, two more small fragments of the Gospel of Mary were discovered. Both of them are part of the original Greek text, and neither of them contain material from the missing half of the Coptic text. So, while they give us a better sense of what the original text looked like, they don't provide any additional insight into the content of this unusual document.

The Coptic text from the Berlin Codex belongs to the fifth century, although it is impossible to date the Greek manuscript from which it was translated. The two fragments in Greek have been dated to sometime in the second century, and this establishes an early date for at least some form of the Gospel of Mary.

A Sin-cere Question

Since the first six pages are missing, we are dumped right at the start into the tail-end of a dialogue between Jesus, who was called the Savior, and a group of his disciples. Later hints in the text indicate that this was a post-resurrection appearance, a common setting in all kinds of early Christian literature. Part of the Jesus story that seems universal in early Christian literature is the claim that, following his resurrection, Jesus spent some length of time instructing his followers more completely than he had prior to his death. These post-resurrection appearances then became the venue for each group to expound its own interpretation of Jesus as if taught by Jesus himself. Post-resurrection teaching or revelation is key to several of the Nag Hammadi documents that we'll be looking at later in this book, so keep an eye out for it.

All that's left of the dialogue in the Gospel of Mary is a pair of questions. The first questioner (whose identity is unknown because of the damage to the text) wanted to know the eventual fate of the material world. Jesus told them that, like everything else, the material world is rooted in its own nature, and eventually all things will return to their own nature. Right now, everything is mixed together so that it is hard to distinguish what is lasting from what is passing away. Since the material world is, at its root, temporary it will eventually sink under its own weight and dissolve away. Only that which is by nature eternal will remain, and in the Gospel of Mary that is the spirit alone.

The second question, asked by Peter, concerns the definition of sin. If the material world is perpetually fading away into nothingness, then where is sin coming from? In response, Jesus shocks us with the assertion that there is no such thing as sin, per se. Sin isn't a separate thing with its own energy and existence. Rather, it is the result of our inordinate, unwarranted attachment to this unstable physical existence. Sin, Jesus tells Peter, is a "love for what deceives you" that causes us to pursue what "is contrary to nature," namely, the Divine Image in which we are created as spiritual beings.

Words to the Wise

The Gospel of Mary explicitly avoids all description of God except as Good. The Savior's teachings are aimed at freeing people from suffering and death, not punishing them for their sins. The Gospel of Mary has no notion of hell. There is no intrinsic value in the atoning death of Christ or the martyrdom of believers or the punishment of souls because there is no such thing as sin. This theology stands in clear contrast to that of other Christians, however much their language and themes resonate with each other.

—Karen King, *The Gospel of Mary of Magdala*

Sin, then, arises out of an adulterous mixture of flesh and spirit that causes sickness and death. It is the result of taking the body seriously and catering to its needs and desires. Our focus is entirely on what is passing away. Rather than incurring guilt for which there needs to be atonement—the orthodox Christian view—the Gospel of Mary prescribes a turning of the heart toward the Good (meaning God in Christ), who is entirely spiritual. And it is precisely for this reason that "the Good" came "pursuing the good." The Savior's mission was to make us all aware of our true nature as spiritual beings with eternal significance.

As he wound up the dialogue, Jesus made three statements.

♦ First, Jesus offered a blessing of peace ("Peace be upon you") and encouraged them to seek peace within themselves.

♦ Second, Jesus warned them not to heed anybody who tries to tell them that he—Jesus—will come again in a literal fashion. Rather, they should look within themselves to find the Son of Man (or, as scholar Karen King has translated it, "the child of true Humanity")

♦ Finally, the Savior commanded them to go preach the good news, but to be careful not to add to it any "rule" or "law" above what he himself had laid down. Otherwise, he warned, they "might be dominated by it."

With that, he left them.

She Talks to Angels

The disciples were deeply shaken and disturbed at the prospect of going out to preach Jesus' message. They were afraid that they would suffer the same fate that he did. Their fear literally paralyzed them.

It was Mary Magdalene who stood up and began to comfort them all. She encouraged them by reminding them all that the Savior's grace "will shelter you." We should praise him, she counseled them, because "he has prepared us and made us true human beings." (The Greek fragment that parallels this section has "he has united us" in place of "he has prepared us"). She turned their hearts "toward the Good," meaning toward God, and their spirits began to lift. Encouraged, they began to discuss what the Savior had taught them (namely, the preceding dialogue that we have so little of).

Peter asked Mary to offer them her words. Because Jesus loved her more than all other women, he says, she should have access to teachings that the rest of the disciples had not yet heard. Mary agreed to tell them about "what is hidden from you." She related to them a vision she received in which Jesus came to her.

Twenty-Twenty Vision

In her vision, Mary saw Jesus but was not startled by his appearance to her. Jesus was pleasantly surprised by her ability to see him and commended her character because she held her composure at his appearance. He told her that her mind was pure and firmly oriented toward God, and this both enabled her to receive this vision and to be calm and at peace in the midst of it. There was no visceral quality to the prophetic imagination in the Gospel of Mary, no hysteria or ecstasy.

Jesus' words prompted Mary to question the source of the prophetic vision: do we see visions with our soul or with our spirit? Neither, Jesus replied. Visions are perceived by the mind, which exists between the soul and the spirit. It may seem like an odd or even trivial thing to inquire about, this question about where prophetic vision is located, but wrapped up in that question and the answer that Jesus gave is a whole host of assumptions about the nature of humanity that were hotly disputed within the early church.

In practice, this question still troubles church members today: are we spirits who happen to have bodies or are we naturally physical beings? As scholar Karen King has pointed out, that's the larger question that lies behind Mary's query about visions. Within the early church, there were those who championed the idea that our physical existence is critical to our humanness. Without a body, these folks argued, we aren't whole beings. Bound up in that idea is the insistence that who we are physically, including our gender (and this a the critical point for the author of the Gospel of Mary), is as much a part of our eternal nature as who we are spiritually. We are a package deal, so to speak.

Not so for the Gospel of Mary. According to that document, the body is a purely temporary thing, something that will eventually be sloughed off and done away with. Anything that belongs to the body, including gender, is therefore secondary to what is eternal about us as human beings. Spiritually speaking, we are ungendered, neither male nor female. And that means that any walls that we create between ourselves on the basis of difference in sex—say, for example, not allowing women to participate fully in the worship life of the church—are based on a deception. Those kinds of attitudes, the Gospel of Mary would allege, are part of that adulterous nature that confuses the physical with the spiritual.

It's Mind over Matter

There is yet another aspect to the Savior's assertion that it is mind that perceives visions. If visions are perceived by the soul, which is a product of our physical existence, then not just anyone is capable of such spiritual experiences. There is a connection, in such a view, between a person's physical purity or sinlessness and his or her capacity to receive revelations from the Divine. This view of the soul fits very well with the view commonly held in mainstream Christian communities on the importance of the sacraments in worship.

According to the Gospel of Mary, however, the human mind bridges our sensory experiences in time and our spiritual vision of God. This vision of God can come only to the pure, but it is not a ritual purity we are talking about here, but a purity of viewpoint and intention. Mary "sees" God because her purity consists of an "unwavering" orientation toward God—not some legalized notion of sin. It should be noted that there were orthodox Christians, such as Clement and Origen, who would have agreed with this view.

Jesus continued to flesh out his answer to Mary, but unfortunately this is where the text ends, with the next four pages missing. When it picks up again, we're in a completely different realm.

Going Up!

As part of her vision of Jesus, it seems that Mary began an ascent of the soul. This is another common teaching technique in ancient literature, and appears in all kinds of Christian literature from the first few centuries. The Apostle Paul, of course, is famous for having been "caught up to the third heaven" (2 Corinthians 12:2), where he saw and heard things "not lawful to mention." The Revelation of John, the last book in the New Testament, is entirely the record of one man's experience of being drawn into the heavens.

> **From the Source**
>
> After this I looked, and there before me was a door standing open in heaven. And the voice I had first heard speaking to me like a trumpet said, "Come up here, and I will show you what must take place after this."
>
> —The Revelation of John 4:1 (NIV)

For gnostics, the ascent of the soul had a specific purpose beyond mere revelation. Bound up in the gnostic view of the world is the conviction that the ultimate goal of each truly spiritual human being is a rejection of physical existence and a reunification with the Divine realm. We've already seen some of that in the Gospel of Mary.

Standing in the way of that goal, however, are sets of powerful beings that we've already mentioned—archons or rulers who seek to hold humanity in bondage. What gnostics longed for was a way to evade or defy those rulers and make it past them to God. Knowledge of how to do so came principally through an experience called "heavenly ascents," where an individual was lifted into the spiritual realms through a trance. During these experiences, the gnostic would be taught how to circumvent the rulers. Through the course of this book, we'll see several examples of this kind of revelation.

Who Goes There!

When the text picks up again, its obvious that we've been dropped right into the middle of just such an ascent experience. Mary was relating the experience of "the soul" as it rose upward through what appeared to be four powers. The first is missing from the text, but may have been called Darkness (from hints later in the text). The second is named Desire, the third Ignorance, and the fourth is called Wrath.

At each stage, the soul is impeded from further progress by one of the powers. Each of the powers in turn interrogates the soul in some way. We don't know what is said because the text is missing. Desire refuses to believe that the soul originates from anywhere but the physical world. "I did not see you descend" from the Divine realm, so therefore the soul must belong to the physical world. The soul defies Desire, claiming that Desire only saw "the garment I wore," meaning the body, rather than the soul's true nature.

Ignorance has a different tactic. The soul cannot go free because it is "bound by wickedness." Guilty in its sinfulness, Ignorance argues, where does the soul get the right to judge the powers? The soul, ever feisty, responds that it is not beholden to the powers at all. It is not sin that anchors the soul to the material world but the illegitimate rule of the powers that holds the soul in bondage. The soul goes free because it is not of the same nature as the powers; it doesn't seek to bind anyone else, so it cannot be bound.

The last Power, Wrath, seems to be a summation of all of the powers. It takes seven forms: darkness, desire, ignorance, zeal for death, the realm of the flesh, foolish wisdom of the flesh, and the wisdom of wrath. A second look at that list makes the character of the powers absolutely clear. These are not benevolent beings by any stretch of the imagination.

Wrath accuses the soul of its own tendencies: violence and domination. It calls the soul a "murderer" and "destroyer of kingdoms" and demands to know where the soul is going. The soul takes these accusations as honorable titles, reveling in its freedom from the illusions that held it bound. It contrasts the failings of material existence, and the evils of its subjugation to the powers, with the eternal realm of rest to which it is returning. And so it passes the final Power, and the vision ends.

The Odd Couple

Mary's story was not what Peter had expected to hear. Both he and his brother Andrew responded with incredulity at Mary's vision. I don't know what anyone else has to say, Andrew began, but this all sounds way too strange for me. Andrew certainly spoke for many early Christians who had a hard time with the kinds of gnostic teachings that the Gospel of Mary expressed. It is interesting that, despite the gospel's obvious intention to defend Mary, Andrew's question was never answered. Instead, the focus shifted immediately to Peter. Peter picked up on his brother's skepticism and extended it beyond just the content of the vision. For Peter, the greater concern was why Jesus would have communicated such a deep teaching to a woman.

Words to the Wise

The Gospel of Mary was written at a time when the truth of Christian teaching could not be settled by appeal to a commonly accepted "Rule of Faith" or canon of gospel literature, let alone an established leadership. The Gospel of Mary framed the issue as a matter of character: Who can be relied upon to preach the gospel? The argument for the truth of its teaching is based on a contrast between Mary's character and Peter's. Peter represents the error of assuming that simply having heard the teaching of Jesus is enough to ensure that one has actually understood it.

—Karen King, *The Gospel of Mary of Magdala*

By the way, if you are under the impression that Peter has suddenly changed his tune, you get extra credit. Where previously Peter asked Mary to tell them about teachings that the rest of them may not have known, now he rejected her vision. It wasn't the manner in which she received the teaching that she had shared, but the fact that it came through a woman that really disturbed him. Would Jesus have really spoken privately to a woman about such things, he asked, and would he expect the rest of the (male) disciples to "turn around" and follow her instruction?

Mary was driven to tears by their response. She just couldn't believe that Peter and Andrew would turn on her so quickly or accuse her of lying. Another disciple, Levi, came to her defense. You're being a hothead, he told Peter, like usual. Jesus loved Mary more than he did the rest of the disciples, and he knows her well. If he was pleased to share this vision with her, who is Peter to object, Levi asked?

Instead of arguing about things, Levi continued, we should "put on the true Human being" and go preach the gospel without adding laws or rules. In other words, Levi essentially restated Jesus' parting instructions to the disciples. The Coptic version ends with all of the disciples dispersing to preach. The Greek fragment that parallels this passage has only Levi leaving. In either case, the reader is faced with the disturbing prospect that at least some of the disciples might not have been prepared to present Jesus' true teachings.

Who Gets to Lead

So did Mary and Peter have a big fight? Who knows, but that's not the point. The Bible is honest enough to frequently point out the conflicts that tore at the early church. The disciples argued among themselves about who would be greatest in the Kingdom of God. Paul had conflicts both with his partner Barnabas and with Peter, not to mention frequent run-ins with those who disagreed with him on the question of whether Gentile Christians needed to be circumcised. So it shouldn't come as any great shock if it were proven that Mary Magdalene and Peter happened to have a falling out at some point. It's only speculation, though. That the two are so often pitted against each other in so many of these newly-discovered texts is intriguing, but still far too flimsy to consider as historical evidence.

More important than any alleged break between two of the best known of Christ's original followers is the way that different groups took such a conflict for granted and used it to interpret their own place in the emerging Christian movement. We should beware of automatically associating the historical figure of Mary Magdalene with the teachings that are put on her lips or expressed in her name. Certainly Mary must have been a powerful symbol to marginalized people. As a symbol for them, she could integrate them into the Jesus story, investing someone like them with significance and authority.

Neither Male nor Female

Salvation is available to both men and women. On that, all Christians would agree. The Apostle Paul, writing to the church in Galatia, penned these words: "There is neither Jew nor Greek, slave nor free, male nor female, for you are all one in Christ Jesus" (Galatians 3:28). For Paul, neither ethnic distinction, social class, nor gender is a bar to receiving the life of Christ. All well and good, but what about participation in the leadership of the Christian community?

Right away, both Gentiles and slaves were active in the leadership of the church, the first through heated theological discussion and the second by simple demographics (many early Christians were slaves). Their redemption alone qualified them for service. The role of women within the church, however, has been a hotly debated topic almost since the beginning.

Many readers have found in the Gospel of Mary renewed evidence of both the fact and the desirability of female leadership within the church. It communicates a theology of ungendered spirituality, where physical traits like sex are no bar to whether or not a person is fit or qualified to exercise authority within the church. Although orthodox Christians will have serious disagreements with the rationale that is offered to justify that egalitarianism, they may be able to sympathize with the ideal that the writer of the Gospel of Mary was trying to bolster: a Christian community where spiritual maturity and intimate communion with Christ, not external criteria, are the hallmarks of leadership.

The Least You Need to Know

- The Mary of the gnostic book, the Gospel of Mary, was not the prostitute that tradition has made her out to be, but the first witness to the resurrection and an apostle to the apostles.

- We only have about half of the gospel text available to us.

- Sin, in the Gospel of Mary, arises from loving the material world as opposed to realizing that it is temporary and will soon dissolve away.

- Mary's vision laid out a plan for escaping from the powers that rule the world and hold the soul in bondage.

- By suggesting a leadership role for Mary, this gospel portrays a conflict between Peter and Mary that has larger implications for the way the Christian movement apportioned authority in its development.

Chapter 8

The Gospel of the Egyptians

In This Chapter

- One version of the gnostic mythology
- Why Seth was more important than Adam
- The role of baptism in gnostic beliefs
- Ritual incantations for accessing the divine

Although it is better known as the Gospel of the Egyptians, the book itself gives us a different title, The Holy Book of the Great Invisible Spirit, and that largely defines its contents. The Gospel appears twice in the Nag Hammadi library (Codex III,2 and IV,2).

The two copies were translated from different Greek originals, which means that at least two versions of this gospel were in circulation, although there don't appear to be any really significant differences. Scholars can't agree on when or where the Gospel of the Egyptians was written. It's important to point out that this is not the same Gospel of the Egyptians that Clement of Alexandria referred to in some of his writings.

In the Beginning ...

Like the Gospel of Thomas and the Gospel of Mary (see Chapters 6 and 7, respectively), the Gospel of the Egyptians really doesn't fall into the literary category of a true gospel. Although it does tell a story (unlike Thomas), that story has little to do with the life of Jesus of Nazareth. Instead, it presents a gnostic myth, an attempt to tell the reader (or, probably in this case, the hearer) how the world came to be the way that it is and where it is going from here. Fundamental to gnostic spirituality appears to have been the mythology that they constructed to explain the nature and structure of the universe. For gnostics, knowing the pattern of the eternal realms was a necessary means of injecting meaning into the present moment. If you believe that you are from an eternal realm and that you are returning there, knowing the lay of the land is crucial to living properly.

Of course, the myth differs from one account to another. The Gospel of the Egyptians contains one form, but we'll see others as well. There was a kind of classical gnostic myth, which we'll get to know a bit better in Chapter 13, but there was also a specifically Valentinian version that had some crucial differences. We'll get to know the Valentinian myth better in the next chapter when we look at the Gospel of Truth.

Ineffable, Unknowable, Invisible

Right away in the Gospel of the Egyptians, we're dropped into the middle of an inscrutable place. We are told that the Divine being is absolutely unknowable, beyond all definition, and lives in eternal light. This Divine being is self-originating, meaning that it looks to nothing else as the cause of its existence.

From the start, we're confronted with one of the difficulties of gnostic mythology. If you claim that God is indefinable, that no words can suffice to explain, explore, or delimit the Divine, then how helpful is it to make the effort to explain who and what God is like? The gnostics didn't let this difficulty stop them.

The Gospel of the Egyptians, in particular, has difficulty navigating the limits of language to adequately explain the Divine. Over and over again, the gospel tries to find ways of verbalizing who God is. We'll see later in this chapter some of the more clever ways that the text tries to go about this. For now it's enough to say that, despite the vast number of names and epithets in the book, none of them are thought sufficient to adequately address God. In other words, everything about this gospel is a partial answer.

Ring Around the Deity

Returning to the gospel, we are told that a series of emanations, or powers, grows from the "Divine Parent." The first set of "powers" is three in number: the Father, the Mother, and the Son. Except that these three are one. If that multiplicity doesn't confuse you, try this: each of these powers is itself a collection of beings or characteristics (the gnostics didn't distinguish between the two at this level). The Gospel refers to them as "octets" or groups of eight. So the Father, Mother, and Son each have eight characteristics or qualities associated with them.

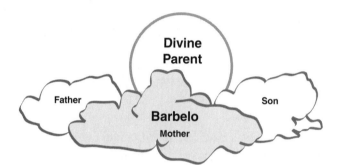

The Divine Parent emanates the Mother/Father/Son.

The text is too damaged to list the Mother's characteristics except that she is called the Barbelo, though that name really applies to the three of them together. The Barbelo becomes a big deal in Chapter 13, so we won't ruin the surprise by saying more now. We do find a list of the Father's characteristics. Here they are:

- Thought
- Word
- Incorruptibility
- Eternal life
- Will
- Intellect
- Foreknowledge
- The androgynous Father

> **Words to the Wise**
>
> For Jews and Orthodox Christians (to solve a huge problem with inappropriate simplicity), God just is, ever was, and created the universe. But for Gnostics, God was both ever existent and self-evolving. The Gnostic God had a prehistory.
>
> —Keith Hopkins, *A World Full of Gods* (256)

The Son's characteristics aren't listed explicitly. We are simply told that from him emanated "seven powers of the great light, which are seven vowels." These seven vowels are an "invisible symbol," which is the name of God. We'll take a look at these vowel constructions (there are more than one) later in this chapter when we look at the power of ritual speech and the use of magical incantations in gnostic literature. From these seven sounds comes "the Word."

At the end of this section of the gospel, we are told that the Father, the Mother, and the Son lifted up praise to the Divine Parent. This is another favorite theme found in the Gospel of the Egyptians, the act of worship. At each successive stage of the emanations, the gospel sums up the new round of creations by having the newest members of the heavenly realms—the Pleroma, you'll recall, is what this refers to—lift up praise to those who have come before them. This devotional side to the Gospel of the Egyptians is missing in other texts.

Rounding Out the Team

The gospel then goes on to describe a whole series of emanations that follow this original threefold manifestation. Not all of them are readable in the text due to damage to the pages. One of the beings who comes into existence is the Christ, who is called "the invincible power." This Christ is not the person we know as Jesus Christ. Rather, this power is an eternal being emanated directly from the Divine Parent through the Father-Mother-Son or Barbelo. Don't let all of these biblical terms confuse you. The author of the gospel is speaking of higher realities, beings that take on the character more of a force of nature than anything else.

The Christ shines out from the Barbelo.

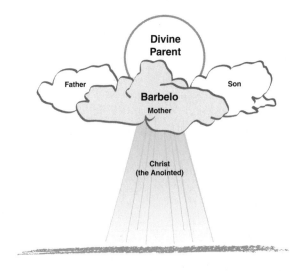

Another of the beings who comes into existence at this point is referred to simply as "the five seals." We'll discuss this more when we talk about the Gospel of Philip, because the five seals are very important for explaining gnostic worship rituals. We'll leave it there for now, but if you just can't wait, head on over to Chapter 10.

First Person, Plural

Just as before with the appearance of the Mother, Father, and Son trio and the powers that derive from them, we now get a new barrage of names, aeons, and emanations. The Divine realm is an intensely fertile place, with beings coming into existence one after the other. The Divine Parent seems to be constantly in motion, always producing. And with each new cycle of creation, there is a renewed burst of praise.

This time around, we get the first human being. If you're thinking that it's Adam, think again. The physical Adam comes later. Right now, the gospel writer is talking about the spiritual being that the later, material Adam will simply echo. This fellow is called Adamas, and like most of the characters that we're encountering, he will show up again in other versions of this myth.

The gospel tells us that there is, inexplicably, "a lack" somewhere in this utopian existence. Something is missing, and Adamas was emanated "for the obliteration" of it. The author doesn't really address what caused this lack, but other versions of the myth tell the story of Sophia, one of the many aeons, who broke with the Pleroma (either knowingly or accidentally, depending on which version you read) and gave birth to either the material world or the Demiurge (who is, you'll remember, the "craftsman" or "maker" who shapes the chaotic material world into its present form and rules over it). The Gospel of the Egyptians doesn't include these details in its telling of the gnostic myth, but it obviously assumes that some such event occurred.

Adamas gets a lot of time at center stage in this version of the myth. He is "light," "the first human being." He is the source of all things, and the person for whom all things exist. Sounds like the kind of guy you would want on the job, right? Just in case you thought he wasn't up for it, though, he's getting some help. Adamas becomes one with the Word, the divine name that came into being out of the Son. The two of them together (Adamas and the Word) take the form of, and thereby create, human reason.

Son of a Son

Adamas wanted to be a daddy, and he requested from the Divine Parent that he be allowed to produce a child. Over and over again, we see emanations coming only in cooperation with the Divine Parent who is at the center of this all. This highlights the fact that, ultimately, each and every aeon and angelic being is an expression of the Divine. It also reinforces the orderly process by which the gnostics believed that creation took place and continues to take place. In other versions of the myth, we'll see later, it was Sophia's failure to work in conjunction with the Divine Parent that got her into trouble.

Adamas' son was named Seth, and he was destined to be the central figure in the story. The gospel makes it clear that Seth was intended to be "parent of the immovable and incorruptible race." This race of beings, which comes into existence a little later in the text, would include all those human beings who are spiritually alive. The gnostics understood themselves to be part of that immortal race, and therefore took Seth as their ultimate ancestor. The story of that race becomes the focus of the action in the Gospel of the Egyptians, but not before Seth got a few friends to help him out.

The emanations from the Christ.

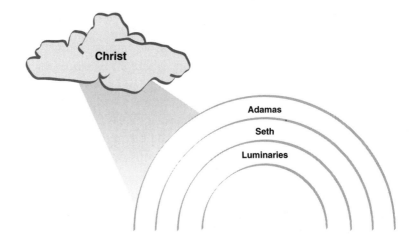

Armies of Angels

What's a king without a court? Every father of an immortal race should have a retinue, and Seth was no different. Along with Seth, we are told, four "luminaries" emanated. These four beings appear repeatedly in the gnostic myth and must go back to some common tradition, perhaps in Jewish speculation about angels. A female counterpart or "consort," an attendant, and the attendant's consort accompanied each of the luminaries. Their names are listed in the following table.

The Four Luminaries and Their Attendants

Luminary	Consort	Attendant	Attendant's Consort
Harmozel	Loveliness	Gamaliel	Memory
Oroiael	Perception	Gabriel	Love
Daueithe	Intelligence	Samblo	Peace
Eleleth	Prudence	Abrasaks	Eternal Life

With the emergence of Seth and his entourage, the Pleroma was complete. Thrones were created for the four luminaries to sit on, and from which to rule over four eternal realms. The "incorruptible spiritual church," Seth's "immortal race," began to flourish within these four realms. A final act of praise was lifted up to the entire Pleroma, as the immortal race began "praising and singing, all glorifying with one voice in unanimous from with a never-silent cry" to the entire Divine realm.

Seth Saves the Day

When scholars first began to examine the Nag Hammadi findings, they noticed a curious similarity in some of the texts. Several of the new documents seemed to assign a special role to Seth, the son of Adam. In these texts, Seth was first and foremost a divine being who was only partially resident in the actual son of Adam named for him. Seth's responsibilities included fathering an immortal or eternal race of people who would be marked out by their special relationship to the Divine. It appeared that at least some gnostic groups saw themselves as the fulfillment of, or at least part of the fulfillment of, that divine race.

This tradition of seeing Seth as something more than just a footnote to a genealogy in Genesis goes back prior to Christian gnostics and finds its roots in Jewish speculation about the beginning. There were certain groups, for example, who argued that Cain (and, in some cases, Abel as well) was not the son of Adam. Instead, he was the result of Eve's dalliance (or rape) by angelic beings. This tradition certainly crept into gnostic literature, and we'll see examples of it in Chapter 13.

According to those same gnostic and Jewish groups, Seth was the true son of Adam. These groups contrasted the line of Cain with the line of Seth in Genesis 4–5, and they speculated that Cain was the father of the line of the wicked, while Seth was the father of the just and godly race. Philo of Alexandria put his own allegorical slant on this story, viewing Seth as the father of all those who are of pure heart and virtuous life. It was only a short hop from there to promoting Seth to the level of a savior. The larger myth structure devised by the gnostics created precisely the right setting for elevating Seth.

Managing Chaos

All you bureaucrats, take heart. Even divine beings delegate. The gospel relates that "Chaos and Hades" appeared out of nowhere, though they had probably been there all along (this is definitely a theology that most bureaucracies can relate to). The Greek philosopher Plato, whose ideas experienced a certain resurgence of popularity in the second century, said that matter was eternal and inherently chaotic. It's possible that that's what was assumed in the gospel as well. It is certainly clear that neither chaos nor Hades were the creation of the Divine Parent.

Wherever Hades comes from, the luminary Eleleth decided that somebody (but not him) needed to take care of the chaotic mess. The text here is a little spotty because of damage to the papyrus, but we do know that Sophia made a very brief appearance at this point. The text refers to her as "material Sophia," which may be a reference to the belief that Sophia, when she realized her great error, essentially split in two. One part of her returned to the Pleroma, but the other part of her was left behind in the physical world that she had helped to create. This trapped part of Sophia, who was originally part of the Divine, is the "lack" that exists in the Pleroma.

The Gospel seems to say that Sophia had come into being to rule over chaos and Hades, but that isn't entirely clear. Immediately after Sophia appears in the text, the gospel tells us that the angels Gamaliel and Gabriel also decided that someone needed to look after things (again, not them—it's a true bureaucracy at work). Perhaps out of Sophia, which would be consistent with the other versions of the myth, Sakla came into being. This is the Demiurge that we've already mentioned. Sakla means "fool" in Aramaic, but we'll get to know him by a different name in Chapter 13.

A Devil of an Angel

Sakla went to work right away, bringing some order and organization to chaos and Hades. He appointed 12 angels, who were listed by name, to rule over various parts of his realm. At first, all seems to go well. Whether he realized it or not, Sakla was working according to the will of the Pleroma.

Maybe Sakla didn't realize that there were beings higher than him in the spiritual food chain. That's how other versions explained his behavior. Or maybe it all just went to his head. Either way, he got himself into some very hot water when he declared to his angels, "I am a jealous god, and nothing has come to be except through me." This boast appears in nearly every version of this myth, and must go back to whatever sources are behind its creation. It reflects an early association of the Demiurge with the Creator God of the Jewish Scriptures, and this association reflects general gnostic hostility toward the God of Israel.

From the Source

Sakla's boast is very similar to the kind of language used by God in the Hebrew Scriptures. The earliest appearance of God's jealousy appears in the Exodus version of the Ten Commandments:

You shall not make for yourself an idol in the form of anything in heaven above or on the earth beneath or in the waters below. You shall not bow down to them or worship them; for I, the LORD your God, am a jealous God, punishing the children for the sin of the fathers to the third and fourth generation of those who hate me, but showing love to a thousand generations of those who love me and keep my commandments.

—Exodus 20:4–6 (NIV)

Sakla didn't get far with his boast. A voice from heaven reminded him that Adamas and his son Seth existed as well. In other words, he was seriously outranked. Along with the voice came an "image," which was a kind of shadow or reflection of the heavenly human being Adamas and his son. This image was an active thing, and it created a physical body for itself, Adam. In this way, it created a race of "earthborn aeons," the seed of Seth coming to Earth as human beings, "so that … the lacks might be completed." (This differs from other versions of the gnostic myth, where it was the Demiurge who created the human body.)

All Out War

Without giving any real details (though we find them in other versions; see Chapter 13, for example), Sakla and Adam each had sons. Sakla, here called "the demon-begetting god," had Cain, while Adam sired a son just like the divine Seth. The text mentioned both of these briefly before passing on, but we know from other texts that this division is fundamental to the gnostic self-identity. Gnostics thought of themselves as the seed of Seth, born of the line of Adam, while others came from Cain's line and were the children of Sakla. Trust me, given how the story ends, it's much better to be a child of Seth.

Being of the seed of Seth turned out to be a good thing, but right away it didn't look so good. The seed of Seth—which included everyone descended from Seth—had a pretty rough going at first, since Sakla wanted to destroy them. Because of them, the flood came. Because of them, "conflagrations came upon the earth." Because of them, plagues and famines came. Because of them, deceptions and false prophets came. It's hard to imagine why they were so unpopular, isn't it?

Finally, it was time for Seth himself to intervene. He could see that Sakla's whole program of destruction and persecution was set to backfire on him. So he called for an army of guardian angels, and 400 of them descended to the earth to watch out for Seth's people. But it didn't stop there, because Seth himself was coming to Earth to deal with Sakla once and for all.

Third Time's a Charm

If the sources that were used to write the Gospel of the Egyptians really were primarily Jewish, then this was the most obvious point at which they had been adapted to a Christian viewpoint. Seth came down now "through the three advents"—the flood, the "conflagration," and the judgment of the rulers—to take up residence in a human body that had been especially prepared.

Earlier in the text, we are told that Seth had set up his coming by preparing a body born of a virgin. Now he descended to that body, which was Jesus, called the "reason-born being." According to the Gospel of the Egyptians, Seth "put on" Jesus the way you would put on a jacket. Through Jesus' death he "nailed down" the rulers. Seth came to "save the race that went astray." The key to his plan was the institution of baptism, which was "higher than the heavens."

Living Waters

The third and final section of the Gospel of the Egyptians presents what some think is a baptismal service. It makes sense in some ways. The entire gospel has been leading up to this moment! The baptism instituted by Seth finally became available! Believers now had access to the gnosis of God! By concluding the myth with the ritual, the book demonstrated that there was no easy dividing line between gnostic theology and practice. Whether or not the baptismal service that is outlined was ever actually used, it shows that baptism was an experience to be desired.

> **Words to the Wise**
>
> It is in their rituals of ascent that the Gnostic sects most effectively blended their practices of ritual power with the visions of the mystics. The rite of baptism, which began as a Jewish ceremony of purification, developed into a rite of heavenly initiation.
>
> —Richard Smith, *Ancient Christian Magic* (61)

Baptism was associated with the mysterious five seals, which we'll talk more about in Chapter 10. Whatever form these seals took, either spiritually or as a ritual observance, they were clearly significant to gaining gnosis and achieving a transcendent experience. In Chapter 15, we'll look at Zostrianos, an account of one gnostic's ascent to the heavens, and we'll see just how important the idea of baptism was to receiving a highly coveted mystical vision.

The act of baptism was accompanied by a hymn sung by the believer in response to the vision that he or she was supposed to receive. The song began with exclamations of praise that focused on aspects of the Divine; "O living water" was one, "O name of all glories" was another. "Having known you, I have now mixed with your unchanging nature," the believer confessed. The "fragrance of life" was now in the believer, because it was mixed in with the waters of baptism.

Names, Names, Names

Like the rest of the Gospel of the Egyptians, the third section contains a lengthy list of spiritual beings, aeons, and angels who were involved in the act of baptism. Apart from names that we have come to know already, such as the four luminaries, there were beings who watched over the waters themselves, those who presided at the baptism, and those who chaperoned the believer in his or her spiritual ascent into the heavens.

Part of the key to gnostic revelation is its insistence on knowing the path that lies before the believer. Navigating the spirit's escape from this life involved more than just good luck and a prayer. Better to see the lay of the land before you have to travel it, gnostics believed. Baptism prepared a believer by equipping him or her with an experience of ascent that established a renewed communion with the Divine.

But the Divine refers not only to the ineffable Parent at the center of the gnostic Pleroma, but to the whole divine realm of beings named—often with mind-numbing precision. And yet, even these names are not entirely accurate. It had to have been obvious to at least a few gnostics that many of the names—Cain, Abel, Seth, and Gamaliel, to name just a few—that they used were drawn from the Hebrew Scriptures (what Christians call the Old Testament) and the Christian gospels.

These names are mythological, and were not meant to be taken as historical figures. They represented elemental spirits, not your next-door neighbors. The actual names of these beings were not important. Gnostics would have claimed that they named these spiritual beings in ways that highlighted certain truths. However, their orthodox opponents frequently accused the gnostics of multiplying angels and inventing names to give their myths more substance than they were worth. They reserved particular scorn for the mystical names that gnostics used for God.

What's That Racket?

All through the Gospel of the Egyptians, you'll see these very odd sentences full of vowels that have no apparent meaning. Here's an example. These are the seven vowels sounds that are emanated by the Son:

```
IIIIIIIIIIIIIIIIIIIIIII
_____
EEEEEEEEEEEEEEEEEEEEEEEE

OOOOOOOOOOOOOOOOOOOOOOOO

UUUUUUUUUUUUUUUUUUUUUUUU

EEEEEEEEEEEEEEEEEEEEEEEE

AAAAAAAAAAAAAAAAAAAAAAAA
_____
OOOOOOOOOOOOOOOOOOOOOOOO
```

What on Earth is going on here? Well, since the Divine is indefinable and inexpressible, this may be one way of "naming" the Divine visually. The letters, their position, and the frequency of their occurrence each lend itself to a symbolic interpretation, which add up to a kind of picture name for God. For example, each of the vowels appears 22 times. This number—22—is the same as the number of letters in the Hebrew alphabet. Is that a coincidence, or deliberate? Probably deliberate.

When read in columns, the first four letters form the word "Ieou." This is possibly a version of Yao, itself a shortened form of the Hebrew name for God, Yahweh, which was frequently used in Jewish magical incantations. The remaining two letters, alpha and omega, are the first and last letters of the Greek alphabet. In the Revelation of John in the Bible, Jesus used them to describe his eternal existence ("I am the Alpha and the Omega, the first and the last, the beginning and the end" Revelation 22:13). In other words the Greek alpha and omega formed part of a palette from which writers of various revelations drew to paint their pictures of the divine realm.

From the Source

In the sacred formulas they inscribe, purporting to address the Supernal Beings—not merely the Soul but even the Transcendents—they are simply uttering spells and appeasements and evocations in the idea that these powers will obey a call and be led about by a word from any of us who is in some degree trained to use the appropriate forms in the appropriate way—certain melodies, certain sounds, specially directed breathings, sibilant cries, and all else to which is ascribed magic potency upon the Supreme. Perhaps they would repudiate any such intention: Still they must explain how these things act upon the unembodied: They do not see that the power they attribute to their own words is so much taken away from the majesty of the Divine.

—Plotinus, Sixth Ennead (Tract. 9.14), decrying the Gnostic practice of addressing the Divine powers through exclamations and incantations

Several more of these vowel constructions appear in the baptismal hymn, which leads one to speculate whether they were not merely tools for meditation or revelation but were meant to be spoken aloud as an exclamation of praise. What effect this would have had on the worshipper is unknown. Was it designed to accompany (or even induce) an ecstatic state of some kind, one that might be conducive to receiving a vision?

To suggest that the gnostics were bargaining with the spiritual beings whom they addressed through their rituals, both public and private, hardly makes them unique. Scads of amulets have been discovered bearing Coptic incantations for protection or blessing. The use of "magic" was common among average folks, even those in orthodox Christian churches. Gnostics may have elevated the use of these techniques in their own rituals, for which Irenaeus and Tertullian censured them, among others, but they didn't invent the practice. Nor did it die off with their disappearance.

Signposts

The Gospel of the Egyptians ends with two postscripts. The first is part of the text itself, and tells how Seth himself wrote this book and placed it on top of the mountain Kharaksio. It's possible that this was intended to establish some authority for the gospel, attributing it not to a human source like an apostle but instead to a Divine source.

The monk who copied the text apparently added the second postscript. It appears at the end of the copy of the gospel in Codex III, and claims to be the words of "Eugnostos"—which means "good-knower" in Greek. He adds his name "in the flesh"—Gongessos, an Egyptian/Coptic-sounding name which was probably his "real" name among people. Our friend the copyist praised the words of the gospel that he had just finished transferring, and ended with the claim "of divine authorship is the Holy Book of the Great Invisible Spirit! Amen!"

The Least You Need to Know

- The gnostic's basic mythic story begins with a perfect realm of a Divine Parent—about whom we can say nothing—but it grows immensely complex with "aeons" as gods and demi-gods, along with various greater and lesser powers, all of whom have specific offices and personalities.

- A being named Seth becomes the origin and then savior of a perfect race, to which the gnostics felt they belonged.

- For gnostics baptism meant far more than a ritual. It was an experience designed to open the believer to a transcendent experience.

- Gnosticism included the use of magical texts and incantations as a means of accessing the Divine.

Chapter 9

The Gospel of Truth

In This Chapter

- ◆ Proclaiming the gnostic "good news"
- ◆ The Valentinian origins of the gospel
- ◆ The Gospel of Truth's take on the gnostic myth
- ◆ Allegorizing the orthodox canon

The word "gospel" literally means "good news," a reference to the essence of the message that Jesus' followers were commissioned to spread. It also refers to a literary genre, a type of writing created by the authors of Matthew, Mark, Luke, and John as they formulated the works that eventually appeared in the New Testament. Gospels are narrative works. They tell the story of Jesus, including his teachings, his acts, and his passion. By that second meaning, most of the so-called Gnostic Gospels don't qualify. The Gospel of Thomas (see Chapter 6) is a just a collection of sayings, while the Gospel of Mary (see Chapter 7) is, in part, an account of a post-resurrection dialogue. The Gospel of the Egyptians (see Chapter 8) doesn't even come close. It resembles Genesis more than it does a gospel.

The Gospel of Truth is not like the four gospels we know, either. But its author might very well argue that it is a gospel in the original sense of the word—the proclamation of "good news." The Gospel of Truth is actually a sermon delivered to a gathering of Christian believers. Whether those believers happened to be gnostics or not is one of the questions we'll explore in this chapter.

The Text

When this text was first discovered, many scholars attributed it to Valentinus, the second-century gnostic genius who we met in Chapter 4. The title corresponds to a reference in Irenaeus's *Against Heresies* to a document called the Gospel of Truth that was used by the Valentinians. The sermon's argument corresponds to what little we know of Valentinus's teachings, so it certainly comes from him or one of his followers. Yet it doesn't have any of the complexities that came later as Valentinus's students expanded upon his ideas.

From the Source

But those who are from Valentinus ... boast that they possess more gospels than there really are. Indeed, they have arrived at such a pitch of audacity as to entitle their comparatively recent writing "the Gospel of Truth," though it agrees in nothing with the Gospels of the Apostles, so that they have really no gospel which is not full of blasphemy. For if what they have published is the Gospel of truth, and yet is totally unlike those which have been handed down to us from the apostles, any who please may learn, as is shown from the Scriptures themselves, that that which has been handed down from the apostles can no longer be reckoned the Gospel of Truth.

—Irenaeus, *Against Heresies* 3.11.9

The style of writing in the Gospel of Truth is similar to the admittedly small fragments of Valentinus's writing that are excerpted by some orthodox writers as part of their refutation of his thinking. What is a more convincing case for attributing authorship of the text to Valentinus, though, is the difficulty of imagining anyone else in the Valentinian camp who could pull off such a feat of rhetorical brilliance. At this point, however, we have to say that, while it's quite possible that the Gospel of Truth was penned by Valentinus himself, there is no way of proving it. Assuming that Valentinus did write it, the gospel would date from sometime in the middle of the second century.

Two copies of the Gospel of Truth were discovered at Nag Hammadi. The first, Codex I,3 is in fairly good shape. The second, Codex XII,2 is very fragmented.

Valentinus and His Movement

We've already talked about Valentinus briefly, but a fuller examination of the man and the movement that he started will help us better understand this text. As mentioned in Chapter 4, Valentinus originally came from Alexandria in Egypt. Having imbibed deeply of the gnostic thinking that thrived there, he moved to Italy. While historians differ on the precise dates and details, it seems that Valentinus spent the better part of two decades teaching in Rome both by involving himself in the public life of the church and by running a private school.

In the second century, if you were a Christian serious about growing into a mature spiritual life, you would join a school or *didaskaleion*. These were small groups of men and women who would gather around a teacher, often for years, in order to fully digest that person's teachings and lifestyle. Such groups flourished around the Mediterranean world as a forum for instruction but also as a means to create a sense of community.

Such groups are mentioned in the New Testament. The original disciples of Jesus gathered around him in a manner that, later, non-Jewish believers would have interpreted as a school. During his missionary endeavors in the city of Ephesus, Paul rented the hall of Tyrannus for two years, offering public lectures and undoubtedly attracting non-Jewish students as followers (Acts 19:9). Later, mainstream Christians also followed this pattern. Justin Martyr, a contemporary of Valentinus, lived above a bathhouse in Rome where his students would come and learn from him. The School of Alexandria, which we discussed in Chapter 3, ran along similar lines.

> ### Word Knowledge
>
> The **didaskaleions** were small gatherings of men and women who attached themselves to an individual teacher in the hopes of being mentored into a deeper spiritual life.

> ### Words to the Wise
>
> Small study-circles were the powerhouses of the Christian culture of the second and third century. The extraordinary intellectual ferment of the period is unthinkable without them.
>
> —Peter Brown, *The Body and Society*

The independent nature of these schools made confrontations with the established churches almost unavoidable. To the clergy, preaching to the faithful gathered together on Sunday, these autonomous, charismatic teachers were dangerous. The schools were under no authority; therefore there was no assurance that their teachings adhered to the "Rule of Faith." Depending on how secretive these private groups were about their actual teachings, it might actually take quite a bit of time for these conflicts to develop. Valentinus and his followers were content to remain within the larger Christian community, using its Scriptures and joining in its confessions, while all the while reinterpreting them to fit their own needs in the hopes of converting orthodox Christians to their own views.

The School of Valentinus

During his lifetime, Valentinus and his followers remained a part of the larger Christian community. For some time afterward, this state of affairs continued. In the two decades between Valentinus's passing and the publishing of *Against Heresies*, Valentinus's system had developed into two basic camps, the Eastern and the Western Schools. Their influence was widespread. When Irenaeus wrote his *Against Heresies* he attacked not only Valentinus but several of his students as well.

As we'll see in the next chapter, the Valentinians were already beginning to develop their own unique and separate understanding of the meaning of baptism and the celebration of the eucharist, central acts of worship in the early Christian community. In addition, the Valentinians began to place a great deal of emphasis on their own kinds of sacramental acts, rituals not observed in other Christian circles. It was probably inevitable that they would eventually drift away and form their own version of Christianity.

By the time that Constantine issued his edict in A.D. 326 forbidding heretics, including the Valentinians, from meeting, it was clear that the Valentinians had already established an identity of their own. We know that a mob destroyed a church building used specifically by Valentinians in the Syrian city of Callinicum in A.D. 386. This was just a couple of decades after the Nag Hammadi library is believed to have been buried. Valentinians continued to exist as a discrete group for several centuries, but they had been successfully removed from the Christian community.

The Western School

Also known as the Italic School, some of Valentinus's students continued his work in and around Rome. Their principal difference with their Eastern brethren seemed to have been a disagreement over the nature of Christ's body. The Western Valentinians took the position that the Demiurge (the "god" of the physical world) created a body for Jesus out of the psychic or soul substance. It was upon this body that the Savior came at Jesus' baptism in the Jordan River, investing Jesus with a spiritual nature as well. This also seems to have been the view of Basilides and others in the Alexandrian gnostic community, so there may be a continuing influence there from Egypt.

The best known of the Western Valentinians was Ptolemy. Although we know next to nothing about him personally, Irenaeus devoted considerable space to outlining the system that Ptolemy taught. It seems that it was Ptolemy's teaching and its influence over certain members of Irenaeus's congregation in Lyon that motivated Irenaeus to write his monumental work, *Against Heresies*. Ptolemy was also the author of a very well-written work called the *Letter to Flora*.

From the Source

I intend, then, to the best of my ability, with brevity and clearness to set forth the opinions of those who are now promulgating heresy. I refer especially to the disciples of Ptolemy, whose school may be described as a bud from that of Valentinus. I shall also endeavor, according to my moderate ability, to furnish the means of overthrowing them, by showing how absurd and inconsistent with the truth are their statements.

—Irenaeus, *Against Heresies* 1.preface.3

Ptolemy is an unusual name for a Roman, so scholars have long speculated that he may be the same as a man named Ptolemy (mentioned by Justin Martyr) who was executed sometime around A.D. 152 for attempting to convert a Roman matron to the Christian faith. If both the identification and the date are accurate, that puts Ptolemy's death during the time that Valentinus was teaching in Rome, which hardly makes him a good candidate to be Valentinus's successor. It also takes Ptolemy out of the picture more than 20 years prior to Irenaeus's urgent rebuttal.

Another famous name from the Western School is Heracleon. Clement of Alexandria called Heracleon "the most distinguished of the school of Valentinians." Heracleon is best remembered as the author of what may well have been the first complete commentary of one of the gospels. While it no longer exists, Heracleon's commentary on the Gospel of John inspired Origen's own work on the subject. Written principally to refute Heracleon's interpretations, Origen's comments on the Gospel of John quote extensively from Heracleon and in many ways adopt his interpretive methods.

The Letter to Flora

Written by Ptolemy to a Roman woman named Flora, the Letter to Flora was pre-served for us when Epiphanius of Salamis quoted it in its entirety in the fourth century.

The letter was an attempt to convert a presumably orthodox Christian woman to the Valentinian perspective. The central focus of the letter was how a Christian ought to read and understand the Old Testament. Is it divinely given and therefore something that every Christian should read and observe, and is it truthful information about God, Christ, and humanity? Is it demonic, designed simply to mislead the hearer? Or is there a third option? Ptolemy claimed that there was.

Ptolemy had complex ideas about the Law of Moses. Though incomplete, he held that the Mosaic Law was basically "just." He rejected the notion that it could be the work of a demonic being set on the destruction of the human race. He argued further that the Old Testament cannot be the revelation of the Divine Father of Jesus Christ, who is perfect and perfectly good. The Hebrew Scriptures contain contributions from Moses and other men in addition to what comes from God. In addition, not all that comes from God demonstrates perfection. Some parts are good but await fulfillment in Jesus. Other parts are not entirely just, such as the decree allowing divorce, and will be set aside by Jesus. Other parts are symbolic, such as circumcision, and will be spiritualized. The author of the Law of Moses, then, is an imperfect but just God. This position is similar to that outlined by Marcion in his break with the rest of the Christian community.

Ptolemy claimed that his benchmark for reading the Old Testament as imperfect stemmed from the teachings of Jesus himself. By comparing what Jesus revealed of the Father, it was clear to Ptolemy that the Father and the God of the Jews was not the same being. He promised Flora an additional letter that would go more fully into depth and discuss the Divine Father and how all these things came about. Presumably this letter or series of letters would have described Ptolemy's version of the gnostic myth that Irenaeus detailed.

Unfortunately, those additional letters were never written or they have not survived. This single letter, however, makes it clear how gnostic teaching would be persuasive and attractive to non-Jewish converts to Christianity. Ptolemy's style was lucid and straightforward. The letter is compact but presents its argument well. If most of the Valentinian teachers were of this caliber, it is easy to see why they posed such a threat to the orthodox viewpoint.

The Eastern School

Another bastion of Valentinian thought was based partly in Alexandria and in the eastern parts of the Roman Empire such as Syria and Asia Minor (modern-day Turkey). The Eastern (sometimes called the Oriental) School took a different tack with regard to the nature of Jesus' body. For the Eastern teachers, the Savior was born only of spiritual substance. In doing so, they bought into the docetic view of Jesus as a being incapable of suffering (for more on docetism, see Chapter 3).

Two names are of interest in the Eastern School. The first is Theodotus, about whom we know almost nothing. Much of what we do know of Theodotus comes from Clement of Alexandria's *Stromata*, which includes a section known separately as the Excerpts from Theodotus. While it can be difficult to separate Clement's own notes from the selections he has taken from Theodotus's writings, it is an invaluable resource for exploring the Eastern form of Valentinianism. We'll look more closely at it in Chapter 10, where we discuss the Gospel of Philip.

Another popular gnostic teacher from the Eastern School was Mark. Irenaeus told us a great deal about him, very little of it flattering. According to Irenaeus, Mark was quite the womanizer. He took literally the idea of the "bridal chamber," which we'll look at in the next chapter, and used it as an opportunity to seduce women into having sex with him. Accusations of this kind were common rhetorical devices used to discredit someone as a reputable teacher, so there may be no truth to them. On the other hand, it wouldn't be the first time that a religious leader used his authority and charisma for sexual gratification.

The Valentinian System

Trying to describe precisely what form of gnostic myth Valentinus composed is an exercise in educated guesswork. Irenaeus gave us a quick thumbnail sketch, but only as part of a kind of mythological archaeology. He began with the teachings of one of Valentinus's students, Ptolemy, and peeled away the layers to follow it back through Valentinus to the classical gnostics and finally (Irenaeus asserts) to Simon the Magician (see Chapter 4 for more on Simon the Magician). Using Irenaeus's descriptions along with fragments of Valentinian writings preserved in the various Valentinian texts discovered in the Nag Hammadi library, scholars have attempted to reconstruct Valentinus's system, but there is no way to be certain that our picture is accurate. Apart from other considerations, there is no way to know how often or how drastically Valentinus may have altered or developed his own ideas during the course of his career. With those qualifications, let's take a look at the Valentinian version of the gnostic myth.

Unlike the classical gnostic myth, which introduced us to a single Divine Parent, Valentinus began with a pair. There was a masculine Father who Valentinus called Primal Depth (bythos). This being was joined by the feminine Silence (sige). Together they emanated a pair of aeons, the Intellect (nous) and Truth (aletheia). These four together emanated two more pairs: Word (logos) and Life (zoe), and Man (anthropos) and Church (ekklesia). These eight beings together brought forth the rest of the Pleroma, 10 coming from Word and Life and 12 more coming from Man and Church. All together, Valentinus outlined 30 aeons (15 male/female pairs), different from the more complex gnostic myths that preceded his.

A Newer, Friendlier Sophia

As with previously discussed myths, the last of the aeons is Sophia. Usually Sophia is portrayed as being at fault for trying to create without her consort. Valentinus emphasized instead that the entire Pleroma longed to know the Divine Parent. According to the Valentinians, only the Intellect had knowledge (gnosis) of the Divine parent. Sophia attempted to move toward the Divine, but was rebuffed by something called Limit or Boundary, which divided the rest of the Pleroma from the Divine parent. In her despair at being unable to know the Divine, Sophia became separated from the rest of the Pleroma.

The Pleroma immediately emitted another Boundary, to separate what was outside the Pleroma from what was within. Sophia was left on the outside. Next, the entire Pleroma emanated two new beings, Christ and the Holy Spirit. They served both to stabilize the rest of the Divine realm and to rescue Sophia from her exile.

Sophia was returned to the Pleroma by Christ, but in the process, her thinking and emotional distress became separated from her and left behind outside the Pleroma. This division between the "upper" and "lower" Sophia is a unique part of the Valentinian myth. The "lower" Sophia is also called Achamoth.

This is one of those points at which the Valentinian myth gets complex, and it will be helpful to keep in mind that Valentinus is using symbolic language to describe a process of salvation. He knew Christians try to use human, flawed wisdom (our knowledge, insight, and experience)—Sophia—in cooperating with Christ to reach heaven. The Gospel of Truth suggested seeing salvation as part of a larger, more complex movement from Earth to heaven. Think of all of this as symbolic: for

"Pleroma," think "heaven"; for "Sophia/Wisdom" think "flawed human thinking"; for "Achamoth," think "our need for salvation, confused and yet hopeful", and so on.

From the Source

With his trademark biting sarcasm, Tertullian discussed the variety of opinion among the Valentinians about how Christ came to be:

Now, concerning even the Lord Jesus, into how great a diversity of opinion are they divided! One party form Him of the blossoms of all the Aeons. Another party will have it that He is made up only of those 10 whom the Word and the Life produced; from which circumstance the titles of the Word and the Life were suitably transferred to Him. Others, again, that He rather sprang from the 12, the offspring of Man and the Church and therefore, they say, He was designated "Son of man." Others, moreover, maintain that He was formed by Christ and the Holy Spirit, who have to provide for the establishment of the universe, and that He inherits by right His Father's appellation. Some there are who have imagined that another origin must be found for the title "Son of man; "for they have had the presumption to call the Father Himself Man, by reason of the profound mystery of this title: so that what can you hope for more ample concerning faith in that God, with whom you are now yourself on a par? Such conceits are constantly cropping out amongst them, from the redundance of their mother's seed. And so it happens that the doctrines which have grown up amongst the Valentinians have already extended their rank growth to the woods of the Gnostics.

—Tertullian, *Against the Valentinians*

Words to the Wise

Rebellious Wisdom became a frenetic power of mere proliferation. Driven to create out of despair at her separation from God, Sophia formed a redundant universe. Matter came into being, and, with matter, the sad sense, which many second-century thinkers shared with Valentinus, that the material world was an abortive attempt to imitate an infinitely distant, invisible, and ever-elusive model. The world created by Sophia spoke only of the chasm that separated what was from what should be.

—Peter Brown, *The Body and Society*

The process then had to repeat, because the whole determination of the Divine Parent is for a complete restoration of the Pleroma. To heal Achamoth of her "passions," her terrified and grief stricken emotional state, they emanated Jesus the Savior. He removed Achamoth's passions from her, refining them into a pair of different essences. The first, born of Achamoth's grief and fear, was the material substance. From her desire to repent and be restored to the Pleroma, the psychic or soul substance was formed. To these two, Achamoth added a third when, free from her passions, she conceived "out of joy" and brought forth the spiritual substance. Keep these three substances in mind, because they become very significant for the Valentinian view of salvation.

Achamoth used the soul substance to fashion a new being, the Demiurge. He, in turn, created our own universe from the material and soul substances. The Valentinian Demiurge is much less malicious than the one who appears in the classical gnostic myths. In fact, while you might easily conclude that the Demiurge and the devil are the same person according to the earlier gnostic myths, the Valentinians explicitly separate them.

Where Does It All End?

According to the Gospel of Truth, human beings were created by the Demiurge out of the material and soul substances. In addition, Achamoth secretly imbued human beings with a spiritual nature as well. We are told that the spiritual nature of human beings will ultimately be saved and will return to the Pleroma. The material nature, on the other hand, will dissolve away and be destroyed. The soul nature is in between the other two, and tends toward one or the other.

The Gospel of Truth tell us that human beings fall into one of those three categories (we saw these in Chapter 4), so that some folks are spiritual (having body, soul, and spirit) and are guaranteed salvation, while others are irredeemably material (body only, without soul or spirit) and are without hope. It's the people in the middle, the "psychic" or soul people, who need help. They have the free will to decide whether to live for the world or to live for God. To save them, the Savior took on a body and lived a human life. He came upon the man Jesus of Nazareth at his baptism in the Jordan River and used him to reveal the Father to those who were capable of seeing and hearing. At the end, the spiritual nature of the Savior left the human Jesus prior to the crucifixion.

According to the Valentinian myth, the three categories of human beings have a direct reference to existing groups. The spiritual, who are saved on the basis of their nature, are the gnostics. The material folks are those who have no interest in spiritual matters. In the middle, of course, is the soul group or "psychics." They correspond to the regular church folks, who are saved by faith and works. Ultimately, Achamoth will be united to the Savior as a renewed pair of aeons in the Pleroma. Along with them, the gnostics will shed their bodies and souls and ascend to the Divine realms where they will be united with angels (more about this when we talk about the "bridal chamber" in the next chapter). The material folks will simply cease to exist, along with "psychics" who lived for the world rather than for spirit. Those "psychics" who choose to follow the teachings of the Savior will spend eternity with the Demiurge in a place called the "midpoint," a lesser realm that exists outside of the Pleroma.

The Sermon

The Valentinian myth clearly differed from the story that the orthodox Christians were telling about Jesus. For the orthodox, the Father of Jesus and the Creator of the world were the same being, which makes the physical world a pretty important place. Salvation is needed, not because people are ignorant but because they are rebels against the Divine. The cross is the center of orthodox theology. That wasn't the case for the Valentinians. Rather, they held to the gnostic reverence for Jesus as the spiritual teacher who had overcome the powers through stealth and led the way back to the Father. How can these two groups possibly coexist?

The Gospel of Truth was a sermon, likely given to an audience that included orthodox Christians. It demonstrated the lengths to which Valentinus, or one of his most brilliant followers, could go to communicate his teachings in a way that wouldn't immediately turn off their hearers. The Valentinian myth was presented in a very subtle manner, with a great deal of care and sensitivity to mainstream beliefs. The fact that it failed to convince most Christians is certainly not from any lack of trying. The chasm between gnostic and orthodox beliefs was simply too wide to bridge by rhetoric alone.

Speaking Truth

Identifying the author of the Gospel of Truth is tricky, and that problem makes it hard to create a helpful outline of the text. The author glided by one idea, alluding and suggesting, and then moved on to another. Images and parables were as important as concepts. The Gospel used orthodox language; the cross was taken seriously and at one point was described as the moment when the knowledge of the Father was put on display. Sophia appeared, but not by name. Instead, she was called Error. Of the many emanations of the Divine Parent in the gnostic myth, only the Father and the Son made an appearance. Yet, behind it all, you can sense the larger worldview of the author tugging in another direction.

The ultimate goal the author set forth was rest, coming to a state of unity with the Father. "This is the account of the good news about the discovery of the Pleroma," he mentioned toward the end. Coming to a final rest in the Divine presence was the end result of a process that began with the recognition of our ignorance of the Father. The means to ending ignorance is knowledge, not of a factual nature but an awakening to truth. That knowledge comes as the response to a call, a summons from the Father, to which each individual responds. Knowledge brings with it the responsibility to share, but that isn't an onerous duty. From its very first sentence— "The proclamation of the truth is a joy for those who have received grace from the father of truth"—the author sought to convey the creative, life-giving joyfulness of truly knowing the Father.

From the Source

With their emphasis on self-knowledge through an immediate experience of the Divine, it should come as no surprise that Valentinians were eager for visions. Hippolytus preserved this short note about an alleged experience that Valentinus himself claimed to have had:

For Valentinus says he saw a newborn babe, and questioned it to find out who it was. And the babe answered him, saying that it was the Word. Thereupon, he adds to this a certain pompous tale, intending to derive from this his attempt at a sect.

—Hippolytus, *Refutation of All Heresies* (translated in Bentley Layton's *The Gnostic Scriptures*)

Images of Truth

The author knew that a straightforward, academic lecture was not going to be persuasive with his audience. So he used parables and imagery to convey an atmosphere that would more effectively communicate his concerns. Forgetfulness, which is the obstacle to knowing the Father, was described both like a fog and like being drunk. There is a parable of jars that described the differences in people, and insinuated that the loss of some people is not so great a tragedy.

One of the author's most important points was that knowing the Father leads to a capacity to see the physical world as an illusion. To make his point, he offered a hair-raising description of what a nightmare feels like. Sometimes a person imagines being chased by unseen forces, he says, or falling from a high place, or committing some unspeakable act, like murdering one's neighbors. While the person is dreaming, it seems completely real and logical. But when one wakes up, one realizes that he or she was dreaming. The person is free from the logic of the dream, and also from its consequences. What happens in the dream, stays there. To the author, that's what it's like to awaken to the Father.

The use of imagery was intended to evoke a kind of gut-level recognition, a sudden "a-ha" moment. The author was fishing for those who "have ears to hear" and the curiosity to seek out greater understanding. Using images and experiences helped to keep the author from running afoul of the local heretic-hunters while still suggesting a different way of looking at things.

Your Personal Universe

Valentinus took the classical gnostic myth and turned it inward in a manner that we would now view as psychological. We don't want to be too anachronistic, reading our own modern concerns into what Valentinus was doing, but it is clear that he had taken the features of the gnostic mythological universe and had begun to turn them inward. It's no surprise that famed therapist Carl Gustav Jung found the gnostics particularly insightful in terms of his own archetypal psychology.

This psychological aspect emerged at points within the sermon. For example, the idea that a man who has knowledge "is his Pleroma" bespoke a certain blending of the lines between external and internal reality. There was a sense in which each person, being part of the Divine essence in spirit, *is* the Pleroma. Such a person is complete, "being in no way deficient in anything." This demythologizing of the gnostic myth made self-knowledge and self-exploration the key to knowledge of the Divine.

Here's where the image of waking from a nightmare takes on new significance. For the author, the world is not just the product of Sophia's maddened despair. It's not an actual place, but a state of mind. Coming to knowledge is like awakening to find that you were dreaming. The dream world was never anyplace but inside yourself. If "the lack came into being because the father was not known, from the moment that the father is known, the lack will not exist." This world of chaos and destruction, of pain and evil and separation from the Father is an illusion, a nightmare. Wake up, the author wanted to say, and you will find that it is not real.

But the Deeper Meaning Is ...

The Gospel of Truth is one of the oldest texts we are aware of that refers to the canon of Scripture being used by orthodox churches. In order to couch his sermon in terms that would be acceptable to his hearers, the author drew from or alluded to several works from the New Testament, including Matthew, John, Romans, 1 and 2 Corinthians, Ephesians, Colossians, Hebrews, 1 John, and the Revelation. There may very well be others that would make such a list (the Shepherd of Hermas, for example, which did not make it into the New Testament, was very popular in Rome during this period), but the author of the Gospel of Truth did not refer to them.

The author's use of these texts demonstrated how Valentinian gnostics could so easily remain within the larger Christian community, using the same Scriptures and even confessing the same "Rule of Faith." Valentinians used an interpretive technique to *allegorize* those parts of the Scriptures or the church's confessions that they found problematic.

> **Word Knowledge**
>
> To **allegorize** a story means to read it figuratively rather than literally. The characters and places in the story represent certain ideas or experiences.

Allegory was a common, though frequently controversial, means of reading texts in the Greek-speaking Mediterranean world. It goes as far back as the fifth century B.C., and was adopted by such Jewish thinkers as Philo of Alexandria as a way of reading the Hebrew Scriptures in a manner that enabled readers to find Platonic meaning in them. The Apostle Paul famously used allegory in his Letter to the Galatians, when he interpreted the figures of Hagar and Sarah as representative of the two covenants, those who kept the Law of Moses and those who existed under grace through Jesus Christ (Galatians 4:21–31). Orthodox writers used the technique as well, particularly Origen, who effectively demonstrated both the value and the danger of the allegorical method in his own writings. Allegory continued to be a popular means of interpreting stories, Scriptural or otherwise, well into the Middle Ages.

As Bentley Layton describes in his book *The Gnostic Scriptures*, allegorizing Scripture enabled the gnostics to read their own understanding into a text that was already accepted as authoritative to the reader or hearer. At the same time, they could neutralize interpretations that countered their own, not by denying the text out of hand but by rereading it so as to explain it away.

Irenaeus's account of Ptolemy's version of the gnostic myth was filled with examples of the Valentinian teacher's allegorical readings of Scripture. For example, Ptolemy read the Genesis account of Cain, Abel, and Seth as representative of the three natures of human beings: the material, the psychic, and the spiritual. The curing of the woman with the hemorrhage (Luke 8:43–48), who had suffered for 12 years, Ptolemy read as emblematic of Sophia (the twelfth aeon in Ptolemy's system) reaching out for healing from the Savior. The fact that there are 30 aeons in the Pleroma is revealed by the 30 years that Jesus lived prior to beginning his ministry. These are some of the examples of allegorization that Irenaeus reports.

A close reading of the text shows that the author often played with the passages that he was alluding to, reshaping them to conform to the point he wanted to make. This practice demonstrates the gnostic belief that their knowledge made them superior to any Scriptural text. The measure of truth was not the external Scripture but the internal understanding of the nature of God and self.

The Least You Need to Know

♦ The Gospel of Truth is not a gospel in the literary sense of the word. However, its author would certainly have described it as a proclamation of "good news."

♦ Valentinus's students spread all over the world, further developing his system.

♦ Valentinus developed a modified form of the gnostic myth that was more explicitly Christian, though not Christian enough to prevent it from coming under attack.

♦ By embracing allegory, the Gospel of Truth presented Valentinian theology in a form palatable, or at least not deliberately offensive, to mainstream Christians.

Chapter 10

The Gospel of Philip

In This Chapter

◆ The use of anthologies in early Christianity

◆ Were Jesus and Mary Magdalene lovers?

◆ The five gnostic ritual sacraments

◆ A closer look at the bridal chamber ritual

The Gospel of Philip is another oddly named text in the Nag Hammadi library. The Apostle Philip appears only once in this collection of sayings, stories, and sermon quotations, but that was apparently enough to credit him for all of it. It has achieved a certain notoriety for suggesting that more was going on between Jesus and Mary Magdalene than we might otherwise guess, but its true importance is as a source of information about the worship life of the most significant group of gnostic Christians, the Valentinians.

The Text

The Gospel of Philip appears once in the Nag Hammadi library, at Codex II,3. Like all of the other Nag Hammadi texts, it is a Coptic translation from a Greek original. It doesn't tell a story, and in fact has more in common with the Gospel of Thomas (see Chapter 6) than with any of the New Testament gospels. While there are stories about and sayings by Jesus scattered throughout, Philip is really a collection of quotations from a variety of sermons, letters, and other texts, a number of which look to be Valentinian in perspective.

This hodgepodge of excerpts is not organized in any recognizable pattern. At times, certain blocks of material seemed tied together by common catchwords, but this is more likely a coincidence than deliberate. The quotations are not marked or numbered individually, and scholars disagree on exactly how they should be separated.

From the Source

Anthologies were not unheard of in late antiquity. Preserved in the Stromata of Clement of Alexandria is another anthology of gnostic literature. These quotations were probably collected for use during Clement's lectures at the School of Alexandria. The quotations are drawn from the works of Theodotus, a key figure in the Valentinian Eastern School. Because the excerpts are not numbered or set apart from Clement's comments, it is often difficult to separate one from the other.

One selection from the Excerpts highlights what, for many, serves as a handy definition of gnostic thought and experience:

What makes us free is the gnosis
of who we were
of what we have become
of where we were
of wherein we have been cast
of whereto we are hastening
of what we are being freed
of what birth really is
of what rebirth really is.

Word Knowledge

Syriac was the language of Syria during the early Christian period. It was a close cousin of Aramaic, the language that Jesus and his followers spoke on a daily basis.

Two of the excerpts are concerned with the definitions of certain words in *Syriac*. Also, the tenor of the selections seems to favor some of the ascetic and sacramental concerns that were important in Syrian Christianity. This has led some experts to speculate that the anthology as a whole may derive originally from Syria. No date for the collection is certain, though it could not be earlier than the middle of the second century because of the Valentinian content.

What we don't want to assume, as we read Philip, is that everything fits together perfectly in one nice, neat little package. Each of the sources that the editor of Philip used to create his collection had its own discrete theological bent. While we can lump certain passages together because they seem to be saying similar things, we're just going to have to hold any conclusions lightly. Philip can be unexpectedly complex.

The Gnostic Jesus

Although it doesn't focus specifically on the biographical details of the life of the Christ as the New Testament gospels do, the Gospel of Philip contains some interesting tidbits about Jesus and a smattering of sayings attributed to him. Several appear to come from the Gospels of Matthew and John. The text also draws from 1 Corinthians and 1 Peter, and it alludes to other New Testament documents. In addition to those sayings that can be attributed to the New Testament, several sayings are explicitly gnostic. It's very unlikely that any of these are actual sayings of Jesus.

In addition to the sayings attributed to Jesus, Philip also preserved some stories about Jesus. One such story describes how his father, Joseph, had planted a grove of trees to supply wood for his carpentry trade. From that grove, Joseph made the cross upon which his son died. After his resurrection, another passage relates, Jesus was known to appear in many different forms. Sometimes he even appeared to certain people as a mirror image of themselves. On one occasion, he appeared to his followers "in glory upon the mountain." At that appearance, we are told, "he was not small," but assumed a huge stature.

What's in a Name?

We've seen, in the Gospel of the Egyptians (see Chapter 8), how significant names were to the gnostics. The Gospel of Philip is equally concerned with names. "Names given to worldly things are very deceptive," one saying says, "since they turn the heart aside from the real to the unreal." For that reason, the gospel said that those who possess the name of the Son "think it but do not speak it." Much like the Gospel of the Egyptians, however, gnostic writers continued to find ways to speak about the unspeakable.

The gospel details the names of Jesus, perhaps to demonstrate one way that truth reveals itself. Jesus, we are told, is a private name, whereas Christ (meaning the one who is anointed) is a public name. Jesus is just a personal name, but every language has a word for Christ. Christ, then, is a more significant name because it describes a reality that is open to every culture and experience. It speaks to the inner spiritual reality of which Jesus is just one particular expression. A later passage delves into the ways that the apostles supposedly used the various names and title associated with Jesus.

Mother Mary

The Gospel of Philip includes statements about a number of important figures from the Jesus story. There are Marys just about everywhere in the life of Jesus. The name actually comes from the Hebrew name Mariam. Mariam was the name of Moses' sister, who figured so significantly in the Exodus story, and consequently it was a very popular name for Jewish girls. In fact, Mariam was as common a name in Jesus' day as Mary is among Roman Catholics today. So it should be no surprise to find so many Marys in the New Testament.

"Some say that Mary conceived by the holy spirit: They are mistaken," begins one passage about the mother of Jesus. This excerpt clearly came from a Western Valentinian perspective. (Eastern Valentinians, as we saw in Chapter 9, readily accepted the idea that the Holy Spirit was responsible for the birth of Jesus, and that he was therefore born in a body that was entirely spiritual. Western Valentinians, on the other hand, insisted that this was not possible.) "When did a female ever conceive by a female?" the passage continues. In Semitic languages like Syriac, Hebrew, and Aramaic, the word for spirit is feminine gender, so occasionally the Holy Spirit was referred to as "she" (this happens in Syrian Christian literature, such as the Odes of Solomon and the songs of Ephraem). It was natural to ask, therefore, how can a feminine Holy Spirit impregnate a woman, Mary? Instead, Western Valentinians held that the Spirit came upon Jesus at his baptism, and thus bypassed that question.

Jesus and Mary, Sittin' in a Tree ...

The Gospel of Philip mentions at one point that there were three Marys who were constant companions of Jesus. The first was his mother. The second was his sister, who is otherwise unknown. The third was Mary Magdalene, who was called his "companion."

It has been claimed that this word companion, which is sometimes translated as "consort," indicates that Mary had a particularly intimate relationship with Jesus. The speculation has been emboldened by another passage from Philip, which says that Jesus "loved her [Mary Magdalene] more than all the rest of the disciples" and that "he used to kiss her on her [mouth]." It's easy to see why so many people have jumped to conclusions about the possibility of a physical relationship between Jesus and Mary.

But it's important to note that the word "companion" or "consort" does not indicate a sexual relationship in the way that some authors have claimed. In addition, the passage about kissing is fragmented, and the word "mouth" doesn't exist in the text. It has been reconstructed on the basis of certain assumptions, but the reading isn't certain. Even if it is accurate, which it likely is, kissing in ancient cultures (and many modern ones, for that matter) is not always sexual in nature. Kissing is mentioned elsewhere in Philip as a means of receiving grace, a variation on the "kiss of peace," which was a common Christian practice at the time.

> **Words to the Wise**
>
> Valentinians gave their own interpretation to the traditional Christian kiss of fellowship: It was by the light touch of mouth and breath, and not through the hot genitals, that the firmest links in the chain of true humanity were formed: "For it is by a kiss that the perfect conceive and give birth."
>
> —Peter Brown, *The Body and Society*

Finally, both passages should be read in the context of the entire Gospel of Philip, which (as we'll see near the end of this chapter) takes a dim view toward sexual relationships. It seems highly unlikely that Philip's editor would have deliberately included works that alleged a sexual relationship between Jesus and any woman.

Water in the Water, Fire in the Oil

One of the central concerns of the Gospel of Philip is the ritual life of the Valentinian community. The bulk of the material excerpted in Philip has to do with sacramental worship. Various quotations describe the use, conditions, and meanings behind the various practices of initiation celebrated by at least some gnostic groups.

"The Lord did everything in a mystery: a baptism and an anointing, and a eucharist and a redemption and a bridal chamber." With that, Philip outlined the five discreet ritual actions that made up the Valentinian sacraments. Scholars disagree about how each of these five sacraments were celebrated, and some scholars contend that some or all of them were actually folded together into a single act. There's no question that they often overlap in their meanings. The rituals don't stand alone, but are integrally linked by what they purport to symbolize. Still, there is enough evidence to believe that at least baptism, the anointing with oil (often called chrismation), and the eating of the eucharist—three rituals also celebrated in the larger church—were kept as distinct acts. Together, these five acts may be synonymous with the "five seals" often spoken of in other gnostic literature. Or perhaps these are a Christianized version based on the five seals. Let's take a look at what Philip has to say about each of these five ritual acts.

Baptism

The first of the five seals was baptism. Baptism in water already had a history of acceptance among gnostic sects. Baptism, as we saw in Chapter 8, was a central concern for a number of gnostic groups that seem to have come out of a radicalized form of Judaism. These Sethite texts, like the Gospel of the Egyptians, were concerned with the issue of cleansing and taking upon themselves the new reality to which they were ascending. If you are familiar with the New Testament, you will already know about John the Baptist, who baptized Jews who came out to the desert to see him. There were many "Baptist" groups and movements in Judaism during the first century, and it is now believed that some of these continued to develop into gnostic groups with a singular focus on baptism.

So baptism as a ritual act was not unique to Christians in the first and second centuries. What was different was the idea, conveyed by Paul but probably more generically Christian in its source, that the believer was being baptized into the death and resurrection of Jesus.

In the Gospel of Philip, one of the principal meanings of baptism is its connection to the believer's resurrection. Jesus "perfected" baptism by drawing out death, so now the believer enters the waters safe from the destructive powers of "the spirit of the world." One saying compares baptism to the parts of the Temple in Jerusalem. Baptism is the outer, holy place through which the believer proceeds to enter the inner holy place and finally the innermost holy of holies, representing the sacraments of redemption and the bridal chamber respectively (these sacraments are discussed later in this chapter). "Baptism possesses resurrection," the passage asserts. Another excerpt warns the reader that it is pointless to wait, as some do, to die before attaining resurrection. "If they do not receive resurrection while they are alive, once they have died they will receive nothing." How is resurrection attained? "Great is baptism!" the passage concludes, for through it resurrection is available right now.

Here we see that gnostics viewed resurrection as spiritual and individual. No final, general resurrection of bodies for them. Rather, resurrection for gnostics takes place, first, at the awakening of the spirit in the act of coming to knowledge, and then, secondly, when the individual dies and the soul rises, like a spark, to the Pleroma. The reality of this kind of resurrection begins immediately on experiencing it. Resurrection is not a distinct, specific event—a physical resurrection—but an enlightening and enlivening of the inner person.

From the Source

For some ... distort into some imaginary sense even the most clearly described doctrine of the resurrection of the dead, alleging that even death itself must be understood in a spiritual sense. They say that which is commonly supposed to be death is not really so—namely, the separation of body and soul: It is rather the ignorance of God, by reason of which man is dead to God, and is not less buried in error than he would be in the grave. Wherefore that also must be held to be the resurrection, when a man is reanimated by access to the truth, and having dispersed the death of ignorance, and being endowed with new life by God, has burst forth from the sepulcher of the old man, even as the Lord likened the scribes and Pharisees to "whited sepulchers." Whence it follows that they who have by faith attained to the resurrection, are with the Lord after they have once put Him on in their baptism. By such subtlety, then, even in conversation have they often been in the habit of misleading our brethren, as if they held a resurrection of the dead *as well as we*. Woe, say they, to him who has not risen in the present body, for they fear that they might alarm their hearers if they at once denied the resurrection.

—Tertullian, *On the Resurrection of the Dead*

Philip preserved a number of interesting images that enrich the understanding of baptism. In one instance, God was compared to a dyer of cloth. In the same way that good dyes ink into the fabrics that are immersed in them, so God infuses a new reality into the person who is baptized. In a related passage, Jesus entered the dye works run by a fellow named Levi. Throwing 72 different colors into a vat, they all came out white. This was why the son of man came, he tells Levi, to be a dyer. Both passages, and the first one in particular, are very suggestive that Valentinian baptism involved immersion in water much as baptism was performed in the larger Christian community.

Baptism was also likened to taking off old clothing and putting on new "garments of light." That's why initiates strip before entering the baptismal waters, so that they can put on the "perfect human being" in place of their earthly "clothing."

In another excerpt, those who are baptized but don't receive the Spirit in the act are only borrowing the name "Christian." If you do receive Spirit, the gospel argues, then it's yours. Those who legitimately possess the name get to keep it no matter what, but those who are borrowing will eventually have to return what they have taken.

Anointing

A couple of passages in the Gospel of Philip link the sacrament of baptism with the sacrament of anointing. In one, the waters of baptism are compared to a mirror in which a person sees his or her true self. That mirror is meaningless, however, without a light to see by. That light is the chrism, the anointing oil.

The second passage says that "by water and fire the entire place is set apart." The fire is, again, the oil.

> ### Did You Know?
>
> It was a practice in some Christian circles to heat fragrant oil and apply it to believers as part of the baptismal initiation into the Christian faith. Practices differed with regard to how the oil was applied, what words were spoken, and at what point in the process (before or after baptism, for example) to anoint the believer. In most places, anointing seems to have taken place after baptism, but in eastern Syria there was a practice of anointing prior to baptism.

The link between baptism and anointing is located in the accounts of Jesus' baptism by John in the Jordan River. As the Gospel of Mark 1:10–11 relates it, "As Jesus was coming up out of the water, he saw heaven being torn open and the Spirit descending on him like a dove. And a voice came from heaven: 'You are my Son, whom I love; with you I am well pleased.'" Thus, baptism was the occasion for the coming of the Spirit on Jesus. Gnostics interpreted this as the moment when the Savior entered Jesus and began to reveal the Father to human beings. Anointing with oil, also called chrismation, began in Christian circles as a way of symbolizing this event.

"Chrism has more authority than baptism" one passage says. Baptism applies to any number of groups, but only Christians are anointed. It's a play on words. Christians are named for Jesus Christ. "Christ" is the Greek word for the Hebrew title "Messiah," and both mean the same thing: "anointed." So Jesus is the "anointed one" and, therefore, Christians are anointed, also. There even seems to be a pattern here: the passage relates that the Father anointed the Son, the Son anointed his apostles, and the apostles "anointed us."

From the Source

Orthodox Christians also used the imagery of fire to represent the presence of the Spirit in their sacramental rituals. This passage comes from the Hymns on the Faith by the fourth-century Syrian deacon Ephraem of Nisibis:

See, Fire and Spirit were in the womb of her who bore you,

see, Fire and Spirit were in the river in which you were baptized.

Fire and Spirit are in our baptismal font;

in the Bread and Cup are Fire and Holy Spirit.

—Ephraem of Nisibis, Hymns on the Faith 10

Eucharist

The Gospel of Philip says comparatively little about the sacrament of the *eucharist*. The crucifixion was not the central point to the life of Jesus, in the gnostic view, and in some cases was downright pointless. That attitude may have undermined the importance of the eucharist in many gnostic groups. It is certain that, as with other rituals, they redefined the meaning of the act.

Word Knowledge

The **eucharist** is one way of referring to the ritual act of eating and drinking bread and wine as part of Christian worship. The practice was initiated by Jesus at his Last Supper, and from the beginning seems to have been one of the defining characteristics of Christians no matter where they were or what theological camp they belonged to. The word eucharist comes from the Greek "eucharisteo," which means "to give thanks" or "to bless."

We know that, outwardly, the gnostic version of the eucharist ritual seems to correspond to what you might find in an Orthodox Church at the time. Valentinians used the bread and a cup in which wine was mixed with water. According to the Gospel of Philip, these two would clothe the gnostic in the "flesh" and "blood" of Jesus. By flesh and blood they didn't mean a literal physical body. To be clothed in flesh, we are told, is really to be naked. But the gospel takes pains to argue that those who assume that there is no form at all to the resurrected life are also mistaken. In fact, through eating the eucharist the gnostic took on a spiritualized flesh and blood of Jesus, which is "Word" and "Holy Spirit." These two, which are actual aeons in the Pleroma, are the form of eternal life that the gnostic believer adopts.

Philip's comments on the eucharist demonstrate a certain gnostic flexibility in their view of the body. Whereas we often see the gnostics rejecting all interest in the physical body, with regard to the eucharist the gnostics seem to take a more moderate stance. The Valentinians in particular, perhaps under pressure from mainstream critics, adopted a kind of middle way where after death the soul takes on a new kind of body, one that in substance resembles Jesus.

The Redemption

The sacrament of redemption is one of the hardest of the ritual acts to figure out. While the three rituals we've looked at already correspond to similar rituals used by the Christian community at large, redemption (it may also be translated "ransom") appears to be unique to the gnostics and perhaps just to the Valentinians.

The Gospel of Philip actually sheds little light on the subject. Although it mentions redemption several times, it's almost always in the context of something else, and often the passage has no obvious ritual meaning. In those instances where redemption is mentioned, one or more of the other rituals always accompanies it. For example, the image of Jerusalem that we mentioned with regard to baptism describes redemption as the second of those steps into the holiest place of the temple. It follows baptism and precedes the bridal chamber. That alone makes it seem as though redemption is a separate ritual act.

Irenaeus gave us the most detailed information that we have on redemption. He reported in the first book of *Against Heresies* that "They maintain that those who have attained to perfect knowledge must of necessity be regenerated into that power which is above all." This regeneration, as Irenaeus described it, comes after knowledge is attained as a form of confirmation. According to Irenaeus, it was performed in many different ways. As he put it at the end of his report, "But since they differ so widely among themselves both as respects doctrine and tradition, and since those of them who are recognized as being most modern make it their effort daily to invent some new opinion, and to bring out what no one ever before thought of, it is a difficult matter to describe all their opinions."

Some groups melded the ritual of redemption with the ritual of the bridal chamber, which we'll discuss next. Others had a second, subsequent baptism. While the first baptism would probably be into the Father, Son, and Holy Spirit as the standard form, the second baptism was supposedly accompanied by the declaration, "Into the name of the unknown Father of the universe—into truth, the Mother of all things—into Him who descended on Jesus—into union, and redemption, and communion with the powers." Still others would use a form of anointing with balsam oil, similar to the separate act of anointing that we've already discussed. And then there were those who eschewed all outward rituals, and defined redemption as simply the act of knowing.

Redemption was not always a single act. In some cases, it was repeated right up until death. It was thought by some groups that an anointing with oil might provide a guarantee of protection from the various rulers and powers through which the spirit must pass on its way back to the Pleroma and the Divine presence. Along with this, they would learn certain phrases or questions to use (we'll see more of these in later chapters) in order to bypass those same guardians.

The Bridal Chamber

The last element of the mystery described in the Gospel of Philip is the ritual of the bridal chamber. It appears throughout the Gospel of Philip, intruding at times even on descriptions of the other sacraments. As with the previous rituals, but perhaps more than all of them, there is disagreement as to what the bridal chamber is, and how, if at all, it was enacted.

Whether literal or metaphorical, the bridal chamber was intended to point to a restoration of the spirit of the gnostic with the Pleroma. How this was accomplished, and why, requires some explanation.

Sex and Separation

Remember that for the gnostics the source of the physical universe, and the pain and suffering that came with it, was the Sophia's fall from the perfection of the Pleroma. She fell because she chose to create entirely on her own, without the permission of the Divine Parent and without the cooperation of her male counterpart or spouse. The result was a creation that was entirely of female origin. Such a creation, in the minds of ancient people, would be deeply flawed. Females were considered largely passive in the act of procreation. Males provided form for the undirected creative energies of the female. Consequently, anything born entirely of the female would naturally be formless and, therefore, weak.

An attempt was made to rectify that matter in the creation of Adam and Eve. We've mentioned in Chapter 6 the belief that the original human being was an androgynous individual. The male and female were united in one being. That androgyny came to an end with their separation, but with that division came the beginning of death. Philip included one excerpt that made clear that "when Eve was in Adam, death did not exist." The end of death will occur when Adam "reenters" and reunites with Eve. The male-female division must come to an end.

That division had begun to heal with the restoration of Sophia, when she rejoined Christ as her spouse. The result of this union included a race of angels who were male in essence and a spiritual substance that was female in nature. This spiritual element is resident in human beings. Whether physically male or female, all human beings are spiritually female according to the Valentinians. The goal of the bridal chamber is to unify the female spirit of a human being with a male angelic being. These restored androgynous pairs will then arise to the Pleroma when the human being becomes free from the physical body (in other words, when they die).

The goal of the bridal chamber involves a reunification that joins the gnostic with a heavenly being who becomes his or her "spouse." The intention is to restore the male-female pairing of the aeons by pairing spiritual humans with an angelic counterpart, hence the language of marriage.

Heavenly Honeymoon

Now the use of matrimonial language like "bridal chamber" should start to make sense. By reversing the division of Adam and Eve, if only metaphorically, Valentinians presumed that they would find their way into the Pleroma. The sexual imagery was bound to raise questions about just exactly how this spiritual reality was experienced. Their critics were not above pointing out the irony in the situation. Tertullian took a jab when he sarcastically thrilled over the picture of sweaty, bearded men rushing to the bridal chamber so that they might enjoy the hot embraces of an angelic husband.

Unquestionably there were abuses in the use of the "bridal chamber." Irenaeus, in *Against Heresies*, attacked Mark, one of the leaders of the Eastern School of the Valentinians. According to Irenaeus, Mark preyed principally on wealthy matrons, promising them that he could help them learn to prophesy. Once involved with him, Mark encouraged these women to receive from him the power of the Spirit by joining with him physically. Irenaeus described several women of his acquaintance who had reported either having been approached by Mark or having actually been seduced by him. It's one of the sections in *Against Heresies* where you can actually sense Irenaeus' indignation.

The Gospel of Philip, on the other hand, makes it pretty clear that the union in the bridal chamber was entirely spiritual. In fact, by coming into union with their angelic counterpart, Valentinians believed that they would be delivered from sexual desire altogether. One passage from Philip describes sexual temptation like a bar scene. Seeing a man sitting around by himself, female spirits swarm that guy to "fondle him and pollute him." The same goes for women and male spirits. But if you are sitting there with your husband or wife, everyone else stays away. "Just so, if the image [the human being] and the angel join with one another, none dare to make advances to the male or the female."

> ### Words to the Wise
>
> The men and women who had been redeemed by Valentinian teaching and initiation looked toward the stilling of sexual feeling as the outward visible sign of a mighty subsidence that had first taken place in the spiritual reaches of the universe.
>
> —Peter Brown, *The Body and Society*

Freed from the constant barrage of spirits inflaming their physical desires, the Valentinians expected to finally be free from the act of sex itself. Liberation from sexuality was only the first of many changes that they expected to stem from this experience of spiritual union brought about by the ritual of the bridal chamber, but it was a significant one. Sexuality, then as now, carried with it a whole truckload of cultural baggage. Marriage and childbearing were necessary for the maintenance of society, particularly at a time when plagues, wars, and high infant mortality rates could easily devastate the population of a city or nation, threatening its very survival. Having kids was a civic duty.

From the gnostic perspective, however, sex amounted to supporting the evil that was the material universe. "Without marriage," one passage in Philip asserts, "the world would not exist." Gnostics transformed by the experience of the bridal chamber felt that they were empowered to opt out of that system. The procreative desire continued, as well it should for beings preparing to return to the ever-creative realms of the Pleroma. Instead of physical children, however, that desire was redirected toward sharing the knowledge that the gnostic had received. As the Gospel of Philip puts it, "Now, whoever has become free through knowledge is a slave on account of love toward those who have not yet taken up the freedom of knowledge."

The Least You Should Know

- ◆ The Gospel of Philip preserves a collection of Valentinian theological excerpts.

- ◆ The Gospel of Philip contains several sayings and stories about Jesus.

- ◆ The gnostics used a set of sacramental rituals familiar to other Christians, such as baptism and eucharist, but redefined their meaning to fit their own theological concerns.

- ◆ This gospel frequently mentions the "bridal chamber" which may be a ritual, or sacrament, but the phrase certainly refers to a gnostic symbol of reuniting the "feminine" soul of individual humans with "masculine" spirits.

Part  3

The Gnostic Library

The Gnostic Gospels have gotten nearly all the press, but the Nag Hammadi library contained a mother lode of gnostic literature. In the decades since their discovery, these texts have added an entirely new dimension to our understanding of the gnostics and their worldview.

In the coming chapters, we'll take a look at the rest of the Nag Hammadi library by assessing the many ways that they have improved our knowledge of the gnostics. In each chapter, we'll focus on an area of gnostic belief and teaching, and then trace those beliefs through a selected handful of the Nag Hammadi documents.

The Revelations of the Apostles

In This Chapter

 ◆ Paul takes a flight into the tenth heaven

 ◆ Peter sees the true nature of the enemy, and of the Savior

 ◆ A "secret book" about James reveals new sayings of Jesus

 ◆ Everyone's favorite apostle, James, dies twice

Revelations were the stock and trade of the gnostics. Openness to new and fresh insight, provided by supernatural means and the presence of spiritual guides, was part of what made gnostic groups so attractive to outsiders. Mainstream Christian writers railed against the way that gnostic teachers always seemed to have a new dream or vision upon which to base their most recent innovative doctrine. To the gnostics, however, these direct encounters were part and parcel of a life lived in genuine communion with God.

Gnostic Christians insisted on the permissibility of their experiences, citing the Apostle Paul's encounter with Christ while on his way to Damascus in chapter 9 of The Acts of the Apostles and the account of his heavenly ascent in chapter 12 of 2 Corinthians. Their orthodox opponents fired back that Paul had downplayed his own experience of revelation in favor of an ethical life motivated entirely by love.

The texts in this chapter all have in common the attribution of certain revelatory experiences to one or more of the apostles.

The Revelation of Paul (Codex V,2)

The Revelation of Paul is the first of several "revelations" that appear in Codex V. This suggests that the person who put the codex together had a purpose in creating a collection of revelations. The Revelation of Paul preceded the two Revelations of James (we'll look at them later in this chapter) and the Revelation of Adam (which we'll see in Chapter 15). We're not sure exactly who penned the Revelation of Paul. It's possible that the author had some anti-Jewish feelings (see the description of the "old man" below), but that doesn't give us enough to identify what gnostic group may have produced this text.

I'll See Your Three Heavens and Raise You Seven More

The revelation actually picks up on a previous passage from one of the letters of Paul. In the second letter to the Corinthian Church, the Apostle Paul related an experience that he had in which he was "caught up to the third heaven" where he "heard inexpressible things." No further details are given, and this text became the source for a great deal of speculation in Christian circles, particularly among gnostic Christians.

From the Source

I know a man in Christ who 14 years ago was caught up to the third heaven. Whether it was in the body or out of the body I do not know—God knows. And I know that this man—whether in the body or apart from the body I do not know, but God knows—was caught up to paradise. He heard inexpressible things, things that man is not permitted to tell.

—Paul, II Corinthians 12:2-4

The Revelation of Paul actually takes Paul's experience a step further. As he was caught away into the heavens, Paul actually skipped the first three and headed immediately for the fourth heaven and beyond. As much as anything else, this is an indication that gnostics did not feel bound to the Scriptural text the way that orthodox Christians might. They felt perfectly free to continue Paul's journey, to take him beyond where he had gone before. Revelation was an ongoing experience for the gnostic believer. The presence of the Holy Spirit guaranteed that there would be a sufficient guide for the journey.

A Guided Tour

The revelation began with the appearance of a small boy. Paul requested directions to Jerusalem and the boy invited him to "awaken your mind" and move beyond the merely physical journey that he was on. The boy introduced himself to Paul as the Holy Spirit, but at times he also seemed to be some kind of angel or guiding spirit. It was common in Valentinian gnosticism to picture Jesus as a small child, particularly in visions and revelations of this kind. In any event, the child represented someone who shared with Paul the knowledge of the path he or she must take through the heavens.

As Paul and the Spirit/boy leapt into the fourth heaven, the 12 apostles joined them. The apostles never actually said anything, and seemed to be along simply as companions. Both the fourth and fifth heavens appeared to be dedicated to judgment. In the fourth, a man was brought out by angels (these are the archons or rulers who impede the soul's progress) and was interrogated about his sins. He at first refused to acknowledge them until three witnesses came forward to convict him. Whether because he was convicted or found himself guilty, the man descended out of the heavens into a new body. There may have been hints here of reincarnation, which was commonly believed by gnostics. The fifth heaven was more obscure but also more threatening. One angel with an iron rod was accompanied by three others with whips. These spirits herded the souls of humans on to judgment.

A Cranky Old Man

The sixth heaven was a place of great light streaming down from above. Paul spoke to the toll-collector, a character obviously drawn from certain astrological myths, who opened up a door and allowed Paul and his companions to move on to the seventh heaven.

As they entered the seventh heaven, an old man sitting on a throne confronted them. His clothing was white and his throne shined brighter than the sun. The imagery is right out of Jewish apocalyptic literature, such as Daniel 7, where the Ancient of Days sits on a throne and rules creation. Some Christians picked up on this imagery as well; for example, see the so-called Great White Throne judgment scene captured in the twentieth chapter of the biblical text the Revelation of John. To the orthodox Christian, therefore, arriving at the seventh heaven might seem like the end of the journey.

> **From the Source**
>
> As I looked,
> thrones were set in place,
> and the Ancient of Days took his seat.
> His clothing was as white as snow;
> the hair of his head was white like wool.
> His throne was flaming with fire,
> and its wheels were all ablaze."
>
> —Daniel 7:9

It is clear that Paul knew better than that. At the insistence of the Spirit, he ex-changed words with the old man. The old man wanted to know where Paul thought he was going. Paul said, "I am going to the place from which I came." This phrase was commonly found in gnostic formulas for escaping the prison of this physical world. Most gnostics expected that at some point after death they would have to overcome the spiritual being or beings who created and maintained this world. The man on the throne threatened Paul, pointing out to him all the "principalities and power" that would hold Paul back. The Spirit then told Paul to show the old man "the sign" that would allow Paul to pass. Paul did as he was instructed and the old man let him pass.

What sign Paul gave we aren't told. This is where gnostic instruction was personal and intimate. Rarely was it written down, and never for public consumption. It was one of the ways that gnostic teachers drew in their adherents. They promised secret information—passwords, magical incantations, hand signs—that would allow the soul to pass through the powers that control the physical realm and escape. In a time when most people felt themselves at the mercy of powerful spiritual beings that didn't necessarily have their best interests at heart, such assurances were embraced.

Home Sweet Home

Paul was in the home stretch now. The seventh heaven was the final hurdle. The eighth and ninth heavens appeared nondescript, though they were populated with beings that Paul greeted as he passed through. Although he had been traveling with the 12 apostles all along, we are now told that he met them in the eighth heaven. This may indicate that either he or they (or both) had undergone some kind of transformation.

In the final heaven, Paul greeted "my fellow spirits." He had reached the Source of all life and found that he is part of it. There are echoes here of the gnostic insistence that spiritual men and women are not simply children of God but are part of God. Attaining of the tenth heaven is the returning of the spiritual Paul to himself.

The Revelation of Peter (Codex VII,3)

Also known as the Apocalypse of Peter, this document is very different from a previously known book by the same title. Like all of the Nag Hammadi texts, this book is a translation from Greek into Coptic. Unfortunately, the translator appears to have been completely incompetent. The result is that the Revelation of Peter is even more difficult to understand than it might have been otherwise.

A significant theme in the Revelation of Peter is the conflict between orthodox and gnostic Christians. That suggests that it was written after break between orthodox and gnostic Christians became more open, perhaps in the early third century when the line between the two was more explicit. That would also help explain the animosity that the text shows toward the opponents of the gnostics.

Hiding from the Mob

The book began with Peter and Jesus in the Temple. Jesus was encouraging Peter to be strong, because "from you I have established a base for the remnant whom I have summoned to knowledge." This strong emphasis on the leadership and authority of Peter is one of the main themes in this book.

Their conversation was interrupted as a mob of priests and others suddenly charged at them. Peter was surprised and terrified, but Jesus was unflappable. He reassured Peter that their enemies "are blind ones who have no guide." To prove it to him, Jesus told Peter to cover his eyes. When he did, Peter had a vision of an entirely different reality, where a blinding light settled down on the Savior, and the priests started shouting praises to Jesus.

At this point in the story Jesus began to explicitly expound on the conflict between orthodox and gnostic Christians. He advised Peter to be careful about revealing what he had seen and heard, because those without knowledge will "blaspheme." Many people, Jesus told Peter, will start off believing the teaching about the spiritual Jesus. Later, they will fall away and "cleave to the name of a dead man," a reference to the orthodox teaching about the necessity of Jesus' crucifixion.

All of these folks are mortal souls, Jesus continued, created for "eternal destruction." Immortal souls, however, are not like that. According to Jesus, for the time being they look just like mortals. The difference is in their essential natures. The immortal soul "thinks about immortality, having faith, and desiring to renounce" material desires.

Jesus went on to tell Peter that for the time being, immortal souls are oppressed by mortals. Some of these "who name themselves bishops and also deacons" will lord it over "the little ones." In the end, the "never-aging one" will turn things around and turn the rule of things over to those immortal souls.

Jesus or Christ?

Following this lengthy discourse, Peter seemed to see Jesus grabbed by the mob and led off to be crucified. He seemed to be seeing double, though. While he saw one man being nailed to a tree, he saw another who was laughing.

The laughing man was the true Savior, according to the text, "filled with a Holy Spirit," while the one who was crucified was the fleshly body—"a substitute." The blind mortals were unable to see that they were crucifying a meaningless thing. The true Savior was something other than that body, and he had been set free.

The Revelation of Peter presented a vision of a docetic Christ, a Christ whose physical sufferings were not merely meaningless but also nonexistent. The immortal Christian knows that reality is more spiritual in nature.

The Secret Book of James (Codex 1,2)

Also known as the Apocryphon of James, this book is a collection of what we might call "Jesus sayings" grouped together in the form of a dialogue with James and Peter, two of Jesus' disciples. At some point, the entire thing was framed with opening and closing words to make it seem like a letter written from James to another person. This made it all sound more intimate and personal, more like an actual revelation from a teacher to a disciple.

The Secret Book of James isn't quoted in any of the existing early Christian literature. Its secret was well kept indeed. Despite its relative obscurity, certain scholars have suggested that some of the sayings in the book might be old enough to go back to Jesus himself. They make this argument because, in the opening lines of the book, the apostles are all sitting around "recalling" or "remembering" all the words that Jesus had spoken to them. The only people who could "remember" Jesus' sayings were people who had actually heard them, the actual eyewitnesses of Jesus.

Did You Know?

The Apostle James was first bishop of Jerusalem (though he was never called by that title in the Bible) and a significant presence in the early period of church history.

The Acts of the Apostles demonstrates his central participation in the development of the early church. When the Apostle Peter was released from prison (Acts 12:17), he asked the brothers to inform James of his escape. At the all-important Council of Jerusalem, when the church decided not to require Gentile believers in Jesus to keep the law of Moses, it was James who summarized and pronounced the Council's decision (Acts 15:13–21). The Apostle Paul listed James as one of those who received a post-resurrection visit from Jesus (I Corinthians 15:7). Earlier, in his letter to the Galatians, Paul described James, along with Peter and John, as "pillars of the church."

In that same letter to the Galatians, Paul wrote about meeting with "James the Lord's brother." What exactly the descriptive "brother" meant has been a hotly debated issue at certain periods in Christian history. The early development of the belief in the perpetual virginity of Mary the mother of Jesus tended to close off the possibility of considering James a biological brother of Jesus, though Protestants tend to believe that they were both born of Mary. Another early theory described James as a son of Joseph by a previous marriage. Yet another simply called him a cousin of Jesus. Gnostic literature, where it addresses the matter at all, seems to focus on a spiritual kinship rather than a physical one.

James was stoned to death in A.D. 62. but his reputation and authority outlasted his martyrdom. The fact that several of the Nag Hammadi texts used his name suggests that it continued to carry considerable weight in the second-century Christian community. The high view of James often found in these texts makes clear that James was very well regarded, a status amply demonstrated by this passage from the Gospel of Thomas: "The followers said to Jesus, 'We know that you are going to leave us. Who will be our leader?' Jesus said to them, 'No matter where you are, you are to go to James the Just, for whose sake heaven and earth came into being.'" (12)

The word "remembering" is significant, these scholars say, because it is most often found in documents written around the end of the first century and the beginning of the second. Living witnesses to the teaching of Jesus and his apostles were dying out around then, and the various oral stories about things that Jesus had said and done were beginning to settle into written forms. The use of this language in the text is, in the judgment of these scholars, evidence that the sayings in this book represent an oral tradition. It would also indicate that the book was written early in the second century.

Critics of this view suggest that it's just as likely that the writer of the Secret Book used the language of "remembering" precisely because it lends the book a certain antique air and a degree of authority. In that case, it becomes more difficult to assign a date to this book.

Opening Words

When it was originally published, the Secret Book of James was often called the Secret Letter of James. That's because, as noted previously, it actually starts out and ends like a letter. The greeting and introductory remarks and the postscript frame the rest of the book and give it a personal touch.

James wrote that he was sending along this secret book at the insistence of his reader. He alluded to a previous book of secret teachings that he had sent 10 months earlier. He also said that he was writing the current work in Hebrew. Both of these details were designed to add a realistic flavor to the letter format.

According to James, he and the other disciples were sitting around together writing down what each of them could remember about the teachings of Jesus. It was 550 days after the resurrection and Jesus appeared to them. They asked him if he was leaving them, and he told them that he was going "to the place from whence I came." He invited them to come along with him, and they all responded, "If you bid us, we come." Jesus then drew Peter and James aside so that he "may fill them." This began the dialogue portion of the book.

The Sayings

The bulk of the Secret Book of James is a collection of sayings of Jesus, originally separate from any kind of story, crafted into a kind of loose dialogue. James and Peter took turns asking questions of Jesus, and these questions became the occasion for presenting a block of sayings. The following is a breakdown of the different sections of the dialogue:

◆ **First words**. After pulling James and Peter aside, Jesus began with a first block of sayings in which he invited them to "Become full and leave no space within you empty."

◆ **Full and empty**. Peter assured Jesus that he and James were already full. Jesus responded, telling Peter that there were essentially different kinds of being full and being empty. He wanted them to "become full of the Spirit" and not to be preoccupied with human reason.

◆ **Take it like a man**. James told Jesus that they could obey, and asked for help to resist temptation. Jesus told him not to get squeamish about putting his body on the line for what he believed. You haven't even suffered yet, James, Jesus said, and you're pulling back already. You have the Spirit around your life like "an encircling wall," so "scorn death … and take thought for life." Jesus ended by reminding James of his own crucifixion.

◆ **Dying to death**. James recoiled from the memory of Jesus' death. He wanted nothing to do with the cross. But Jesus told him that only those who "believe in my cross" would be saved. They should "become seekers for death," then, because "the kingdom belongs to those who put themselves to death."

◆ **The head of prophecy**. Next came a two-part question. James asked how they would prophesy, or reveal truth, to those who asked. Jesus told him that the "head of prophecy had been removed," and James wanted to know how that could happen. There's a sort of double reference here. Jesus was talking about John the Baptist, who early Christians thought of as the last of the prophets. With his death, then, the line of prophets would have ended. There may be a more subtle but graphic meaning, however. John the Baptist was beheaded.

Did You Know? _____

John the Baptist had run afoul of Herod Antipas, who ruled Galilee and Perea in the northern part of Palestine, until 39 A.D. Herod had married Herodias, who was both his niece and his sister-in-law. John condemned the marriage in truly prophetic fashion, and Herod had him arrested.

The gospel accounts reveal that Herodias was furious with John and determined to do him in. She enlisted the aid of her daughter Salome. In one of the most famous scenes in the entire New Testament, Salome performed a seductive dance for Herod and his court. When he offered her any reward she wanted, she demanded the head of John the Baptist just the way her mother had coached her. Herod was bound by his promise, and John met his end.

◆ **Be saved!** James' question about prophecy kicked off the longest of the blocks of sayings. This section probably contains some of the oldest sayings in the whole document, particularly the Parable of the Date Figs and the Parable of the Head of Grain. The gist of this lengthy passage is Jesus urging them to "hasten to be saved without being urged." Jesus' teachings, he told them, were sufficient for them.

◆ **Body, soul, and spirit**. James and Peter "became glad." When Jesus saw them happy, however, he brought them back down to Earth. They had to realize that they were "foreigners" to this world. Jesus laid out the three basic elements of the human being familiar to gnostic teaching: a corrupt body, a rational soul, and a divine spirit. The body just follows what the soul does, but the soul "kills itself" by caring too much for this life. The body is just a garment that should be disregarded, for "none of those who have worn the flesh will be saved." Rather, "Blessed is the one who sees himself as a fourth one in heaven," Jesus concluded. This final statement was perhaps an invitation to join the divine Trinity (Father, Mother, and Child in gnostic terms) as an equal.

◆ **The missionary call**. Where before they were happy, Jesus' words now distressed the pair. He encouraged them to look to his example. "Do not make the kingdom of heaven a desert within you," he told them. Don't just sit self-contented and proud in your enlightenment. Be like me, he told them, since I was willing to endure all of this for your sakes.

◆ **The Promise of Life**. Peter asked a final, bewildered question. You seem to be encouraging us to pursue the kingdom one moment, he complained, and then pushing us away from it the next. Jesus reassured them that they "have received life through faith and knowledge." They should stop listening to "words of rejection" and instead rejoice in the "promise of life." Not even the Father can cast away those who have received life and become part of the kingdom.

These last words ended the long central part of the book. Jesus told James and Peter to stay with him as he ascended and left them. He wanted them to "pay heed to the glory that awaits me" and to "hear the hymns" that were being sung in the heavens.

Closing Words

James and Peter fell to their knees and followed Jesus with their hearts. At first they heard the sound of battle and trumpets (typical imagery in apocalyptic literature) and then, past that, they heard angels singing and rejoicing. Finally, they tried to push on toward "the Majesty" but they weren't allowed to see or hear anything.

At that moment, the other disciples interrupted James and Peter. They have come in to find out what Jesus had told the pair. The two explained what they received, and the other disciples believed it, but they weren't too happy about the idea of "children coming after us." To keep things peaceful, James sent them all off on missionary journeys. As for himself, James returned to Jerusalem to pray.

> **From the Source** _____
>
> But the same writer [Clement of Alexandria], in the seventh book of the same work, relates also the following things concerning him [James]: "The Lord after his resurrection imparted knowledge (gnosis) to James the Just and to John and Peter, and they imparted it to the rest of the apostles, and the rest of the apostles to the seventy ..."
>
> —Eusebius Pamphilus, *Ecclesiastical History* II,1,4

A few final words made up the postscript to the letter frame. James admonished the reader to share this faith with others so that "you may share salvation with them." It is by proclaiming salvation to others, the children that Jesus has promised, that we are saved.

The Revelation of James

Good titles must have been hard to come by in the second century. In the same codex, two completely different documents are called the Revelation of James. To make matters more confusing, the two appear back to back. For the sake of clarity, scholars have cleverly taken to calling them The (First) Revelation of James and The (Second) Revelation of James. Although at first glance the two have little in common, they both take as their subject matter the martyrdom of James the Just.

The (First) Revelation of James (Codex V,3)

The (First) Revelation is an almost textbook example of a "revelation dialogue." It's a conversation that took place between Jesus and James the Just. They began by talking about Jesus' upcoming crucifixion. Jesus also related to James that he, too, would suffer at some point just like Jesus. This made James understandably afraid, not of death itself but of his apparent powerlessness in the face of the many spiritual beings arrayed against him. Jesus offered understanding, and instructed James that redemption ought to be his only concern. He was to look forward to the time when he was "no longer James" but had become united again with "the One-who-is," namely, God. This would come after Jesus had fulfilled his own task at the cross, which the text brushed over with as little fanfare as possible. In fact, Jesus' crucifixion seemed almost inconsequential.

Overcoming the Archons

In the wake of Jesus' suffering on the cross, James was praying on a mountaintop when Jesus appeared to him. At first, James was relieved and wanted to destroy those responsible for Jesus' death. Jesus brushed aside his anger, explaining that he hadn't really suffered at all. The people of Jerusalem were, he said, a "type of the archons" (recall from Chapter 2 that *archons* are demonic and angelic spiritual beings who rule over the world). Jesus told James that the destruction of Jerusalem would be a means of overthrowing those spiritual beings who worked through the people to crucify Jesus.

> **Did You Know?**
>
> Jerusalem was destroyed in A.D. 70 by the Roman armies of Titus, the son of the emperor Vespasian. The destruction of the city was the culmination of a campaign to end a four-year uprising in Palestine. The event was a catastrophe for the Jewish people, resulting in the loss of the city and the complete destruction of the Temple.

Jesus began to talk to James about James' upcoming martyrdom and how he could escape death to reach the Pre-existent One. First, Jesus said, he would be confronted by three toll-collectors. These three would try to steal his soul by asking him three questions. Unfortunately, the text is damaged here, so we only get to see the first two questions and the answers that Jesus instructed James to give.

As we've already seen, information about what answers to give to the gatekeepers of the spiritual realm was a fundamental part of the gnostic approach to immortality or the afterlife. This question-and-answer script represents just one of several examples of this type of instruction that appeared in gnostic literature and teaching.

A Secret Mission

The remainder of The (First) Revelation of James gets more difficult to read as pieces of the text are missing. However, a few items can be gleaned by a careful reading.

First of all, James was supposed to pass on his secret knowledge to a handful of people. They were named in the text, but were difficult to identify. The first is Addai, whose association with the Thomas tradition we saw in Chapter 5. It's interesting to see Addai mentioned here, because it might indicate that this (First) Revelation originated in Syria, where Addai's name would be meaningful. What's important is the suggestion that James's secret knowledge was to be hidden until after his death. Could this have been a response to critics who were attacking these teachings as new and innovative?

James also questioned the status of the female disciples of Jesus. He mentioned "seven disciples," though he named only four: Salome, Miriam (Mary), Martha, and Arsinoe. Jesus had some kind words to say about these women, but don't get too excited. Their spiritual strength, Jesus said, rested on the fact that "the female element has attained to this male element."

What Jesus seems to be getting at with this reply seems to be the same thing that we saw in the final saying of the Gospel of Thomas (way back in Chapter 6), namely that the "feminine" would have to become "masculine" in order to find salvation. As we mentioned in Chapter 6, there are some passages in the gnostic literature where this call for females to become like males in spirit seems very literal and others where it appears more figurative. This example from The (First) Revelation is one of those passages that seems very literal. Note that James isn't asking about any of Jesus' male disciples. Only the female disciples are considered questionable.

The last thing that James did was "rebuke" the 12 apostles, apparently for some kind of complacency. The end of the text, which is too damaged to read, describes James's death at the hands of a mob. It provides a perfect segue into The (Second) Revelation of James, which goes into much greater detail about the death of James.

The (Second) Revelation of James (Codex V,4)

The (Second) Revelation is a lyrical piece of literature. It contains gnostic elements, but not of the Valentinian variety (see Chapter 9). It is full of prayers and declarations that sound like they might have been used in a liturgical or worship setting. It's sometimes a difficult text to read. It is in fragmentary condition, with the bottom edges of most of the pages missing. Consequently, it is sometimes hard to make out who was speaking, Jesus or James.

The document takes the form of a report given to Theuda, the father of James, about the death of his son. A priest named Mareim, who apparently witnessed what had happened, gave the report. He told Theuda that James, before he was killed, stood up in front of a "multitude of people" to speak.

What James Had to Say

James' speech began with the claim that he had "received revelation from the "Pleroma of Imperishability" (this title is one example of how far gnostics stretched language to try and describe the Divine). He was now "rich in knowledge" or gnosis.

He then shared some of that knowledge as he related part of a discourse given by Jesus in which Jesus claimed, "it is by knowledge that I shall come forth from the flesh." Jesus referred to himself by a variety of standard Christian titles: "the beloved," "the righteous one," and "son of the Father."

This first speech was followed by a second experience, in which Jesus opened a door and came in, addressing James as his brother. Jesus told James that James would be the one to make Jesus known to the people. "Your father is not my father," Jesus told him, "but my father has become a father to you."

Next, James told of a longer discourse by Jesus in which he contrasted the Creator of the physical world, "he who boasted … there is no other except me" and who "imprisoned those from the Father," with the Invisible One who is "life" and "light." The Creator doesn't even know about the Invisible One. James, on the other hand, was invited to know this One, and to become an "illuminator" and a "redeemer of those who are mine."

A Tough Crowd

James ended his speech with a final attempt to persuade the crowd. "Renounce this difficult way," he exhorted them, and "become free men." They were judging themselves when the "kind Father" would happily receive them, and that's why they remained in bondage to the Creator. James' last words to the crowd might be understood as a threat against the Temple which, he said, "I shall doom to destruction."

This final statement didn't go over well with James' audience. Mariem picked up the narrative here, describing in detail how the crowd found James in the Temple and elaborately stoned him to death. Before he died, however, James prayed a remarkable prayer. Although the prayer is associated with James' death, nothing about it demands that it belongs here exclusively. It was almost certainly composed separately and added to this text later. There is no explicit gnostic character to it. Instead, James' last words read like one of the Psalms, asking God for deliverance from "this place of sojourn," redemption from "sinful flesh," and salvation from "a humiliating enemy." It is a fitting prayer for a man facing brutal execution.

The Least You Need to Know

- The Revelation of Paul demonstrates the ways that gnostics taught their initiates to overcome the archons who kept them bound.

- Peter's visions are used to describe a world of conflict between gnostics and other Christians who do not share their views. It emphasizes that, contrary to the orthodox teaching, the real Jesus did not suffer and die on the cross.

- The sayings of Jesus that appear in the Secret Book of James may stem from an entirely different tradition of Jesus' words.

- The two Revelations of James revolve around his suffering and death, demonstrating James' significance to at least some parts of the early church.

12

Acts and Letters

In This Chapter

- ◆ The Apostle Peter finds an unusual way of keeping his daughter home at night
- ◆ A fairy tale journey for the 12 apostles is a revelation
- ◆ A question-and-answer session with the risen Christ and his apostles
- ◆ The multiple Gospels of Mark

Christianity is a historical religion, bound up in the particular words and deeds of Jesus of Nazareth and his disciples. For gnostic Christians, that history often became a source for allegorical interpretation, meaning that they were more concerned with the symbolic meaning than they were with the question of whether or not something had actually happened. Getting to the heart of the meaning of the story was more important than the facts themselves. Nothing demonstrates this better than the books that we're going to look at in this chapter.

The Act of Peter

The Act of Peter is one of a few documents described in this book that does not come from the Nag Hammadi library. The Act actually appears in the Berlin Codex mentioned in Chapter 5. We've already looked at the Gospel of Mary (Chapter 7), and in Chapter 15 we'll get acquainted with The Wisdom of Jesus Christ, a work that appears in both the Nag Hammadi library and the Berlin Codex.

It's generally accepted that this Act of Peter forms the missing first part of the larger Acts of Peter mentioned way back in Chapter 4, when we talked about Simon the Magician. If so, that makes it part of one of the earliest of the many apocryphal Acts that began circulating from about the middle of the second century on.

Easy Come, Easy Go

The Act of Peter begins with an action scene. Peter is busy healing the sick on the Lord's Day when someone in the crowd challenges him. If you have such fabulous healing power, they charge, then heal your own daughter. Peter's daughter, who is with him, is paralyzed on one whole side of her body. We're told that she is a virgin.

In a remarkable display of power, Peter confidently commands his daughter to rise up from her bed. Right away she gets up and walks over to him. The crowd is stunned. When it becomes obvious that they are suitably persuaded of the power of God, Peter tells his daughter to return to her original place. When she does, her paralysis returns and she is right back the way she started out.

Convinced now that Peter has God's power of healing, the crowd begs him to cure his daughter permanently. They are startled by her sudden reversion. Peter quiets them down and explains that his daughter's illness is "beneficial for her and me." He tells them about a vision he received when his daughter was born warning him that she would "wound many souls" if she remained whole. He didn't think much of the vision at the time. Oh, but you know that trouble was coming.

You Think Your Parents Are Strict?

When Peter's daughter was 10 years old, she was so beautiful that many men were interested in marrying her (at the age of 10?!). One day a wealthy fellow named Ptolemy saw her taking a bath and began making advances of his own. He asked for her hand repeatedly, but Peter and his wife kept turning him down.

What happens next is uncertain, since a couple of pages are missing in the text. We get a clue from a book written by the fourth-century bishop Augustine, who mentions a story he knows about the daughter of Peter who was paralyzed by her father's own prayers. That, along with what we can figure out from where the text picks up again, suggests the following scenario: Ptolemy, in a desperate act, kidnaps Peter's daughter. It seems that he intends to sleep with her so that Peter will have no choice but to marry her off to Ptolemy. But before that can happen, in response to Peter's own prayers, the girl is paralyzed. That's where the text of the Act starts again. Ptolemy's men drop the girl off out in front of Peter's house, and that's where her parents find her.

That's not the end of Ptolemy's story, however. As Peter relates to his now spell-bound audience, Ptolemy felt very guilty for what he had done. Somehow, as the result of his constant weeping, he became blind. In despair, he decided to kill himself, but at that moment he had a vision. A great light filled his house and a voice spoke to Ptolemy, telling him that these events were necessary to teach him that God does not give his servants for "corruption and pollution." Ptolemy should have recognized Peter's daughter as his sister and treated her accordingly. The voice sent Ptolemy to Peter's house to receive further instruction and, one hopes, to apologize.

Ptolemy arrived at Peter's house and told everyone what he heard in his vision. Suddenly, both the "eyes of his flesh" and "of his soul" could see again. He went on to become a wonderful servant of God, and many folks came to Christ because of his life. When he finally died, he left a piece of property to Peter's daughter in his will. Peter promptly sold it and gave the money away to the poor.

Peter's story ends with an encouragement to "be penitent," to be "watchful," and to stay in prayer. He distributed bread to the crowd and, presumably with his daughter, went home.

The Value of a Story

The central point of interest in this story about Peter and his daughter is its strict approach to sexual self-control. The story certainly upholds the value of remaining free from sexual relationships. There was a lot of encratite literature (writings by strict moralists in Syria who lived ascetic lives that included renouncing sexual relationships) that went further than this, but this story certainly expressed an encratite view.

Still, why would this story be appealing enough to gnostics to include as part of a collection of literature? Well, most of the gnostic groups taught an ascetic approach to the world. Since the flesh, along with its desires, is corrupt and meant for destruction, having sex could, and did, certainly rank at the top of the list of self-destructive behaviors. At the same time, like all literature of this kind, the gnostics were perfectly capable of approaching the story allegorically to open up all sorts of new meanings much more in line with their view of the world. They could, for example, interpret characters in the story as symbols rather than individuals—thus, Peter's daughter represents the soul of the gnostic believer, Ptolemy represents temptation, and so on. Through these kinds of reinterpretation, ancient readers could bend a story to their own use.

The Acts of Peter and the Twelve Apostles (Codex VI,1)

Written as a polemic against the rich and wealthy within the Christian community, the Acts of Peter and the Twelve Apostles takes the form of a fantasy-like journey across the ocean and an encounter with Christ in a unique disguise. Scholars disagree about when it was written. Some argue for an early date, say in the late second century, while others opt for the early third or even the fourth century.

Taking a Cruise

The first part of the text is missing, so we're not sure how the journey begins or what prompts it. However, it's clear that Peter is narrating the story, and that all of the apostles are present. Contrary to the title, there are only 11 of them.

The apostles headed down to the sea, where they hopped on a ship and sailed for a day and a night until they reached a city "in the midst of the sea." Peter went off looking for a place where they could stay, and asked around to find out the name of the city. One of the residents told him the city was called Habitation.

From the Source

Again, the kingdom of heaven is like a merchant looking for fine pearls. When he found one of great value, he went away and sold everything he had and bought it.

—the Gospel of Matthew 13:45–46

The Pearl of Great Price

During his wanderings, Peter came across an odd-looking man standing around crying, "Pearls! Pearls!" He found out that the pearl merchant was also a stranger to the city, and that he was not having much luck with the wealthy residents of Habitation. They came out when he called, but because they couldn't see the pearls he claimed to be offering—he has no visible bag or purse—they thought that he was pulling their leg. They all headed back into their homes and ignored him.

The poor, on the other hand, were more interested. They didn't have anywhere near the kind of money needed to actually purchase something as valuable as a pearl, but they were very curious to see one. The merchant told them that if they came to his city, not only would he show them pearls but he would also give them pearls for free.

Lions and Tigers and Bears, Oh My!

Peter, eager to learn more, asked for the merchant's name and for directions to his city. The merchant called himself Lithargoel, which he himself translated to mean "the light, gazelle-like stone." As for the way to his city, it was full of all sorts of dangerous obstacles, including robbers, dogs, wolves, lions, and bulls. Each of these would take something away from the traveler, be it food, water, or clothing. There was only one way to get to the city, Lithargoel told Peter. He must forsake everything, and fast every day during the journey.

When Peter was taken aback by the demands of going to Lithargoel's city, the merchant reminded Peter that the name of Jesus was a powerful source of strength for precisely that kind of journey. When Peter asked, Lithargoel told him that the city is named Nine Gates.

There was an odd moment of transition here between the time in Habitation and the beginning of the journey to Nine Gates. Peter suddenly saw the waves and the walls that surrounded Habitation. He struck up a conversation with an old man who explained that the city was inhabited because the people there endured. Peter mused that that was the case with every city and every kingdom. They existed and were habitable because they endured difficulties and hardships. He made a metaphor out of this by concluding that everyone who endures the hardships of a life of faith will be inhabited (by God?) and will be part of the kingdom of heaven.

Medicine Man

The apostles set out on their journey to Nine Gates, successfully avoiding all of the hardships that blocked the way. Rather than being worn out and starving by the time they arrived, they were full of joy and peace. They stopped outside of the city gates and talked with each other about how to avoid "distraction" and to instead keep themselves focused on matters of faith.

While they were chatting, a man walked out of the city. We are told that it was Lithargoel, and that he was in disguise as a physician carrying a box of medicine. Following a brief deception, Lithargoel revealed himself to the apostles as Jesus, whom they immediately began worshiping.

The apostles asked what it was that Jesus wanted them to do. He gave them the box of medicine and told them to return to Habitation and minister to the poor. They were to endure just as he had endured, and to give the poor the best that they could until he kept his promise to give them "what is better."

Peter reminded Jesus (and, of course, those of us who are reading or hearing the story) that they had given up everything in order to follow him. Where, then, could they possibly scrape together the resources to help the poor? My name, Jesus tells Peter, is more valuable than money.

Jesus reiterated his command that they should heal all the poor people who believed in him. Peter is too nervous to ask another question, so he convinced John to do it. How are we going to heal anybody, John asked, if we aren't trained to do that kind of work? If you heal people's bodies without medicine, Jesus responded, then they will trust you for the more important matter of healing the heart.

Jesus' last words, however, were reserved for the wealthy. Since they didn't even see fit to acknowledge his presence (as the pearl merchant) in their city, the apostles were not to have anything to do with them. "Many in the churches have shown partiality to the rich" because they are also sinners, Jesus said. The apostles were not to do that, but were to "judge them with uprightness." With that, Jesus left them.

Did You Know? _____

Clement of Alexandria wrote a short treatise entitled *Who Is the Rich Man Who Shall Be Saved?* in which he deals line by line with the story of Jesus' encounter with the "rich young ruler" in Mark 10:17–31. Clement concludes that the need to give away all wealth and possessions is not so much a command to be obeyed literally but a summons to an interior willingness to let go of anything that would get in the way of following Jesus.

With its moderate approach to the question of wealth, the book was probably written in response to attitudes like those expressed in the Acts of Peter and the Twelve Apostles, which were common in Egypt during Clement's day, and certainly were characteristic of the later monastic communities.

The text has some odd spots in it where it looks like somebody combined several different stories or ideas together into a single narrative. As a result, there are obvious bumps in the story where the pieces don't connect well. For example, the journey from Habitation, a city in the middle of the sea, to the City of Nine Gates is taken on foot, an odd development unless Peter has been teaching the rest of the apostles how to walk on water. It seems that some editor cobbled the Acts together to create a larger narrative that would champion spiritual growth through self-renunciation.

The Letter of Peter to Philip (Codex VIII,2)

Though it begins like a letter, the Letter of Peter to Philip is not a letter at all. Instead, it is an attempt to introduce gnostic ideas into a framework of traditional Christian language. The Letter is thought to have been written late in the second or early in the third century, and the author seems to be very familiar with the Scriptural texts that were in circulation at that time.

"Dear Phil"

The first part of the text does start out like a letter. Peter wrote to Philip, one of the apostles, to summon him to a meeting in obedience to Jesus' commands to them. They were supposed to organize together to effectively teach what Jesus had taught them. Philip's presence was needed at that meeting. The summons to Philip, which he submitted to "with gladness," served not only to set the stage for the coming revelations, but also to highlight right away the authority of Peter. Like the Revelation of Peter (see Chapter 11), the Letter of Peter to Philip really put Peter at the center of the action and accentuated his position in the church and among the 12 apostles.

Questions and Answers

Gathered together on the Mount of Olives, the apostles began to pray first to the Father and then to the Son for power, "for they seek to kill us." This was the first indication that the main theme of this document was the need for some kind of power in the face of persecution. At this point we still don't know who "they" are, but the need for assistance is both immediate and profound.

A great light appeared, and a voice spoke, introducing itself as Jesus. To this dramatic appearance of Christ, the apostles laid out a series of questions. Basically, they wanted to know why the world was so wrong, what the solution was, why they were under attack, and how they could fight back. Let's look at each question, along with the answer that Jesus gave them:

- **Shorthand mythology.** The apostles asked about the "deficiency" in the way things are. Jesus responded by telling them an abbreviated version of the "myth of the mother." The "mother" tried to create without the permission or the sanction of the Father. As a result, she brought forth an "Arrogant One," who imprisoned part of her divine nature into the physical world. Out of pride, the

Arrogant One created human beings. The whole thing seems to be a shorthand version of the basic gnostic myth of origins that we have seen already in previous chapters.

♦ **Send in the cavalry.** So what's the solution? Into this deficient world, Jesus came in the form of a human body. He was on a stealth mission, sneaking into enemy territory to look for "the seed which had fallen away." He was looking for that seed by seeking out those in whom the light dwelled, even if dimly.

♦ **Boxed in.** Why are we being locked away in this material world? Because the Arrogant One and his little minions are determined to keep that small part of the Mother that they were able to capture and contain. The key to freedom is to strip away the corrupt flesh that people continue to live in. This isn't simply a reference to death as an escape, since the apostles were told that if they would strip away corruption, they would be "illuminators" to the people around them. That's the same word that is used to describe Jesus himself.

♦ **Down with the man!** Did they fight back? Absolutely, because they had something that the archons didn't have. They had a final rest from their struggles to look forward to. They had a final goal where they would at last be whole and complete, deficient in nothing. The archons didn't have that.

Fight the Good Fight

At this point it looks like the author decided to expand on the idea of fighting back against the archons. That jibes with the central theme of the letter, which was for gnostic Christians to find power to face those who were persecuting them. The apostles again asked how they were going to fight with those who were "above us."

Jesus first told them that, essentially, they had to fight fire with fire. They were in a spiritual battle, where only spiritual weapons would do. The archons were after "the inner man," so their response would have to match the attacks of their persecutors.

Jesus told them to fight in two ways. First, they were to gather together and teach what he had given them to teach, "the salvation with a promise." This was part of the reason for their gathering together to begin with. Second, they were to put on his Father's power and continue to pray. Finally, Jesus told them to be fearless, because he is with them always.

It's a Rough Life

With those words of encouragement, and a display of thunder and lightning, Jesus made a flashy exit. The apostles departed, heading down the road to Jerusalem. Along the way they discussed what they'd just heard, and somebody asked the question, if Jesus suffered, then shouldn't we suffer as well?

It was Peter who responded, saying that suffering is natural to our current state. Because of the "deficiency" of the world, we are liable to pain and suffering. We have "suffered through the transgression of the mother," he continued, and it is our "smallness" that gets us into trouble, our part in the chaos of this mistaken creation.

From the Source

In the midst of Peter's discussion of suffering, there is what appears to be a creed-like passage that is worth noticing.

Our illuminator, Jesus, came down and was crucified.
And he bore a crown of thorns.
And he wore a purple robe.
And he was crucified on a tree.
And he was buried in a tomb.
And he rose from the dead.

Jesus, on the other hand, did not need to endure such suffering. He was, as Peter points out, "a stranger to this suffering," coming as he did from the fullness of the Divine where there is no deficiency. But because we suffer, he also suffered. In that way, he became the "author of our life."

It's almost surprising to see that there were no docetic qualities (in other words, only appearing to have a body) to Jesus in this letter. He took on a very real body and suffered in a very real way. The ghostly phantom depicted in some other gnostic works is altogether missing here. At the same time, Jesus remained fully divine in every way. He was the one sent down from the Father. This tension is part of what makes the Letter of Peter to Philip so interesting as a part of the larger Nag Hammadi library.

The apostles prayed for and received the Holy Spirit and were empowered to heal people. Jesus offered them a final blessing and assurance that he is with them always. Then they went their separate ways.

The Secret Gospel of Mark

We end this chapter with another document that does not appear in the Nag Hammadi library. In fact, this is a letter unlike any other we've seen. Its interest lies not so much in the letter itself as in what it tells us about another document that no longer exists. That is, if it ever existed at all. Let's take a look.

An Odd Discovery

In 1958, Morton Smith was hard at work in the Greek Orthodox Monastery in Mar Saba, located near Jerusalem. Sitting in one of the cells, he pored over the monastery's manuscript library, using a camera to photograph and catalog what he found.

In a printed copy of the Letters of Ignatius, handwritten on the back of one of the pages, Smith found a document written in tiny Greek script. As he read it, it turned out to be a letter written by Clement of Alexandria to a man named Theodore. In the letter, Clement commended Theodore for "silencing" the Carpocrations, a group of second-century Christian gnostics founded by a fellow named Carpocrates. The group flourished in Alexandria for a time, and orthodox Christians hotly resisted it.

Shh, It's a Secret

According to the letter, the Carpocratians were making certain allegations about the content of the Gospel of Mark. Clement wrote to Theodore to respond to those claims, but in the process he made a startling claim of his own. Clement described for Theodore the process by which Mark wrote his gospel. The shocking part is that Mark, according to Clement, wrote another, spiritual gospel for those who were entering into greater maturity in Christ. This "secret gospel" remained in the hands of the church in Alexandria, where it was available only to those who were going into the "deep mysteries" of the faith.

Clement alleges that Carpocrates got his hands on a copy of the secret gospel and added his own ideas to it, creating a document even more at odds with the publicly available gospel. So now we have three gospels attributed to Mark that were circulating in Alexandria. The first, the original Gospel of Mark, seemed to be pretty much the same as the Gospel of Mark that we use today. The second, the Carpocration Gospel of Mark, was deliberately distorted. The third, the so-called "secret" Gospel of Mark, became the subject of Clement's letter.

In order to help Theodore, Clement noted two passages contained in the "secret gospel" that were not in the publicly available version. The first would appear between Mark 10:34 and 10:35. In this fragment, Jesus traveled to Bethany where a woman prevailed on him to raise her son from the dead. Jesus went into the garden area where the tomb was located, rolled away the stone in front of it, and raised the young man from the dead. This young man, who was described as rich, welcomed Jesus into his home. A week later, Jesus instructed the young man in "the mystery of the kingdom of God."

A second fragment that Clement mentioned is shorter and less consequential. It would appear between Mark 10:46a and 10:46b in the regular copy of Mark. In this fragment, the sister and mother of the young man whom Jesus raised were present in Jericho, but Jesus did not meet with them. As far as the letter goes, those are the only two legitimate differences between the "secret gospel" and the regular one.

A Questionable Find

Controversy immediately surrounded the publication of this new letter. Some scholars went so far as to call it a forgery or a fraud, but these days, most would agree that the letter as it stands is probably legitimate. Arguments now tend to focus on the content of the letter and its claims.

One question revolves around which version of the gospel is the original one. Assuming that what Clement claimed in the letter is true, which version came first? Some argue that the "secret gospel" came second, through a process of additions. Others argue that it makes more sense to see the "secret gospel" as the original, and the regular gospel the product of some judicious editing.

You might ask the question, "What's the big deal?" It's difficult to see what could be so earth-shaking about either of these two texts. Scholars who have argued for the authenticity of these fragments note that already in Mark there were references to a young man who fit the same description as the young man from the parts eliminated from the "secret gospel": Mark 10:17–22 and 14:51–52, for example. That leaves us wondering why someone would take out some references to the young man but not remove all such references. What is so provocative about these two secret sections that required their removal? That's yet to be determined, but one thing is for sure: the Secret Gospel of Mark will continue to fuel speculation and controversy in the future.

The Least You Need To Know

- ◆ The gnostics found value in all kinds of texts, not just their own teachings.

- ◆ In the Acts of Peter and the Twelve Apostles, an apostolic journey became a platform for encouraging Christians to recapture their commitment to the poor rather than to the wealthy.

- ◆ The Letter of Peter to Philip demonstrated that gnostic Christians could comfortably merge traditional Christian language and ideas with decidedly non-Christian teachings.

- ◆ Evidence exists that there may have been two different versions of the Gospel of Mark.

Chapter 13

The Beginning and the End

In This Chapter

- The standard version of the classic gnostic myth of origins
- A manual for warring with the rulers and powers
- Poetic theology at its finest
- A gnostic text that focuses more on the end than on the beginning

We've already gotten a look at how differently the orthodox Christians and the gnostics answered questions of origins (see Chapter 2). The myth that the gnostics constructed to explain their insights and beliefs varied from one group to another, but enough core similarities existed to compare them. In this chapter, we'll take a look at several texts from the Nag Hammadi library that speak specifically to beginnings and endings. We'll spend most of our time looking at The Secret Book of John, since many scholars regard it as the benchmark version of the gnostic myth. Since most texts adhere to the same basic interpretations, when we look at the remaining documents in this chapter, we'll focus primarily on how they add to or deviate from The Secret Book of John.

The (Four Versions of) Secret Book of John

When it comes to describing the classical gnostic myth, The Secret Book of John is widely regarded as the definitive source. Although it may not have been the original version of this myth, it certainly seems to have been a popular version. Between the Nag Hammadi library and the earlier discovery of the Berlin Codex, four versions of this text are now in existence. Three of these versions are found in the actual texts. The fourth version is found in, of all places, Irenaeus' *Against Heresies*. Irenaeus described a gnostic myth, which shows that he was familiar with The Secret Book of John, but a version different from the three that we now have texts for. No one can be sure which of these versions is the original, or if any of them are. Still, it's clear that several different versions of this book were circulating, which points to The Secret Book's popularity. Most English translations seem to stick to the longer versions.

Did You Know?

Gnostic mythologies were heavily influenced by one of the dialogues of Plato titled *Timaeus*. In this dialogue, Plato described the creation of the universe by a divine being, the First Principle. According to Plato, the universe extends outward from the First Principle in concentric circles that are each less perfect than the one before. Matter also exists, but not as part of the First Principle's creation. Instead, matter exists eternally by itself, and it is inherently chaotic.

At some point between this First Principle and the physical world, there was an intermediate being called the Demiurge or Craftsman who was responsible for shaping the pre-existing chaotic matter into a material world in which we live. This benevolent Demiurge fashioned everything according to the pattern that existed in the higher realms, but the inherently flawed nature of matter doomed his efforts.

The gnostic myths clearly drew from *Timaeus*, which had a resurgence of popularity in the second century A.D. However, the gnostic version of the Demiurge was far less benign than Plato's. For the gnostics, the "deficiency" in the world affected not only matter but also the one who shaped matter, the Demiurge. A great deal of the gnostic back-story is spent explaining why that was the case.

In any event, there were a lot of versions floating around in Greek, and at least three of them were translated into Coptic and preserved as part of the Nag Hammadi library. That means that we have a very important document in our hands, one that was well-known and widely used. Attempts to date the work are probably futile, since we don't even know at this point what the original composition looked like, but in one form or another it predated Irenaeus' *Against Heresies* (written around A.D. 185).

A Visit from Me, Myself, and I

The Secret Book of John began, believe it or not, with the Apostle John. He was wandering in the Temple in Jerusalem when a *Pharisee* named Arimanios accosted him. John's opponent attacked his trust in Jesus and told him that he was following lies. Deeply distraught by this verbal assault, John left the Temple and fled to an isolated location (there's a disagreement in the versions as to whether it was a mountain or a desert).

Word Knowledge

The **Pharisees** were one of two powerful Jewish religious parties that existed during Jesus' lifetime. They are often regarded as the principal opponents of Jesus and his disciples, despite the fact that the New Testament often portrays them in a positive light. The Pharisees, despite their debates with Jesus, seemed to have no hand in his execution. Two of their number, Nicodemus and Joseph of Arimathea, buried Jesus' body at great personal risk. Another Pharisee, the highly regarded rabbi Gamaliel, was portrayed as speaking in favor of leniency when the apostles were later arrested for preaching in Jesus' name. The Apostle Paul was a Pharisee prior to his conversion to the Christian faith, and the Acts of the Apostles makes it clear that he wasn't the only Pharisee to make the switch.

Desperate for answers, John prayed a series of questions:

♦ How was the savior chosen?

♦ Why was he sent into the world?

♦ Who sent him?

♦ What would the future world be like?

Suddenly, John's prayer was interrupted by a divine visitation. The heavens opened, a brilliant light shined down, and the earth shook. John saw someone standing in front of him. At first it looked like a little child, then a moment later like an old man, then a young man, and finally like all three at once. This being introduced itself as the father/mother/son, the "undefiled and unpolluted" one who had come to teach him the answers to his prayers. John was to communicate what he learned to the "immovable race," namely fellow gnostics.

M-m-m-my Pleroma

With that flashy introduction, The Secret Book of John began to lay out a kind of genealogy of the Divine. In the beginning of everything, there was a single being. No language or categories can realistically be applied to this being, nor can it be described, since it utterly transcends all description or categorization. It simply is. Nevertheless, John's divine visitor used a number of words to describe this ultimate Parent. It is unlimited, unknowable, immeasurable, invisible, eternal, *ineffable*, and unnamable. That's a lot to say about something that you really can't say anything about.

> **Word Knowledge**
>
> Something is **ineffable** when it cannot be described in words.

So what does an eternal, ineffable, invisible being do with itself all day long? Three interesting images came out of the initial description of the Parent. First, it "gazed upon itself." Second, it was thinking about itself. Third, its eternal existence was a "wellspring" that continually overflowed with life.

The result of these three actions (if you can call them that) was profound. The overflowing life of the Parent generated a partner of sorts. Gazing at itself created a new image or reflection of itself. As it thought about itself, its thought literally became a second being named in the text Barbelo, or Forethought. Barbelo is described as the perfect image of the Parent, whom Barbelo glorified by its very existence. Barbelo was the mother-father of the rest of the Pleroma. It was also called "the first human being" and "the holy spirit." Other qualities include "thrice male" and "thrice-androgynous."

Barbelo didn't exist alone, however. In addition to being a multiform being itself, it existed alongside of several other beings, or aeons. These emanations were different from Barbelo in some ways, and in other ways they seemed to be characteristics or qualities of the Barbelo itself. They were named Foreknowledge, Incorruptibility, Eternal Life, and Truth. Each of these aeons, including the Barbelo, is a dual being. In other words, each of them has a masculine and a feminine side. These five pairs of aeons, according to The Secret Book of John, "constitutes the parent." In other words, the unknowable Parent is expressed in these 10 aeons.

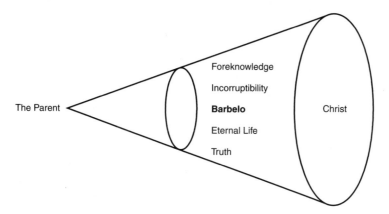

The initial emanations of the Divine Parent.

The action doesn't stop there. The Parent "gazed" at the Barbelo, who brought forth a brand new being, the Only Begotten. The Parent, moved to joy, anointed this new being "with goodness." The Greek word for "goodness" and "anoint" sound alike, so there is a kind of play on words here. This being is also called Christ, which means "anointed one." So thrilled was the Parent with Christ that it set him up to be the "true god" over the entire Pleroma.

Did You Know? _____

Jews and Christians alike were indebted to Philo of Alexandria, the first-century Jewish scholar, for his efforts to harmonize the Hebrew Scriptures and Greek philosophy.

In one of his writings, Philo attempted to synchronize the first chapters of Genesis with Plato's account of creation in Timaeus. In Philo's case, the Logos, or "Word," does the work of the Demiurge. Some scholars see here an influence on the opening line of the Gospel of John ("In the beginning was the Word (logos) and the Word was with God and the Word was God …").

The Christ didn't show up alone, either. A series of aeons emanated with him. As with the Barbelo before it, the Christ "requested" the emergence of its counterparts. Both the Barbelo and the Christ brought forth their emanations by the will of the Parent. We saw the significance of this back in Chapter 8, but it's important to keep in mind because in a moment we'll talk about Sophia and her desire to create without the blessing of the Divine Parent. More about that in a moment.

Following the generation of the Christ, we got the "four luminaries." These angelic beings each represented one realm within the Pleroma. They each had a name, a prototype, and a coterie of additional aeons. See the following table to see how they break down.

The Four Luminaries and their Realms

Luminary	Prototype	Aeons
Harmozel	Ger-Adamas	loveliness, truth, form
Oraiael	Seth	afterthought, perception memory
Daueithai	Seed of Seth	intelligence, love, ideal form
Eleleth	varies	perfection, peace, wisdom (Sophia)

It's important to pause and note a couple of things here. The first two or three proto-types tended to be the same from one version of this myth to another. Ger-Adamas, who was the "perfect human being," and Seth, his son, show up later in The Secret Book of John in relation to the human Adam and his son Seth. Seth and his seed or descendants, who made up the third prototype, we've already seen in the Gospel of the Egyptians (Chapter 10). We'll look at them in greater detail in Chapter 15. The fourth prototype changes from version to version. In this version of the myth, the fourth prototype is the souls of those who did not have gnosis, or knowledge of the Divine, but did repent later. Gnostics reading this story would have identified themselves with the descendants of Seth, and average Christians would have identi-fied themselves with the fourth group.

Altogether, this entire spiritual outline made up the Pleroma. It looks like a flowchart for the heavens, and for a good reason: gnostics were concerned with the makeup of the heavens because that was where they saw their true home. Also, as we'll see later, the shape of the Pleroma was the ideal on which the material world and the heavens surrounding it were based. For gnostics, this physical world is just a cheap knockoff of the real world.

So Sorry, Sophia

Take another look at the preceding table. Notice the last aeon listed—wisdom, also called Sophia. It's Sophia who took this story to the next level. For some reason, Sophia decided to create something entirely of herself, something that didn't come from the will of the Parent. Part of that will involves partnership. Each of the aeons has a counterpart of the opposite gender, so that they make a masculine/feminine pair. Sophia not only brought forth a new being without the consent of the Parent, but also without the cooperation of her male counterpart. And that's where the trouble started.

Gnostics had a couple of explanations for why Sophia would act without the Parent's consent. Some gnostics alleged that Sophia, like all the other aeons in the Pleroma, longed to know the unknowable Parent directly. This longing became so strong in her that it caused her great suffering, and this suffering is what initially separated her from the Pleroma. However, most of the time, including in The Secret Book of John, Sophia was said to have acted deliberately and willfully. She wanted to create on her own, without permission or assistance.

The being that Sophia brought forth, in all versions of this classic gnostic myth, was the Demiurge. Ashamed, Sophia hid her offspring away from all the others in the Pleroma, hiding it in "a luminous cloud." But her child, whom she named *Ialtabaoth*, robbed her of her divine power and began to set up his own realm. Although he wasn't aware of it, the power inherited from his mother enabled him to create a world that was a reflection of the higher realms that he knew nothing about, including his own series of archons, or rulers, to mirror the aeons in the Pleroma.

> **Word Knowledge**
>
> **Ialtabaoth** is one of the names used to describe the being brought forth by Sophia in her separation from the Pleroma. This being, also called Samael and Saklas, was the creator of the physical world and of the bodies of human beings. Ialtabaoth is essentially synonymous with the Demiurge.

Because he was ignorant of the existence of any being or existence higher than himself, he claimed all authority and power. Nearly all the different variations of the gnostic myth have Ialtabaoth saying some version of, "I am a jealous God, and there is no other god apart from me." This is an echo of the Hebrew Bible; when God issued the Ten Commandments in Exodus he spoke of being "a jealous God." This rejection of God as a jealous being was a fundamental part of the gnostic worldview.

The Six-Million Demon Man

Sophia repented. She was sickened by what she had brought forth and by her separation from the Pleroma. Distraught, she appealed to the Parent to be restored, and the entire Pleroma responded. This part of the story was indicative of the gnostic hope for reunification with the Divine. The Pleroma can't be "fullness" if it is missing one of its members. As long as Sophia is apart from the Pleroma, none of them can know any rest.

Things were even worse than they seem, for Sophia was not whole. Her divine power now resided in her offspring Ialtabaoth, who had used it to create a false reality. Any attempt to bring Sophia back without also restoring the power she had lost would be futile. Part of her would still be missing. Any effort to win back Sophia must include the power she lost to her offspring.

So the Pleroma devised a rescue plan. First of all, they recovered Sophia herself. She was elevated to the "ninth heaven," just shy of full restoration. It was a sort of waiting room for her, while the Divine plan moved ahead. Next, they needed to get Sophia's power away from Ialtabaoth.

Playing on Ialtabaoth's almost childish need to create in order to prove itself, the Parent struck upon an idea to con Ialtabaoth into giving up his usurped power. The Barbelo, as the image of the Parent, revealed itself to the material realms in a way that Ialtabaoth and his fellow rulers could see it. They were immediately struck by what they had seen, and gathered their power to recreate the image that they saw.

What followed was an excruciatingly detailed explanation of the creation of Adam. Each one of the rulers had some characteristic or quality that it wanted to impart to their new experiment, and there are hundreds of these rulers. Just to give you a taste of this section, here is part of the list of rulers and the part of the body that they were responsible for.

> "… Bano, the lungs;
>
> Sostrapal, the liver;
>
> Anesimalar, the spleen;
>
> Thopithro, the intestines;
>
> Biblo, the kidneys;
>
> Roeror, the nerves;
>
> Taphreo, the spine …"

And on and on the list goes. No part of the body seemed left out. Even toenails had their own fairy godmother. Then there were rulers who were responsible for making the whole thing work. They were the motivators who got the muscles moving, and there was one for every major part of the body. Finally, there were the spirits who were in charge of the various emotions and passions. Altogether, there were 365 spirits involved in the creation of the first human being.

In the end, however, Adam just lay there. Despite all of their efforts, the rulers couldn't get him up on his feet. After all their work, it looked like Adam's creation was going to be a complete failure.

Falling Up

This was the moment that the aeons in the Pleroma had been waiting for. Angels were sent in disguise to Ialtabaoth, suggesting that he "blow some of your spirit" into Adam. This is an obvious reference to the events of Genesis 2 in the Bible. In this gnostic version, however, when Ialtabaoth breathed into Adam, he ended up breathing out the power he had acquired from Sophia. It passes from Ialtabaoth to Adam, and Adam grew strong and stood up. He was shining from the power that was now in him, and this terrified the rulers, so they cast the hapless fellow into the deepest parts of the material world.

> **From the Source**
>
> The LORD God formed the man from the dust of the ground and breathed into his nostrils the breath of life, and the man became a living being.
>
> —Genesis 2:7

Here the story began to hew more closely to the version that we all know from the Bible, at least in its basic details. Throughout the story, however, the gnostic version turns the orthodox Christian reading on its ear. The Garden of Eden is a prison, the tree of life is a sham designed to poison humankind, and the tree of the knowledge of good and evil is actually the means to breaking free from bondage to the rulers. John's divine visitor actually takes credit for the serpent, which in the orthodox story is a deceiver. In the gnostic version, the serpent is a teacher who acts for humankind's good. The stories really diverge when we get to the creation of woman. As The Secret Book of John tells it, Ialtabaoth decided to get his power back from Adam. The only way he could do that, however, was to find another place to put it. So he pulled part of that power from Adam and created a woman in which to put it. This new vessel for Sophia's power was named Life (the Greek word is Zoe), and Adam immediately recognized her as his spiritual counterpart. The two of them lived together in perfect knowledge, frustrating Ialtabaoth's plan. Furious, the renegade ruler kicked them out of the Garden.

He wasn't done with them yet, however. The Barbelo, concerned for Zoe's safety, sent some spirits who rescued her and removed her from the body of the woman before the assault. Just in time, too, because Ialtabaoth raped the woman (who we can now call Eve, though she isn't named in the text) and had two children with her, Cain and Abel. "And to the present day," The Secret Book informs us matter-of-factly, "sexual intercourse, which originated from the first ruler, has remained." Sex, introduced to the world through an act of violence, is now forever associated with the ugliest side of material existence.

Adam also had a child with Eve. If Adam was the embodiment of the prototypical man Ger-Adamas, then Adam's son Seth was the embodiment of the heavenly Seth. At the same time, Zoe (who had escaped Ialtabaoth's attack by ditching her body) returned now to reside in Seth and in his children. The logic of it all may seem convoluted, but understand that the gnostics weren't writing Genesis from scratch. They were trying to explain Genesis in light of their own very different ideas about the nature of God and the universe, ideas that were not very compatible with the orthodox reading of Genesis.

And the Lucky Winner Is ...

So what do people do in the light of all this? John knew the problem. Now he wanted to know the solution. How do we get out of this mess we're in? John's divine visitor was quick to point out that the truths he had been teaching John were difficult to understand. (You may be agreeing with him right now.) It is likely, he said, that only those of the "immortal race," the descendants of Seth, could grasp them. They are really the stars of the human race, "worthy of eternal, incorruptible life and calling." Okay, all well and good. But what do you do if you weren't born with a silver spirit in your mouth? There is still hope for the rest of us. The spirit of life and the false spirit are duking it out for the souls of women and men. If the spirit of life increases in a person, then when that person dies, he or she will enter into rest, the presence of the Pleroma. On the other hand, if the false spirit grows strong, that person remains bound. When people with strong false spirits die, they fall into the hands of the rulers, who send the spirits back to Earth in other bodies. This round of reincarnations continues until the poor souls wise up.

As for those who have come to knowledge of the Divine and have "then turned away," they will be sent into a prison "where no act of repentance" can take place. They languish there until the end, when they will be "tortured and punished" eternally. Not a pretty picture.

After briefly explaining where the false spirit came from, John's visitor, now revealing itself as the Barbelo, sang a song celebrating its descent into the material world, its act of deliverance on behalf of humanity, and its return to the Pleroma (this poem did not appear in the two short versions). With a final instruction to be careful in teaching what he had learned, the Barbelo left John, who returned to the rest of Jesus' disciples to tell them what he had heard.

The Nature of the Rulers (Codex II,4)

Now that we're familiar with The Secret Book of John and its version of the gnostic myth, we'll move on to other texts from the Nag Hammadi library that illuminate the gnostic story of origins. Our first stop is a work called The Nature of the Rulers. Also known by the older title Hypostasis of the Archons (the titles mean the same thing), The Nature of the Rulers is an origin myth that reflects a gnostic concern with battling the rulers who control the material world and those who live in it. The opening lines of the Nature reflect this concern, referencing the Apostle Paul's comment in the letter to the Ephesians, "For our struggle is not against flesh and blood, but against the rulers, against the authorities, against the powers of this dark world, and against the spiritual forces of evil in the heavenly realms." (Ephesians 6:12) *The Nature of the Rulers* was written, according to its author, because the recipient had asked "about the nature of the rulers" mentioned in Ephesians.

There is a grim quality to this text, almost like a war manual. The powers that rule over humanity are very real and very malevolent. They are prepared to kill, lie, rape, and destroy human beings in their lust for power. Simply put, these are not nice beings, and the gnostic Christian must be armed with knowledge to withstand their deceptions and their assaults.

The Nature of the Rulers follows much the same basic storyline as The Secret Book of John, beginning with the birth of Ialtabaoth and going through Noah's flood. The final section jumps ahead to final liberation of humanity and the destruction of the rulers. Although it's difficult to date, because it may contain some early material, it seems best to put it somewhere in the third century. Certain clues in the text indicate that it may have been written in Egypt.

Who Has the Power?

Perhaps the most noticeable early divergence from The Secret Book of John is the point at which Ialtabaoth lost his grip on Sophia's power. In The Secret Book of John,

Ialtaboath lost it at the moment that he breathed into Adam; The Nature, on the other hand, placed it at the moment when Ialtabaoth "blasphemed" by calling himself the only god. The power left him in that instant and spiraled down into the material world with Ialtabaoth chasing after it.

When Ialtabaoth breathed on Adam later, because the power was already gone, Adam did become an animate being but was unable to rise and walk under his own power. It was only when the "female spiritual principle" came down and inhabited Adam that he got up and moved under his own power.

Woman Power

Like in The Secret Book of John, the rulers tried to remove the Divine power from Adam by separating him and creating a new being, namely woman. They succeeded in draining him of the power, and he ceased to be a spiritual being. Instead, the woman that was created is the new embodiment of the "female spiritual principle" that had originally animated Adam.

Still determined to get their hands on the power, the rulers assaulted the woman. Before they could get her, however, she turned into a tree and left behind a copy of herself, Eve, who was "foully defiled." By the way, if you are disturbed by the casual manner that the gnostic myths seem to gloss over Eve's rape simply because she is not a spiritual person, you are not alone—some of the gnostic's mainstream critics were appalled as well. The implication in the myth seems to be that, because the assault is only against the body, it has little consequence. The spirit is free from attack, and that is what is important.

Free of the woman's body, the feminine spirit entered into the serpent, called "the Teacher," who moved Adam and Eve to eat from the tree of the knowledge of good and evil. Their lack of knowledge became apparent and they realized that they were naked, meaning that they were lacking the spiritual element of their humanity. The rulers come along and, paralleling the Genesis account, cast the man and woman out of the Garden.

Like Mother, Like Daughter ... or Not

The real star of The Nature of the Rulers was Norea, the pure and virgin daughter of Adam and Eve and the wife of Seth. We first saw her indomitable spirit in action when the rulers decided to flood the Earth. They went to Noah, who began to build an ark per instructions. Norea went to him seeking passage aboard the ark, but was refused. So she burnt it down.

Obviously intrigued by this strong woman, the rulers went to see her in hopes of seducing her. The chief ruler, who we know from other texts as the Demiurge or Ialtabaoth, even told her that "Your mother Eve came to us." Norea wasn't having any of it. She proceeded to tell them all what they could do with themselves, which only infuriated them. Frightened, she called out to "the god of the entirety" to save her. Suddenly, the angel Eleleth (you remember him as one of the four luminaries from The Secret Book of John) swooped down to rescue Norea and to teach her about her "root," her spiritual origin. The narrative now changed to first person, as Norea herself began to tell us what the angel taught her.

Norea's Story

What she heard was basically a stripped-down version of what we'd already seen in The Secret Book of John, with one very significant change. When Ialtabaoth began to create his material realm and exalt himself as the almighty, Zoe (whom we met in The Secret Book of John) confronted him and bound him into the abyss. Ialtabaoth was replaced by his offspring, a being named Sabaoth, whom the text equated with the God of the Bible.

Norea, of course, was concerned by what she heard, especially because she believed that she, too, is material. Eleleth reassured her that, in fact, she and her descendants were of the immortal race that is connected to the Divine Parent. Because of this, the rulers could not harm them in any way. For a time, they were to be indistinguishable from the rest of humanity. They were to wait in expectation, Eleleth told her, for the coming of the true human being in bodily form.

The text ended with a poem describing what that final generation would be like. This true human being would teach them everything, give them eternal life, and lead them into the "limitless light." They would trample down the rulers and the power of death. The rulers would be overthrown and all of "the children of light" would know their Parent.

First Thought in Three Forms (Codex XIII,1)

When Codex VI was opened the first time, some pages from an entirely different volume were tucked into the front cover. These eight pages, designated Codex XIII, turned out to be a fragmented copy of a text called The Trimorphic Protennoia, or First Thought in Three Forms.

The text was written in the form of seven poems interspersed with three narrative sections. In selected chunks, these poems recount the history of salvation from the emanation of the Barbelo all the way to the crucifixion of Jesus Christ. The First Thought, or Barbelo, was presented in three forms, as Father, Mother, and Son. As the story unfolds in the poems, the Barbelo descended into the material world three separate times to rescue those who were spiritual. Finally, the narratives appear to be divided into three topics. The first focuses on the emergence of the divine emanations, the second on the redemption of Sophia, and the third on the overthrowing of Ialtabaoth and the punishment of the rulers.

First Thought is significant as a form of poetic theology, and it's possible that it was used in a worship setting. Most intriguing is the baptismal poetry the makes up much of the final poem. We've already talked a bit about baptism in previous chapters, and in Chapter 17 we'll look at a selection of gnostic texts that, in part, deal with baptism. Suffice it to say for now that the act of baptism in the First Thought is a very serious, very real act portrayed as part of a beautiful process that includes stripping, clothing, baptizing, enthroning, glorifying, and "being caught up" (possibly a way of describing the experience of a heavenly ascent). The so-called "five seals" are mentioned in relationship to this process, but whether the two are synonymous is hard to tell.

The Concept of Our Great Power (Codex VI,4)

The Concept of Our Great Power is an unusual document for a gnostic library. It's a salvation history that begins with the creation of the world and continues until the end. The end, in this case, is an Armageddon-like final conflict between light and darkness. Prior to the discovery of the Nag Hammadi library it was assumed that, given their mystical bent and allegorical reading of Scripture, gnostic *eschatology* would focus almost entirely on the personal salvation of individual spirits rather than on cosmic showdowns.

Word Knowledge

Eschatology is the teaching or belief in final or last things, usually dealing with death, the afterlife, divine judgment, and the Second Coming.

The Concept challenges that assumption. From its first lines, the book calls its readers to escape the coming conflagration, when the physical world will be destroyed by fire. It has little to say about how the universe is constructed, a topic thoroughly explored by other gnostic writers, but focuses entirely on a gnostic imagining of the end of the world.

It's difficult to date The Concept. Hints in the text indicate that it was composed in the fourth century. Where it was written, and by whom, remain a mystery.

History in The Concept of Our Great Power is divided up into three aeons or ages: the Age of the Flesh, the "psychic" age or the Age of the Soul, and a third unnamed age that is to come. It's not really all that cut and dried, however. Certain events seem to take place more than once, for example, and at times it's difficult to figure out what the author is getting at. One thing is clear; "Our Great Power" is this document's name for the Divine Parent, and knowing the Great Power is the key to salvation from the coming apocalypse. The world, according to the author, is moving toward a final reckoning, passing through its ages and coming to an end. Let's look more closely at each of these ages.

The Age of Flesh

The first age, as we already mentioned, is the Age of the Flesh. It begins with an account, in terms somewhat difficult to understand, of the creation of humankind. It is very helpful to keep in mind the more detailed version of this myth, which we have seen in The Secret Book of John. The author of The Concept seems to take much of that backstory for granted here. In some ways, the account given in this text feels like a thumbnail sketch of the gnostic myth.

As the story begins, it seems that "darkness" and "Hades" have somehow acquired "the fire" of the Great Power, a reference to the Great Power's creative ability. With it, the powers of the physical world are brought into being. The Great Power reveals its image to the various powers of the physical world, and "the soul" of man is created as a result.

In the briefest of sentences, the story follows the "fall" of the first humans, by which the author means that they "entered into the flesh." The Demiurge pops up here as well, referred to as the "father of the waters." Water is a symbol for the physical world or for matter in general. Interestingly, The Concept here seems to differ with The Secret Book of John by attributing Noah's ark to the work of the Great Power. The Secret Book of John, you'll remember, made the ark out as the Demiurge's plan.

The Age of Soul

The Flood brings an end to the Age of the Flesh and the beginning of the Age of the Soul. We are told that the "psychic" aeon, as the Age of the Soul is also called, "is a small one." The "first defilement of the creation," evidently another reference to the being we've been introduced to already as the "father of the flesh," unleashes all sorts of awful things on human history: wars, hatred, lying, sorrows, and long list of similar calamities.

During all of this "the mother of the fire," a reference to Sophia, "was impotent." In contrast to other versions of the gnostic myth, she played almost no role at all in the redemption of humanity. In comparison to, say, The Nature of the Rulers where the Sophia spirit plays a very visible role in superintending events as they unfold, in The Concept that did not appear to be the case.

During the age of the soul, a man will come "who knows the Great Power." This man will speak in parables, talk about the age to come, and perform miraculous acts. The rulers get one of this man's followers to betray him, but they can't touch him. They are unable to harm the man in any way. Instead, he ascends back into the heavens. If you're thinking that this sounds a lot like Jesus, you are probably right.

The Age to Come

With the coming of the Christ, all out war breaks loose. The rulers go berserk, destroying cities and shattering mountains. An antichrist figure emerges to lead the world astray. Finally, nature itself seems to dissolve, with all sorts of apocalyptic language being used: stars fall, rivers stop flowing, there are earthquakes and droughts. It's not exactly a day at the beach.

At last, Christ rescues "everyone who will know me" and takes them to a safe place where they are no longer hampered by their flesh. The rest of the material universe is not so lucky. Christ sets it on fire and burns it until there is nothing left. Still, the text ends on a hopeful note, as Christ releases "the souls that are being punished," souls that are now becoming pure. Eventually, even these souls become part of the "unchangeable aeon." Everyone likes a happy ending.

The Least You Need to Know

- The perfect Pleroma was made up of a series of emanations from an unknowable Divine Parent.

- In gnostic literature, the creation of the physical world was a mistake that needs to be remedied.

- The gnostics considered themselves spiritual because they possessed a part of Sophia as their spirit.

- The eventual goal is the complete restoration of Sophia's dispersed essence to the Pleroma. When this happens, the physical world will cease to exist.

Chapter 14

The Divine Feminine

In This Chapter

- ◆ The role of the "feminine" in gnostic mythology
- ◆ The conflicted attitude toward women in early Christian history
- ◆ Five Nag Hammadi documents with a feminine bent

In Chapter 7 we took a look at the Gospel of Mary, which argues for sexual equality in the leadership of the Christian communities. And all along we've seen a lot of feminine terms being used for both the soul and the Divine being, the kind of thing you don't hear much of in church on Sunday morning. The gnostic texts in this chapter, while all fairly short, demonstrate the use of feminine language for the soul and for the Divine.

The Feminine Mystique

The use of feminine imagery for God is not unique to gnostic Christians. Chapter 49 of the prophet Isaiah, for example, uses the image of a nursing mother to describe God's great love and care for Israel. Nevertheless, the predominance of "male" language for God in the experience of many Christians in the modern church has made us all very sensitive to the apparently egalitarian quality of gnostic writing.

From the Source _____

But Zion said, "The LORD has forsaken me,
the Lord has forgotten me."

"Can a mother forget the baby at her breast
and have no compassion on the child she has borne? Though she may forget,
I will not forget you!"

—Isaiah 49:14–15 (NIV)

While the use of feminine metaphors for God and the soul have been widely embraced by modern readers of the gnostic literature, these metaphors are not entirely positive. It's not enough to say that the female side of things has a place in the Divine. You have to ask, "What role do female persons or beings play?" When we begin to explore that point, some troubling issues arise.

The Female Aeons

The gnostic texts from Nag Hammadi are full of descriptions of the Divine that include feminine imagery. The Barbelo, for example, is often spoken of as Father, Mother, and Son, and the Mother image quite frequently takes the lead. The Valentinian myth, as we've seen in Chapter 9, teaches that the Divine is a male-female pair. The texts that we will examine in this chapter all speak of the soul as female—no great shock there—but they also speak of God as female. See "The Thunder, Perfect Mind (Codex VI,2)" section later as one clear example.

Most of the references to God as feminine, however, concern Sophia. That may not be as flattering as it sounds. Spiritual beings are most commonly described as pairs—coupled male-female beings. It seems that the gnostics wanted to overcome the duality in nature through the constant unification of the two gendered opposites. The linking of males and females is not intended to blend the two together into one form. Rather, gnostic mythology is seeking to make sense of the human condition (our split in terms of sex) by elevating it into the heavenly Pleroma (the perfect fullness of the Divine realm). The masculine and the feminine are intended to cooperate in the process of creation, and when they do so, all is harmonious. Both the masculine and the feminine contribute something crucial to the final creation. And that is where the problem starts. The Sophia myth places the blame for the shattering of that harmony on a female aeon who sought to conceive or to create without recourse to her male counterpart, who is described as both her spouse and her brother. Modern champions of gnostic thinking often deride orthodox Christians for blaming Eve for the fall of humankind. It's difficult to see the Sophia myth as anything less than Eve on a cosmic scale.

At nearly every stage, the gnostic mythology parallels many of the ways that women were viewed in the ancient Mediterranean world. Within that culture, chaos and destruction occur because a female character decided to act on her own. Then she is redeemed or restored through some form of marriage to her male counterpart. (Remember the bridal chamber?) We will see exactly this story told in "The Exegesis of the Soul (Codex II,6)" the last text we'll see in this chapter.

Words to the Wise

Whilst both sexes seem to have been allowed to play an equal part in religious practice and discussion, the ultimate aim of the gnostic was to achieve a state which eliminated sexual difference—which in effect meant that women had to lose their femaleness in order to be subsumed into the larger "male" group, whose actual sex was no longer significant. The gnostics' use of the terms male and female to describe the division between spirit and matter, and their further equation of these terms with good and evil, inevitably leads to the association of women and sexuality with evil.

—Susan Haskins, *Mary Magdalene: Myth and Metaphor* (42)

It's not all bad news, by any means. Gnostic literature, generally speaking, is more likely to use positive images of the feminine than most orthodox writers are. And who can deny the power of texts like The Thunder, Perfect Mind (the first text we'll review in this chapter) as an expression of a powerful female aspect to the Divine.

Gnostic imagery for God could be shockingly unconventional in terms of its language. In many ways, however, the imagery and basic assumptions about male-female relationships could be very traditional.

Disciples of Jesus

The gnostics did not restrict their high regard for the feminine to aeons and spiritual beings in the Pleroma. Gnostic literature contains numerous positive references to the female disciples of Jesus. Women like Salome and Martha appear often, and Mary Magdalene (whose gospel we saw in Chapter 7) figures prominently in many of the texts where Jesus dialogues with his followers about spiritual matters. The gnostics were not shy about portraying the female disciples of Jesus as strong leaders within the early Christian community.

At the same time, these positive images stand out precisely because of their uniqueness. Most gnostic literature, like orthodox literature, focuses on the male followers of Jesus. In those instances where women appear, even when they hold their own, they are always outnumbered. The Gospel of Mary, for example, presents Mary Magdalene as alone with the 12 apostles. While she receives deeper insight and revelation than the rest of the (male) disciples, it is still the men who go out and preach the gospel.

New Testament Feminism

Tension over the role of women in the church goes as far back as Paul's letters to the church in Corinth. In 1 Corinthians, Paul responded to a situation in which certain women in the community had decided that, because they were now "spiritual" (gnostics considered themselves the "spiritual" ones, remember?), they were no longer bound by any social constraints arising from their gender. It's possible that their behavior was damaging the reputation of Christians in Corinth.

Paul responds not by suggesting that the women are wrong in their understanding of their new spiritual state, but by summoning them to a mature ethic of love. Truly spiritual people, Paul tells them, don't flaunt their freedom at the expense of those around them. It might be worth asking what it was in Paul's preaching that initially gave the Corinthian women the idea that the gospel brings about equality between the genders. Paul, so often accused of misogyny, expresses no animosity to women at all. Rather, he summons them to limit their freedom so that the gospel can be preached without hindrance in their city.

Although the Corinthians certainly did not hold to the kind of well-developed gnosticism that arose in the second century, their use of the term "spiritual" to describe themselves suggests that some later gnostic groups may have inherited many of the same ideas about gender equality that the Corinthian Christians heard in Paul's teaching. If so, they may also have inherited the Corinthian overemphasis. In any event, the question of gender equality in the church was bound to cause conflict even if the gnostics were following Paul to the letter. Not all early Christian groups embraced Paul's idea that in Christ there was "neither … male nor female." (Galatians 3:28)

Myth and Reality

The real question is, "What did this emphasis on the female mean for the average woman in a gnostic group or church?" Did the gnostic view of the feminine filter down to the average gnostic woman in positive or negative ways? Some scholars have embraced the gnostic emphasis on the female as positive; others have criticized its darker side. Both sides have assumed that there is a direct correlation between how the gnostics viewed the nature of God on the one hand and the ways that women in gnostic communities lived out their lives on a day-to-day basis.

Some popularizers of the gnostic texts make it sound as if gnostic societies were utopias of egalitarian sexual equality. Orthodox writers like Tertullian, complaining about the behavior of some gnostic groups, inadvertently lent some credence to the idea of gender equality. Tertullian decried certain "heretics" who opened their doors to almost anyone and who allowed even women to preside at the celebration of the eucharist, a priestly function reserved to men. How accurate was his accusation? That women participated in every facet of gnostic worship and community life seems to be the case. How often, and in what numbers, is another question altogether.

Despite the feminine references to God, and despite the frequent references to women involving themselves in gnostic worship, nearly every gnostic teacher that we hear about is a man. It is possible that Helen, Simon the Magician's paramour, was integrally involved in the leadership of whatever community gathered around the two of them. Irenaeus mentions Marcellina, a follower of the Egyptian gnostic Carpocrates, who began teaching in Rome around A.D. 150. Other than that, however, very few women are mentioned as leaders within the gnostic community. Although women were very active in the gnostic communities, the top spots still seem to have been held by men.

We should also be careful not to overplay the differences between how gnostic and orthodox communities treated women. The same Tertullian, for instance, who was scandalized at the freedom exercised by "heretic" women, also wrote with esteem and even affection about a woman in his church who exercised the gift of prophecy, receiving visions of angels and even of the Lord and freely sharing them with others in the church. Often, orthodox fears about women were not fears *of* them so much as fears *for* them. Irenaeus, for instance, was indignant when he recounted the way that the Valentinian Mark used the promise of spiritual gifts as a means to seduce unsuspecting Christian women. Female members of Mark's group were allowed to preside at the eucharist, and some were invited to attend rituals that would enable them to

prophesy. Irenaeus' concerns stemmed from dealing with women in his own congregation who had allegedly fallen victim to Mark. Fears that women would be
exploited or manipulated by gnostic teachers figured prominently in orthodox
writings.

The actual status of women in gnostic communities continues to be an unsolved
puzzle. We have some of the pieces, but not all of them. The picture that we get
is at times contradictory. That stands to reason, since gnostics were no more consistent on this issue than orthodox Christians were. Both gnostics and orthodox could
act in ways not easily predicted on the basis of their writings alone. It is to the gnostic
writings that we now turn.

From the Source

And do you not know that you are (each) an Eve? The sentence of God on this sex
of yours lives in this age: The guilt must of necessity live, too. *You* are the devil's gate-
way: *you* are the unsealer of that (forbidden) tree: *you* are the first deserter of the divine
law: *you* are she who persuaded him whom the devil was not valiant enough to attack.
You destroyed so easily God's image, man. On account of *your* desert—that is,
death—even the Son of God had to die.

—Tertullian, On the Apparel of Women, Bk.I.1

The Thunder, Perfect Mind (Codex VI,2)

Let's be honest right from the start. Almost nobody knows what to do with this
document.

The text is almost entirely intact, except for some damage to the tops of the pages.
No date for the work can be determined from the text itself, although it certainly had
to have been written prior to its inclusion in the Nag Hammadi library in the mid-
fourth century.

The Thunder, Perfect Mind is perhaps the most unusual book in this library of
out-of-the-ordinary texts. First of all, its title is an interesting intersection of ideas.
Thunder was often associated with the voice of God in the Semitic world, and the
voice of God was often personified as the Logos, or Word, of God. So the intent is
to convey the idea that the Divine is expressing itself, communicating to humanity.
Perfect Mind, on the other hand, suggests a Greek source. Linking the two together

like this in one title suggests that the author is attempting to bridge these two different ways of looking at God.

The text begins with a summons. "Do not be ignorant of me," the Thunder said, and then began to describe herself. The entire text is a monologue spoken in the feminine voice. She seemed to enjoy speaking in "I am" statements and antitheses. For example …

> For I am the first and the last.
>
> I am the honored one and the scorned one.
>
> I am the whore and the holy one.
>
> I am the wife and the virgin.

Many of these pairs are purely paradoxical:

> I am the bride and the bridegroom,
>
> and it is my husband who begot me.
>
> I am the mother of my father
>
> and the sister of my husband,
>
> and he is my offspring.

At its end, Thunder summed up her lengthy resumé with a promise to those who would put aside "the pleasant forms" of "sins," "passions," and "pleasures," and "become sober." Those who do so enter rest, find life, and never die.

The text has a hymnic quality to it, so perhaps it was used at some time in a liturgical setting. Nevertheless, it is one of the most difficult of the Nag Hammadi texts to make sense of in any rational way. As the entry in the *Anchor Bible Dictionary* puts it, "Among the gnostic texts of the Coptic Nag Hammadi Library … few can match The Thunder, Perfect Mind in philosophical inscrutability." And that may very well be the point.

Hypsiphrone (Codex XI,4)

Hypsiphrone is another very short text, named after the female being who is its main character. Her name may mean "exalted thought" or "high-minded one." No date is known for this text.

Hypsiphrone appears to be the account of a being descending from "the place of my virginity" in the heavenly realms to the world. While there she met another being, a male named Phainops, who "breathed into her fount of blood." This may have something to do with the creation of humanity, since the name Adam has some association with the word "blood." The text here is very short, has some damage that makes reading even more difficult, and ultimately trails off without concluding. At the end, we saw Hypsiphrone, "in great fear," leaving with Phainops, who was giving her some kind of instruction regarding "the fount of blood that is revealed by setting afire."

The Thought of Norea (Codex IX,2)

The Thought of Norea is one of the shortest texts in the entire Nag Hammadi library. It contains just 52 lines, and is not titled. The title that we're using comes from within the body of the text itself. The document has some damage, but none that impedes reading the text in its entirety.

The Thought of Norea reads like a prayer or a plea. It begins with an address to the Father-Mother-Son, three-personed God that we have seen before in gnostic mythology. The one lifting up this prayer was Norea, whom we have met before (see the review of the Nature of the Rulers in Chapter 13).

Norea appears several times in gnostic texts. She was the daughter of Adam and Eve and the sister and wife of Seth. As such, she was the mother of the line of Seth, which was the gnostic race. As we saw in the Nature of the Rulers, Norea was about to be attacked by the rulers when she cried out to God and was saved by Eleleth. Here again we saw Norea crying out.

Did You Know? _____

Norea's name appears to be a version of the Hebrew name Naamah. That's significant, since Naamah appears in the book of Genesis. Her name appears in the fourth chapter, and in the sixth chapter the Bible relates that angels and humans had sex together and produced some bizarre offspring. When compared with the gnostic myth of Norea, who is almost raped by the rulers but escapes and keeps her virginity intact, it seems that Naamah may be the source for Norea, but with her original story now turned inside out.

Because Norea cried out, she was saved and returned to the Pleroma. In fact, "she beholds the Pleroma," meaning that she dwelled in complete fullness. Well, sort of. Norea's enlightened state seems to come and go. "There will be days," she is told, when she would see the Pleroma and would be free from "deficiency." The knowledge of the Pleroma would unfold in her life over time, and she would grow in understanding. Aiding her in this were the four luminaries that we have seen over and over again in the gnostic mythology. These beings "intercede on her behalf."

Out of her relationship with the Pleroma, Norea began to "speak the words of life," which indicates that she participated in the Divine plan for redeeming humanity. Norea's rest could not be a selfish or self-centered thing. Out of her own fullness she brought life to others. She was a "saved savior," a common idea in these texts.

Authoritative Teaching (Codex VI,3)

Finally, after a handful of very short documents, we get to a text of some length. And what a text it is! The Authoritative Teaching is a very imaginative work, filled with all sorts of metaphors to describe the pitfalls and perils that the spirit faced as she sought to navigate this life. The language that it uses suggests to scholars that it was written sometime in the second century.

Pretty Pictures

The soul in this text sought to be restored to her rightful place in the "invisible, ineffable worlds" from which she came. For now she was "cast into a body," a creation of those "dealers in bodies," which was susceptible to all kinds of indignities and pains. She was tied up in adultery, we are told, because "the body came from lust, and lust came from material substance."

The soul was pictured variously as a whore imprisoned in a brothel and as wheat that has been mixed up with chaff that contaminates it. By losing her knowledge, she had fallen into "bestiality." She didn't know what to do or say. She dwelled in "a house of poverty," while "matter struck blows at her eyes."

In a really vivid set of images, she compared life to being a fish. The devil keeps trying to entice you into biting the food that he dangles before your eyes. It has a hook in it, however, by which he will drag you back into his power "that he might swallow us." The foods that he uses start out with "a pain in your heart ... on account of a small thing." Following that comes desire for things—love of money, pride, and envy—but the worst of all are "ignorance and ease." Refusing to bite the foods that you are offered is the key to freedom.

The text goes on to describe life as like living with a bunch of nets that are laid out to snare you. If they catch you or trip you up, they will drag you down to the "maneaters."

So Where's the Honeymoon?

Thankfully, the soul was sent a bridegroom, her brother, who would save her. He came to give her the right kind of food. He daubed her eyes with the medicine of "the word" so that she could see with her mind. Once she regained her sight, she would know who she belonged to and would "learn about her root," her true nature. All this happened so that "she would cling to her branch" and "renounce matter."

The soul seeking redemption refused to stop looking for the answers she sought. She "wearied herself in seeking." Ultimately, the soul found what she was looking for. She got to eat of "immortal food" and meet her bridegroom in the bridal chamber. Through that union, she entered into "rest from her labors."

The Exegesis on the Soul (Codex II,6)

The content of the Exegesis of the Soul ought to be familiar to you by now. The soul, originally pure and virginal, fell into material existence and suffered many pains. Coming to her senses, she repented and cried out for deliverance. The Divine sent a savior, who made possible her return. It sounds like a pretty standard Sophia myth.

Ah, but presentation is everything. Despite its somewhat bland title, the Exegesis of the Soul is a fascinating attempt to communicate that same basic story through the medium of a novel. Well, not exactly a novel, but definitely a storybook kind of approach accompanied by a running commentary of sorts. Okay, so maybe it's not Oprah Book Club material, but somebody must have enjoyed it.

The soul was portrayed as a young maiden who was living quietly and chastely in her father's house. She fell into a body, however, and "into the hands of many robbers." Unprotected and far from home, she was repeatedly violated by rapists and lovers alike, forced upon by some and seduced by others. Eventually the soul was left "a poor desolate widow," surrounded by her crippled children who were "dumb, blind … sickly … feebleminded." In her distress, she sighed and repented, and her father heard her longing for redemption. He sent her bridegroom to her, "her man" and "her brother," to save her.

" " From the Source _____

As long as the soul keeps running about everywhere, copulating with whomever she meets and defiling herself, she exists suffering her just deserts. But when she perceives the straits she is in and weeps before the father and repents, then the father will have mercy on her and he will make her womb turn from the external domain and will turn it again inward, so that the soul will regain her proper character. For it is not so with a woman. For the womb of the body is inside the body like the other internal organs, but the womb of the soul is around the outside like the male genitals, which are external.

So when the womb of the soul, by the will of the father, turns itself inward, it is baptized and is immediately cleansed of the external pollution which was pressed upon it, just as garments, when dirty, are put into the water and turned around until their dirt is removed and they become clean. And so the cleansing of the soul is to regain the newness of her former nature and to turn herself back again. That is her baptism.

—The Exegesis of the Soul

The soul's redemption involved a reunification, spiritual marriage, with her brother-savior. She "gave up her former prostitution" and prepared herself in the bridal chamber to receive him. "And she dreamed of him like a woman in love with a man." Their marriage would bring about good children, as she received from him "seed that is the life-giving spirit." Eventually, "when she became young again" she ascended back to the house of her father.

In case the story itself wasn't an obvious enough allegory, throughout the entire text the author interrupted the flow of the narrative to add passages of Scripture and even quotations from Homer's *Odyssey* with the intention of commenting on and unpacking the storyline. The text ends with a call to repentance. "If we repent, truly God will heed us, he who is long-suffering and abundantly merciful …" This has been the focus of the Exegesis all along.

The Least You Need to Know

- Gnostic literature portrays the Divine in feminine language, but its portrayal of females is not entirely positive.

- Women had a great deal of freedom in gnostic communities, but the principal teachers and leaders of the movement continued to be men.

- Some of the most powerful feminine language for the Divine appears in places where the Divine speaks for itself, such as in The Thunder, Perfect Mind.

- Gnostic appreciation for the feminine didn't prevent them from frequently portraying the female soul as helpless and naive.

15

The Sethite Literature

In This Chapter

- ◆ Adam reveals a hidden truth to his son Seth
- ◆ A volume of Sethite prayers gives us a glimpse of gnostic worship
- ◆ A suicidal Zostrianos ascends to the heavens for a guided tour
- ◆ A gnostic revelation that turns inward
- ◆ A text that gives tips for prayer and vocal lessons at the same time

In Chapter 8, we were introduced to the Gospel of the Egyptians. That text was one of several from the Nag Hammadi library that displayed an interest in the unique role of Seth, one of the divine beings that came into existence in the Pleroma. In this chapter, we'll take a look at several more texts from Nag Hammadi that evidence this Sethite focus. As with all of these topical chapters, these aren't the only books from Nag Hammadi that concern themselves with Seth, but they are representative.

The Revelation of Adam (Codex V,5)

It is likely that The Revelation of Adam is an example of Jewish specula-tion about Seth. The text contains no certain indications of Christian influence (though there are some hints that might be read that way, as we'll see in a moment). If it really does stem from a Jewish background, The Revelation of Adam may very well be the kind of source that the author of the Gospel of the Egyptians used to write his more Christian account of Seth and the immortal race. Aside from the possibility that it may predate the Gospel of the Egyptians, nothing substantive is known about the date or place that The Revelation was written.

The Revelation tells an account of the gnostic myth, given by Adam to his son Seth, in which he related knowledge that he received from three beings that he saw in a vision. Adam takes us on a swift and not entirely detailed ride through a gnostic rereading of the first chapters of Genesis. It differs little from other versions of the gnostic myth, presupposing some of the same basic elements. Its lack of detail at certain moments may indicate either that it is earlier than other versions (like the Gospel of the Egyptians) or that it assumes the reader will already be familiar with those details.

Listen up, Son

Adam began his story with a brief account of his own creation, skipping over the detailed cosmic flowchart of aeons and angels that takes up so much of the account in texts like the Secret Book of John (see Chapter 13) and the Gospel of the Egyptians (see Chapter 10). Instead, Adam got right into the action.

He and Eve came into being, Adam said, made out of Earth by "god." The Revelation uses the same word for both the Demiurge and the Divine Parent, which can be disconcerting at times. At the beginning, he and Eve were like "the great angels." From Eve, he gained knowledge about "the eternal god," from whose realm they really originated.

Up to this point, Adam told Seth, he and Eve were physically joined together. As was mentioned in Chapter 6, this idea that Adam was originally both sexes in one being was a commonly held idea in the early Christian period. In Adam's account of events, the Demiurge stepped in and separated the two humans out of anger and jealousy, because he realized that they knew they were superior to him.

The glory and the knowledge that had been their possession left them. It passed "into the seed belonging to great aeons," namely the seed of Seth. Because of that experience, Adam told his son, "I named you after that divine being who is the origin of that race." For Adam and Eve, however, life became ordinary. They were lacking in knowledge, and were easily dominated by the Demiurge.

It was during this time Adam, "asleep in the thinking of my heart," experienced his vision. In it, he saw three people standing in front of him. They weren't named, but it seems pretty certain that this was the Barbelo, or the Father-Mother-Son as they are described in some versions. They began to reveal to Adam the vision that he related to Seth in the rest of the text. Meanwhile, Adam continued, the Demiurge had his violent encounter with Eve that resulted in Cain's birth (see this more fully explained in Chapter 13). Adam and Eve then had Seth. Adam described how, in the wake of his desire for Eve, they lost what little knowledge that they had left and began to age. Once again, we see sex and death yoked together in the gnostic account of the origins of humankind.

Rewriting History Ahead of Time

With that prologue, Adam launched into telling Seth the future events he was shown during his vision. The events described in that vision demonstrate a great deal of negative feeling toward the standard Genesis story. All of the heroes of Genesis, like Noah and Shem, end up looking like dupes, puppets of the Demiurge. He used them to oppose the progress of this other race. In this version, the story of Noah's flood and the restoration afterward parallels the story of "those people," the immortal race.

The flood itself was an attempt by the Demiurge to destroy those who would stand in his presence "in some other glory." The Demiurge definitely didn't like competition. His plans were thwarted, however, when angels in clouds came swooping down to whisk the immortal race away to a safe land. They would dwell there for 600 years, Adam said, "uncorruptible in knowledge."

Foiled Again!

In the meantime, the Demiurge struck a deal first with Noah and then with Noah's son Shem: absolute loyalty in exchange for blessing. It's an interesting development, since Shem was the ancestor of all Semite peoples, most especially the Jews. So as far back as Shem, The Revelation of Adam puts the Jews in a league with the Demiurge.

Noah's other sons, Ham and Japheth, created 12 kingdoms and began to populate them. In an odd development, 400,000 of their people (they populated rather quickly, don't you think?) left them and joined up with the immortal race of Seth, who were safe and secure in their own land. Not for long, though. The "god of the aeons," the Demiurge, rustled up his forces and attacked the chosen race, raining down fire and brimstone on them. The Gospel of the Egyptians associated Seth's race with Sodom and Gomorrah, so it's quite possible that what we're reading is a retelling of the destruction of those plains cities in Genesis 19, with the people of Sodom as the heroes.

> **Did You Know?** _____
>
> Sodom and Gomorrah were two legendary cities that, according to Genesis, were literally blasted off the face of the earth by God. Genesis 18-19 tells us that God, angry with the sins of Sodom and Gomorrah, warned Abraham of his plans to destroy those cities. Abraham, whose nephew Lot lived in Sodom, talked God into sparing the cities if as few as ten "righteous men" could be found living there. Apparently, there weren't even that many. Angels sent from God rescued Lot and his family, and shortly afterward "the Lord rained down burning sulfur on Sodom and Gomorrah".
>
> As one of the more dramatic and memorable stories in Genesis, Sodom and Gomorrah quickly became synonyms for sinful communities everywhere.

Once again, armies of angels in clouds descended to gather and protect Seth's people. Names familiar to readers of other Sethite texts appear here: Abrasaks, Samblo, and Gamaliel (remember them from Chapter 8?). These angels transported the immortal race outside of the physical world and thus out of the range of power of the Demiurge and his rulers. They dwelled in light with the angels, whom they would come to look like, we are told.

Does He Get Frequent Flier Miles?

After the flood and the fire, you would think that a guy would deserve a break. But here came Seth a third time, looking for someone else to save. Everyone who was left lived "under the authority of death," but those who opened their hearts to knowledge wouldn't die. Seth tried to help things along by doing "signs and wonders" to show up the rulers who oppressed humanity.

Although it's very obscure, Seth seemed to take up a body and become a human being with miraculous powers. That is confirmed by the reaction of the Demiurge, who wanted to know who is this human being "who is superior to us?" Not content with an answer, he attacked Seth. Again, the wording is a bit ambiguous, but it seems to say that the spirit of Seth would leave his human body and go to safety. Meanwhile the rulers, who were blind to his departure, "chastised the flesh of the human being upon whom the holy spirit has come." To add insult to injury, the rulers began to spread lies about this human. They "made use of the name deceitfully," a charge that other gnostic texts would take up against orthodox Christians.

If you can't help but think that sounds an awful lot like Jesus, you're not alone. This section is the one point at which The Revelation sounds like it might have some Christian influences. It's not conclusive, however, and there are other ways of explaining it.

What follows is a poem or song in which each of the 12 kingdoms of Ham and Japheth offered an explanation for who this human being was and where he came from. Each of their stories was different, but each one ended with the phrase, "And it was thus that he arrived at the water." This might be a reference to baptism; no such phrase shows up in the last two stanzas. Finally, we hear from that crowd of 400,000 people, the ones who had left the kingdoms of Ham and Japheth. The final stanza of the song comes from the chosen people themselves. The text seems to imply that, out of all the different explanations offered in the song, only the chosen race had an accurate understanding of who Seth was.

The Final Reckoning

Well, enough of that. It's time for a showdown. The final part of The Revelation of Adam details the last struggle between Seth and the powers that ruled the world. It's not what you would expect, though. The worst that happened was that "an obscure cloud" came over everyone.

The people began to acclaim the immortal race of the seed of Seth, recognizing them as knowing the truth. For themselves, the people were also aware that they were worthy of nothing but damnation because they had opposed "the god of truth." They knew that their souls were going to die. The angels who presided over baptism—Mikheus, Mikhar, and Mnesinous—chimed in and confirmed that, indeed these folks were in for it.

There's a curious passage in the angels' accusation that bears scrutiny. The angelic keepers of baptism accused these other people of "having defiled the water of life." Were they judging folks who had been baptized? The author of The Revelation of Adam would certainly not have agreed with the orthodox belief in baptism as a release from sin. Given the gnostic emphasis on baptism as an initiation into gnosis, other forms of baptism might have been viewed as blasphemous. Is this, therefore, an attack against orthodox Christians for their failure to properly approach baptism?

It's difficult to say, largely because we still don't know if there is any Christian influence on this text at all.

The next-to-last paragraph contains an implicit criticism of those who looked to written books to find the words of God. Instead, Adam implied that those who truly know God receive their revelation directly from angels. With that, and a closing paragraph from Adam in which he equated gnosis with baptism, The Revelation of Adam comes to a close.

The Three Steles of Seth (Codex VII,5)

The Gospel of the Egyptians shows us two sides of the Sethite literature. On the one hand, the literature has an interest in detailing the genealogy of the immortal race, the seed of Seth. The Revelation of Adam expresses that interest as well. On the other hand, there is a ritualistic or liturgical focus. Sethite texts are often concerned with proper forms for prayer, praise, and worship. The documents called The Three Steles of Seth fall into this second category. All of these texts are united by their common mythology (particularly the recurring names of certain angels) and their exalted view of Seth. The Three Steles purports to be a revelation that was given to a fellow named Dositheos. His name is familiar to us since he is sometimes mentioned as the teacher of Simon the Magician (see Chapter 4), and therefore has a kind of gnostic resumé. That the text is attributed to Dositheos suggests that it comes from a Jewish background, though there are some hints of a Neoplatonic connection as well. (The two are not incompatible.) Because of these connections, the text should probably be dated sometime in the early third century.

Word Knowledge

A **stele** is a large upright stone tablet or pillar, usually inscribed with a text of some kind. Often, steles were used as memorial stones to some royal achievement or as a means to publish a code of law or rules regarding worship in a temple. Steles were meant to be permanent records, lasting through the ages.

In a vision, probably as part of an ascent into the heavens, Dositheos supposedly saw three *steles* that were set up by Seth himself. He memorized them and wrote them down after he returned. Each of the steles was inscribed with a prayer to one of the Divine beings, from the lowest to the highest. Seth offered up the first prayer to his progenitor Ger-Adamas (or Adamas). The second worship was offered to the Barbelo. Finally, the third stele presented praises to the Divine Parent itself as the final part of threefold ascension to the heavens.

From the Source

In the Gospel of the Egyptians and again in The Three Steles, we hear that Seth set up writings in stone that were intended to stand the test of time. Where did such an idea come from? This passage from the first-century Jewish historian Josephus offers an intriguing clue:

> Now this Seth, when he was brought up, and came to those years in which he could discern what was good, became a virtuous man; and as he was himself of an excellent character, so did he leave children behind him who imitated his virtues. All these proved to be of good dispositions. They also inhabited the same country without dissensions, and in a happy condition, without any misfortunes falling upon them, till they died. They also were the inventors of that peculiar sort of wisdom that is concerned with the heavenly bodies, and their order. And that their inventions might not be lost before they were sufficiently known, upon Adam's prediction that the world was to be destroyed at one time by the force of fire, and at another time by the violence and quantity of water, they made two pillars, the one of brick, the other of stone: They inscribed their discoveries on them both, that in case the pillar of brick should be destroyed by the flood, the pillar of stone might remain, and exhibit those discoveries to humankind; and also inform them that there was another pillar of brick erected by them. Now this remains in the land of Siriad to this day.

—Josephus, *The Antiquities of the Jews* (Bk.I. 2.3), trans. William Whiston

The First Stele

In the first stele, Seth extolled the attributes of his Father, Ger-Adamas. Adamas's descent from (probably) the Barbelo was repeatedly praised, as was his eternal nature. The stele ends with, "Thou art perfect! Thou art perfect! Thou art perfect!"—one of many three-fold repetitions in the prayer. These repetitions were inspired by and reflected the three-personed nature of the Barbelo: Father, Mother, and Son.

Over and over again, Adamas was exalted as the father of "another race," implying the immortal race of the seed of Seth, and this is important in part because the prayer was not merely offered by Seth to Adamas. Instead, the entire community of believers, convinced that they were part of this immortal race, joined in the praise. There was a shift in the last few paragraphs of the text from the singular "I bless his power ..." to the plural, "We bless you eternally ...." This, incidentally, is where the bulk of the repetitions occurred ("You have saved, you have saved, you have saved us, O crown-bearer, crown-giver!"). The nature of these repetitions reinforces the idea that this was a script for communal worship.

The Second Stele

Stepping up from Adamas, the second stele focused its attention on the Barbelo, the three-personed first emanation of the Divine Parent. There is a lot of feminine language in this stele, as the Barbelo is repeatedly addressed as "she." For instance, "She who is called 'perfect'" is one of the opening phrases, and another sentence essentially describes the Barbelo as "the she of the he." It's a theme that continues throughout the prayer.

The Barbelo is presented as "the first shadow of the holy Father," and this language repeats over and over again. That the Barbelo derives directly from the Divine Parent makes he/her/it the object of tremendous affirmation and praise. The Barbelo's nature is rooted in its relationship with that first being.

What's important to the gnostic believer is that the Barbelo is the Divine Parent made visible. Therefore, it allows access to the unknowable Divine center: "For we are each a shadow of you as you are a shadow of that first pre-existent one." That the Barbelo gives believers access to the Unknowable also explains why the Barbelo is time after time described in the text as "empowering" something or someone.

The Third Stele

The last stele contains the prayer to the Divine Parent itself, "the Unconceived." If the gnostic character of The Three Steles was ever in doubt, the sentence "Knowledge of you, it is salvation of us all," should put them to rest.

Here, the language of command becomes important. "Present a command to us to see you, so that we may be saved," reads one passage. Another says, "For you have commanded us, as the elect one, to glorify you, to the extent that we are able." Ultimately, redemption seems to rest in the actions, the commands, of the Divine. The reception of those commands brings life, so the Sethites prayed to be commanded.

The final part of the text seems to indicate that these prayers were part of some kind of ascension ritual. Each of the three sections of worship—to Ger-Adamas, to the Barbelo, and finally to the Divine Parent—are like steps on a staircase leading up to complete union with the Divine. By praying through each of these prayers step-by-step, each individual was opened to the possibility of a transcendent experience. The three-step nature of the prayers already points to that, but the text explicitly mentions ascension into silence, which is the eternal realm. Then the group steps down the way it came—from the third "step" to the second and, finally, back to the first. "The way of ascent is the way of descent," it instructs. Whether the text of The Three Steles contains the entire ritual or if there were additional steps or techniques used is unknown. It does offer us, however, a rare and intriguing glimpse into the life of a gnostic worship community.

Zostrianos (Codex VIII,1)

Named for a near relative or associate of the Persian sage Zoroaster, the document entitled Zostrianos is one of the longest texts in the entire Nag Hammadi library. Unfortunately, Codex VIII suffered damage both prior to and after its discovery. Nearly every page is deficient in some way, and in some cases we are left with only small pieces of text. Obviously that makes reading and understanding Zostrianos very difficult. Since Plotinus was aware of the text in the middle of the third century, we can probably date its composition to around that time or a bit earlier.

From the Source

Orthodox Christians weren't the only opponents of the gnostics. The philosophers of Neoplatonism also opposed the gnostics on a variety of issues. Plotinus, the founder of Neoplatonism, was familiar with the texts Zostrianos and Allogenes, as seen in this passage from a biography written by one of his students:

Many Christians of this period—amongst them sectaries who had abandoned the old philosophy, men of the schools of Adelphius and Aquilinus—had possessed themselves of works by Alexander of Libya, by Philocomus, by Demostratus, and by Lydus, and exhibited also Revelations bearing the names of Zoroaster, Zostrianus, Nicotheus, Allogenes, Mesus, and others of that order. Thus they fooled many, themselves fooled first; Plato, according to them, had failed to penetrate into the depth of Intellectual Being.

Plotinus frequently attacked their position at the Conferences and finally wrote the treatise which I have headed *Against the Gnostics*: He left to us of the circle the task of examining what he himself passed over. Amelius proceeded as far as a fortieth treatise in refutation of the book of Zostrianus: I myself have shown on many counts that the Zoroastrian volume is spurious and modern, concocted by the sectaries in order to pretend that the doctrines they had embraced were those of the ancient sage.

—Porphyry, *Life of Plotinus* (16)

Since the text is autobiographical, Zostrianos is defining himself, and portrayed himself basically as a spiritual seeker. He asked a series of questions about the nature of existence and the Divine, many of which echoed questions asked by the Neoplatonic school. Deeply depressed at finding no resolution to his dilemma in any of the spiritual options around him, he fled to the desert with the intention of killing himself. As he was preparing to do himself in, an angel appeared and invited him to take a journey to the Divine realms. Zostrianos gladly accepted, departed from his body and ascended past the realms of the Demiurge and his rulers to the various aeons of the Pleroma.

What followed was a series of ascensions from one aeon to another. Between the self-existing Invisible Spirit at one end of the spectrum and the material world at the other end lay the realms of the Barbelo. These realms occurred in three sections, or aeons, each with significant names. The first section wore the label: "Self-made," or "Self-begotten"—"Autogenes" in Greek. The second section proclaimed itself: "Protophanes"—"First-appearing." The last, and highest, section was not surprisingly called: "Kalyptos"—"Hidden." Each of these three basic sections further subdivided into angels, powers, and "glories."

Throughout his ascension, Zostrianos had to be baptized in order to take on the characteristics of those beings that dwelled in the next level. This process ended up amounting to dozens of baptisms over the course of the text. These were obviously not physical baptisms, and some have suggested that Zostrianos belonged to those gnostics who eventually abandoned all physical sacraments and rituals in favor of mystical ones. We've already seen a couple of texts that suggest that gaining gnosis is baptism.

Zostrianos's vision sounds almost like a travelogue. His main concern seemed to be collecting names and plotting out how each being was related to the others. At each point he pestered the beings of that aeon with philosophical questions about the nature of existence and how the eternal, self-sufficient Invisible Spirit ever came to generate any other being outside itself. In other words, why did the Spirit suddenly one day decide to begin emanating aeons? Such questions smack of Neoplatonism. Since Plotinus and his students were aware of, and critical of, Zostrianos and Allogenes (the next text we'll look at), you have to wonder who was influencing who?

At the end of his whirlwind tour of the heavens, Zostrianos returned to his body in the material world (after stopping to inscribe three tablets with the gnosis he had gained—sound familiar?). He immediately commenced preaching his newfound knowledge, and he gained a large following. The text ended with a short sermon, which included the following passage: "Do not baptize yourselves with death nor entrust yourselves to those who are inferior to you instead of to those who are better. Flee from the madness and the bondage of femaleness and choose for yourselves the salvation of maleness. You have not come to suffer; rather, you have come to escape your bondage." It's easy to see how gnostic Christians could have been attracted to this text.

Allogenes (Codex XI,3)

If you had been shopping for a copy of Allogenes in your favorite third-century codex store, you would probably have had to check out the "Self-Help" section. The title means "stranger" or "of another race," which certainly fits in with the Sethite focus on the immortal race. The title "Allogenes" is occasionally used in Sethite texts to refer to Seth himself, so we might be justified in seeing the "stranger" in this book as Seth in disguise. In the text, Allogenes was a revealer, sharing his insights and revelations with his disciple Mennos. The text invites the reader into the place of Messos, encouraging readers to hear from the teacher and adopt his truths. Allogenes, like Zostrianos, must have been written prior to Plotinus's criticism of the gnostics in the middle of the third century.

> **Words to the Wise**
>
> In the Sethian texts there are different figures of the Revealer-Saviour called upon to perform an identical function: to illuminate that part of the spiritual substance fallen into the world of darkness.
>
> —Giovanni Filoramo, *A History of Gnosticism* (115)

The first part of Allogenes is an account of a revelation received from an angelic being named Iouel. The revelation consisted of an introduction to the structure of the Pleroma that we are all familiar with by now from the Secret Book of John (see Chapter 13) and other versions of the gnostic myth.

> **Did You Know?**
>
> Like most Sethite texts, Allogenes tends to gloss over Sophia's fall. Sethites seemed more interested in the solution than they were in what caused the problem in the first place.

Iouel denied a vision of the unknowable Divine Parent to Allogenes, however. Iouel basically told him that he was not ready for it yet. Wait 100 years, Iouel told him, and you'll receive a revelation about these highest truths. So Allogenes waited and prepared himself.

That's where the text takes an odd turn and becomes more than just another romp through the heavenly realms. In the wake of his revelation, which included an out-of-body experience just like Zostrianos, Allogenes turned "inward toward knowledge," and found within himself the Barbelo. What so often is an ascent became, in Allogenes, a psychological descent into his self.

What Allogenes saw inside himself was a vision of the unknowable Divine. He immediately attempted to comprehend what he had seen, but was warned not to try too hard to do that. At the heart of this text is a recommendation toward spiritual passivity. The seeker is advised to receive revelation without too much active reflection or that new spiritual understanding might be lost. There is a tension in the Sethite texts like Zostrianos and Allogenes between the gnostic attempt to gain gnosis through intimate, instantaneous experience of the Divine, and the philosophical attempt to reason through to an understanding of the Divine. Allogenes embodies both, first by advising simple reception of the gift of revelation, and then by engaging in a discussion of the nature of the Divine that would be at home in any book on Plato.

Allogenes was instructed to write down what he had learned, and to hide the book on top of a mountain to be guarded by an angel (again, does this sound familiar?). He had been authorized, however, to share these things with you, "O Messos my child." Don't you feel special?

Marsanes (Codex X,1)

Codex X has suffered a great deal of damage so it's hard to be certain how long it was, but it's reasonable to conclude that Marsanes was the only document in it. Even the title is difficult to tease out. With so much of the text gone, often all we get are isolated phrases and paragraphs. The structure of the text is largely gone. No date can be assigned to Marsanes.

There are basically three chunks of the text that are still intact. The first section describes details of an ascent experience of some kind. The aeons are described as 13 "seals" that one moves through in a progress from the "worldly" and "material" all the way to the "Silent One who was not known."

The second major section is a sometimes-fascinating, sometimes-mind-numbing discussion of the nature of the sounds of letters and their relationship to the shape of the soul and the mysteries of the Divine realm (the Zodiac is mentioned several times). These vocal sounds are tied up with the naming of angels and divine beings. It's too bad that the text is so damaged, because this section of Marsanes may hold the key to understanding the use of vowel sounds in chant and prayer texts like the ones we saw in the Gospel of the Egyptians. Who would have thought that instruction in prayer would include a vocal lesson?

The third, and final, section of the text is more fragmented. It seems to focus on the presence of revelatory knowledge in public worship settings. Baptism is mentioned, though the details are impossible to nail down. The text mentions the angel Gamaliel, which suggests that this is a Sethite text. Like many of the Sethite texts, there doesn't appear to be anything distinctly Christian about Marsanes.

The Least You Need to Know

 ◆ Jewish speculation most likely lies at the historical roots of the Sethite literature.

 ◆ Sethite communal worship was part of the process of ascension to the Divine realms.

 ◆ Zostrianos echoes profound questions about the universe—questions which Neoplatonists were asking at the same time.

 ◆ Allogenes tells us that gnosis could be turned inward to find the Pleroma within the self.

 ◆ Marsanes might have held the key to understanding chants and vowels sounds, but it is too damaged to be of much value.

Chapter 16

The Soul's Journey

In This Chapter

- Were the gnostics libertines or ascetics?
- A "sequel" to the Gospel of Thomas takes the Jesus' sayings a step farther
- A collection of ancient proverbs turns up in the Nag Hammadi library
- A teacher tries to introduce his student to a gnostic view of the resurrection

A fundamental part of religious teaching of any kind involves the question of morals and ethics. What we believe about God, the world, and one another shapes the way that we live and behave. Gnostics were no different. Their teachings had immense ethical implications. None of the texts in this chapter are, strictly speaking, gnostic in their teaching. However, the fact that they were included in the Nag Hammadi library makes it very likely that they were in harmony with gnostic beliefs.

Ethical Dilemmas

Their enemies often accused the gnostics of being libertines, of sexual perversions. The evidence for this charge was often a collection of rumor and innuendo backed up by the standard accusations trotted out by any group in late antiquity that was trying to discredit another. It's also possible that the orthodox writers occasionally confused certain metaphorical language for literal practices. The Valentinian "bridal chamber" (see Chapter 10) was one such term certain to raise eyebrows and start rumors. Still, some of the stories the orthodox writers told were things that they themselves had seen and heard. Irenaeus, for instance, made his accusations against the Valentinian teacher Mark after hearing stories from women in his own church who had been involved with the gnostic teacher (see Chapter 14). Epiphanius reported on many of his own encounters with gnostic groups that he met during his travels, and he revealed practices in some gnostic communities that are simply too graphic to mention here. These kinds of eyewitness accounts can't be entirely dismissed.

Words to the Wise

The rejection of the creation and the simultaneous appeal to the possession of celestial knowledge led to a rejection of the conventional conceptions of morality. Two contrary and extreme conclusions could be drawn: the libertine or amoralistic and the ascetic. Both expressed the same basic attitude: a protest against the pretensions of the world and its legislative ruler; a revolution on a moralistic plane. Which of the two fundamental views is the older and more appropriate remains up to the present an unsolved problem.

—Kurt Rudolph, *Gnosis: The Nature & History of Gnosticism*

If orthodox writers were quick to believe the worst about the gnostics, it was largely because they were convinced that the very nature of gnostic teaching lent itself to moral laxity. For Irenaeus and others, the logical question was this: if you tell people that the world doesn't matter, that you are either saved or damned based on your nature (are you spiritual? psychic? fleshly?) rather than on your beliefs or behaviors, then how can you expect them not to act accordingly? If a person is taught that sin is an illusion, they reasoned, what kind of behavior will result?

If the Nag Hammadi texts represent gnostic groups across the Mediterranean world, however, ascetic conduct, rather than immoral behavior, seems closer to the standard gnostic practice. Little in the way of libertinism can be found in works like the Gospel of Thomas or The Nature of the Rulers (Chapters 6 and 13, respectively). Quite the contrary, both are filled with stories and teachings that assume that the gnostic tended to flee from worldly things; sex and marriage, certain kinds of foods, and the rampant acquisition of wealth all come under fire at some point. Rather than feeding the flesh, the gnostics who wrote and read and collected the Nag Hammadi texts sought to deny it. This interest in living an ascetic life shows up in the very contents of the Nag Hammadi collection itself, which includes several documents that are highly ascetic but not identifiably gnostic. We'll see a few of those in this chapter. Since orthodox Christians were equally concerned with ascetic practices, some historians have suggested that this mutual concern for holiness formed a bridge point between gnostic groups and the larger Christian community.

Although they seem to have been vigilant in terms of dealing with personal desires and behaviors, the gnostic approach to service and love of neighbor is a little more ambiguous. The Gospel of Truth (Chapter 9) has a short paragraph on how one ought to behave in light of Valentinian teaching, which includes an exhortation to caring for the sick and feeding the hungry. Even here, however, the focus is on the individual gnostic, and how caring for others is a means of "strengthening", but it is unclear whether that means strengthening others or one's self. Orthodox Christians, with their greater emphasis on community life and centralized authority structures, seem to have had an edge in teaching their people to extend charity and hospitality.

In terms of social and political ethics, gnostic thought seems almost paradoxical. On the one hand, the denigration of worldly powers would seem to have extended to political authorities as well. By its very nature, gnosticism critiques all existing political and economic structures as just another expression of the "mistaken" physical world. The radically individualistic nature of the gnostics' spirituality would, you might reasonably expect, make them into revolutionaries. That doesn't appear to have been the case, however. Instead, they avoided conflict with the governing powers. Gnostics, for example, were nowhere nearly as eager to embrace martyrdom as orthodox Christians were. Their ability to avoid this blatant act of civil disobedience gives us a glimpse of the nature of gnostic rebellion against the powers of the world. What ultimately mattered, according to the gnostics, was not the judgment and overthrow of Roman tyranny but the return of the self to the Pleroma. Gnostic rebellion against authority principally amounted to a withdrawal from the obligations of society in order that the individual might concentrate on his or her reunification with the Divine. Why get involved in politics if all of this is an illusion anyway?

Words to the Wise

Gnosis, at least according to the present state of our knowledge, took no interest of any kind in a reform of earthly conditions but only in their complete and final destruction. It possessed no other "revolutionary" programme for altering conditions, as they appeared to it, than the elimination of earthly structures in general and the restoration of the ideal world of the spirit that existed in the beginning.

—Kurt Rudolph, *Gnosis: The Nature & History of Gnosticism*

One caution is that despite the monumental nature of the Nag Hammadi collection, it really only scratches the surface. We know, for instance, that some portions even of this collection of texts were destroyed after they were discovered. Also, if the library did indeed come from the nearby Pachomian monastery, we would expect that it would be skewed toward having a more ascetic set of texts. It would be fascinating to find a gnostic library kept by a group living, say, in downtown Rome. You might expect to find more libertine teachings, if they existed, in that kind of setting. Just because the majority of the Nag Hammadi texts suggest an ascetic lifestyle doesn't prove that gnostics elsewhere were so ascetically inclined.

The Book of Thomas the Contender (Codex II,7)

When we looked at the Gospel of Thomas in Chapter 6, we took a good look at the legends surrounding Thomas's missionary endeavors in the East. Several important texts came out of that developing tradition, beginning with the Gospel of Thomas and culminating with The Acts of Thomas. Sandwiched in between those two is The Book of Thomas the Contender. The Book of Thomas the Contender is a mid-point in the evolution, from collection of Jesus' sayings like the Gospel of Thomas to a romantic epic like The Acts of Thomas, with its focus on the story as a means of relating the teachings of Thomas. Consequently, it's safe to date at least part of the final version of the book to the end of the second century or perhaps the very beginning of the third.

The Book of Thomas the Contender is a dialogue. We've seen examples of this before (the Secret Book of James, for example, in Chapter 11, and the Dialogue of the Savior, in Chapter 17). The book is an attempt to reconfigure a collection of sayings by Jesus into a question-and-answer format where the questioner, in this case Thomas, elicited revelation from the master, in this case Jesus. These dialogues are usually said to have taken place during that brief period of time between his resurrection and final ascension, when he instructed his disciples more openly than he had in life, and that seems to be the case in the Book of Thomas the Contender.

The opening line of the book calls it the "secret sayings that the Savior spoke to Judas Thomas, which I, even I Matthew wrote down." The mention of Matthew may be a reference to the widespread tradition in the early church that the Apostle Matthew early on recorded many of Jesus' sayings. Judas Thomas we know, of course, from the Gospel of Thomas. Because Jesus referred several times to Thomas as "my twin and true companion," "my brother Thomas," and "my brother," we can confidently trace the origin of this book to Syria, as this identification of Thomas as the twin brother of Jesus was uniquely part of the Eastern Syrian tradition.

The term "contender" that appears in the title of this work can also mean "wrestler" or "struggler," someone who fights against something. In this case, that something is the passions, "the fires," of the body. As The Book of Thomas describes it, the body is on fire, burning with the flames of Hell, and set to disintegrate upon death. The body is animalistic, born of the earth and integrally tied to it. The soul that gives in to the body and its desires will share in its fate. Only by denying the impulses and passions of the body can a person rise above the bestial nature of human life and enter in the rest that God gives after death.

> **Did You Know?**
>
> In late antiquity, it was commonly believed that eating red meat raised the temperature of the body and stimulated sexual desires. Ascetics of all stripes routinely cut meat out of their diet as a means of disciplining their bodies and averting their passions.

Jesus' driving point in The Book of Thomas the Contender seemed to be that each of us must choose between being a human or being an animal. Animals are described as being subject to constant change. They are temporary, devouring one another to survive and having sex to renew their species. People who live like that, we are told, will perish just like animals do. On the other hand, disconnecting from the material world through an ascetic lifestyle that includes celibacy and vegetarianism is the pathway toward redemption. Jesus rejected sex, in particular: "Woe to you who love intimacy with women and polluted intercourse with them," he pronounced. The word "Fire" appears in the text repeatedly. The fires of the passions, we are told, will eventually consume the soul just as they do the body.

The book contrasts the fool, who is ignorant of himself, to the wise man, who lives intentionally. Self-knowledge is the key to knowing God, for "he who has known himself has at the same time already achieved knowledge about the depth of the All." Jesus gave Thomas three pursuits that ought to characterize his spiritual quest for self-knowledge: "learn who you are, in what way you exist, and how you will come to be." Like the Gospel of Thomas, The Book of Thomas evinces no interest whatsoever in the cross or the resurrection of Jesus. Instead, Jesus is portrayed as the Revealer, the one who came to bring light and illuminate our darkness. The important point is, that light is only here to gather up the chosen ones, or the "elect." Once they have all "abandoned bestiality," the light will return to the one who sent it.

The Book of Thomas is highly ascetic, but is it gnostic? A close reading of the text fails to find the basic elements of the gnostic myth, although a great deal fits nicely within the gnostic view. The Book of Thomas seems to avoid speculating about why things are the way that they are. It tells us that the body is an evil from which the soul needs to escape, and knowledge of this peril is necessary for salvation, but there is no mention of where the body comes from or why it is evil. Instead, the book focuses on how a person aware of these things should live. In that sense, it is a very practical book that falls short of being explicitly gnostic.

Sentences of Sextus (Codex XII,1)

The Sentences of Sextus is one of the Nag Hammadi texts that was already known to scholars. Copies of it exist in several different languages. The Sentences are a collection of Greek proverbs and wise sayings assembled by a Christian editor sometime around the end of the second century. They were widely circulated.

The actual pages we have from Nag Hammadi are in rotten condition. Only a quarter of the original manuscript survived, and even that portion is pretty beaten up. The standard version of the Sentences has 451 sayings. In the Nag Hammadi copy fewer than 120 are still readable, and because of the damage to the manuscript it's impossible to know how closely the missing portions match the other existing copies. However, what we can read does match well with the versions that were already known.

The Sentences are not gnostic, but they are evidence that ethical strictures and ordered living were not alien to the gnostics. Evidently the owners of the Nag Hammadi library were not libertines. The maxims are loosely grouped around various catchwords. For example, the first set of maxims in our version revolve around speech—when to speak, what to say, and the like.

From the Source

Selected proverbs from the Sentences of Sextus:

He who is victorious through deceit is defeated by the truth.

After God, no one is as free as the wise man.

The fear of death grieves man because of the ignorance of the soul.

It is not possible for you to know God when you do not worship him.

Know who God is, and know who is the one who thinks in you; a good man is the good work of God.

The Teaching of Silvanus (Codex VII,4)

The name Silvanus is known from the New Testament, where he served as a secretary and partner to the Apostle Paul during many of Paul's missionary journeys. Whether or not the author intended to attribute his work to the biblical Silvanus is unknown. The name was not uncommon in the early church. The text itself leads scholars to conclude that it was written late in the second century or early in the third, probably in Alexandria.

Silvanus is difficult to outline. The first part of the text dished up all sorts of spiritual metaphors designed to encourage the reader to take a strong and uncompromising stand in pursuit of salvation. There was nothing exclusively Christian about the thinking presented here. It resembled a lot of Greek wisdom literature. The second portion of the text focused on salvation rather than wisdom. It placed emphasis on Christ as the revealer who illuminated for us the means of redemption in his own life.

Castles and Diplomas

The Teaching of Silvanus begins by telling the reader that the soul is like a city that needs to be well guarded. All sorts of militant verbs were tossed around: abolish, acquire, intensify, guard your camp, and arm yourself. The reader is told to throw the robbers out and set torches around the gates. Other commands instruct the reader not to show his or her back to the enemy; and be the hunter, not the hunted. If you do these things, the author says, you will have "a quiet life." If not, you will be like the city that has been captured, ransacked, and abandoned to wild animals. The city "which is your soul will perish." All of these images are meant as metaphors. The torches at the gate are "words" and the guards are "counsels." The animals are "thoughts which are not good." The mind should be the "guiding principle" in this whole defense. The mind is the "guide," and "reason is the teacher" who will bring you "out of destruction and dangers."

Shifting from a military metaphor to an educational one, the author encouraged his readers to "put on the holy teaching like a robe." Don't "acquire ignorance" but "accept with joy" education and teaching. That way you won't "lead your people astray." "Evil death" is nothing but "ignorance," and "evil darkness" is "forgetfulness."

The Wise Ascetic

The author taught that "you have come into being from three races," which he identified as the material, the psychic, and the spiritual. These three elements are present in each person. Mixing these elements, the reader is told, is what leads to "inferiority." Instead, we are instructed to "live according to the mind," which is the spiritual element. To live according to the psychic element is to "become male-female," to "cut off the male part" and become "the female part alone." Even worse, living by the material element leads to animalistic life, devoid of the rationality that is the hallmark of the spiritual man or woman.

Part of living a wise life is to dwell in a solitude that, if not literal, is at least all-encompassing. "Do not trust anyone as a friend," the author advised. "If you wish to pass your life in quiet, do not keep company with anyone." The truly wise person needs only God and Christ, without whom God cannot be known. This emphasis on solitude for the sake of personal growth would seem to work well within the parameters of gnostic spirituality as described in the opening section of this chapter.

> **Did You Know?**
>
> Solitude was prized by others besides the gnostics. The so-called Desert Saints—Christian women and men who lived in the Egyptian desert seeking union with God—were fond of solitude as a spiritual discipline. As one of them said, "Unless a man shall say in his heart, 'I alone and God are in this world,' he shall not find quiet."

The author wrapped up the work with a lengthy exhortation to ethical living. The reader is advised to "Let Christ alone enter your world," since he becomes the power that will cleanse the soul. If the reader is a temple, then Christ will "cast out all the merchants" that pollute the body and mind. "Fight the great fight as long as the fight lasts," the author encouraged his readers.

There is some question as to whether or not The Teaching of Silvanus qualifies as a gnostic text. Certainly there are elements that seem to fit. Talk of the "deficiency," for instance, and Christ as an "emanation" of the Father might seem to fall into the orbit of gnostic teaching. On the other hand, Christ is described as the maker of everything, and he created as the "hand of the Father." This affinity for creation as the act of the Father is squarely at odds with the gnostic separation of the Father and the Creator. This connection is made even plainer by the statement, "Let no one ever say that God is ignorant. For it is not right to place the Creator (Demiurge) of every creature in ignorance." Clearly the author associated God with the Creator, and then insisted that the Creator could not be ignorant, in clear contrast to every gnostic myth. We are safe, then, in concluding that the Teaching of Silvanus is not essentially gnostic, but instead falls into the category of ascetic literature.

Treatise on the Resurrection (Codex 1,4)

A very well-preserved document, the Treatise on the Resurrection appears as a short letter written from an unnamed teacher to his student Rheginos to answer some questions about the nature of resurrection. The teachings presented in the letter are Valentinian in origin, which suggests a date sometime late in the second century. There were some suggestions early on that Valentinus himself may have written the Treatise. Most scholars find that unconvincing now.

A teaching on the nature of resurrection might seem odd in a chapter on the ethical nature of the gnostic life. But it's important to keep in mind that gnostic ethics are rooted in a particular belief about the final destiny of all human beings, and of gnostics in particular. Looking at a person's behavior alone doesn't tell you enough to know what he or she considers important. One person may live an ascetic life of regular fasting and voluntary poverty out of a commitment to social justice, believing that no one has the right to more of the world's resources than anyone else. Another person may live the same kind of life out of the conviction that unrestrained desires get in the way the spiritual life and distract a person from reaching heaven. The same manner of life, but two distinct goals. Knowing what the gnostics valued, in ultimate terms, illuminates their ethical teaching.

The Dead Shall Arise ...

Let's be clear, our author told his student, the resurrection is no illusion. "The Savior swallowed up death," he declared. Like beams from the sun, if we live our lives "wearing him," we will be drawn to heaven unimpeded at "our setting, that is to say our death in this life." This, he claimed, is "the spiritual resurrection," which is better than the "fleshly," or bodily resurrection, and "swallows up the psychic." Remember, the Valentinians objected to a purely physical resurrection, but believed that "psychic" Christians could continue to dwell eternally with the Demiurge. They themselves, of course, looked for a "spiritual" resurrection wherein they would be reunited with the Pleroma. The teacher is encouraging his student not to settle for anything but the best.

The author goes on to say that philosophers can't comprehend the resurrection. It is beyond their methods to understand. That's because there is no scientific or rational proof for eternal life. "For it is the domain of faith … the dead shall arise!" No amount of persuasion will convince someone of that truth. We who believe have been "elected to salvation" and "predestined from the beginning not to fall into the foolishness of those who are without knowledge."

... So Get Busy Living

So what is resurrection, the author asked rhetorically? It is, he told his student Rheginos, "the disclosure of those who have risen." The author reminded Rheginos about Elijah and Moses, who stood with Jesus on the Mount of Transfiguration, to demonstrate that life and identity continue after death. Moses is still Moses, the author argued, and will not cease to be Moses. His particular identity has not been lost to him, and the same for Elijah and even for Rheginos. Better to "say that the world is an illusion" than to deny a resurrection that maintains this sense of personal identity. Resurrection is "transformation" and "transition." It is the imperishable coming on the perishable, and light swallowing up darkness. It is the Pleroma filling "the deficiency."

Since this is all true, the teacher encouraged, run away from all the divisions and from bondage to the world "and already you have the resurrection." If you know that you have already died and been raised, how ought you to live? Should you spend your life fearing death or trying to deny that physical death will come, he asked? No, rather it is "fitting for each one to practice in a number of ways" preparing ourselves for our eventual death. This "exercise"—which must have included disciplines, prayers, meditations, and the like—have the double benefit of keeping Rheginos steadfast in his beliefs and of making the ultimate transition that much easier.

Finally, the teacher signed off, mentioning that what he knew he "received from the generosity of my Lord, Jesus Christ." He told Rheginos that he was not the only student, but had "brothers" who were "looking into this which I have written to you." The teacher told Rheginos that he was confident that what he had written would strengthen them, but he offered to clear up any misunderstandings with regard to his teaching.

The Least You Need to Know

- ◆ Gnostics focused their ethics largely on living a life disconnected from bondage to this material world.

- ◆ Both gnostic and mainstream Christians shared an interest in ascetic living, though not exclusively.

- ◆ The Nag Hammadi library contains several texts that are not so much gnostic as an encouragement of an ascetic lifestyle.

- ◆ The ultimate purpose for gnostic ethics was the desire to enter into the resurrection, meaning the eternal life of the spirit.

17

Prayers, Liturgies, and Initiations

In This Chapter

- ◆ Ritual and sacrament in gnostic worship
- ◆ A gnostic prayer attributed to Paul
- ◆ A "book of quotations" used to introduce gnostic Christians to baptism
- ◆ How one group of Valentinians celebrated the sacraments
- ◆ The many sources gnostics drew on for worship

As little as we know about how the gnostics thought, we know even less about how they lived, organized their communities, and worshipped. Some information comes from the orthodox Christian writers, and we get hints from the Nag Hammadi documents. In this chapter, we look at a group of works that tell us a bit about how gnostic Christians might have prayed, taught, and celebrated faith together.

Worship, Gnostic Style

No matter how we go about it, human beings seem to have an innate need to translate our religious convictions and beliefs into physical and social actions. These ritual functions mark out the boundaries that both limit and guide our interaction with the Divine. Sometimes these rituals are integrated seamlessly into our daily lives, like saying a prayer before a meal. Other rituals are only for special moments, such as weddings and funerals. In either case, rituals are our way of bringing the sacred into our lives in a tangible fashion. Often, those religious acts reveal as much (or more) about our beliefs as do our words.

The Christian gnostics, like the larger Christian community, celebrated a series of ritual acts that were intended to make accessible the spiritual realities that those acts symbolized. It's almost impossible to speak definitively about rituals and rites used by all gnostics, since each sect or group had its own secret wisdom and its own manner of enacting spiritual realities through its *liturgy*. We've already discussed the Valentinian approach to baptism in Chapters 8 and 9, and we'll see another text from that group in this chapter. We also took a good look at the "five seals" mentioned in the Gospel of the Egyptians back in Chapter 10.

Word Knowledge

Liturgy literally means "the work of the people." In religious terms, it refers to the prescribed rituals and forms of public worship.

Ritual, Smitual, I Wanna Be Spiritual

Ritual and belief go hand in glove. Separating them can be downright impossible, and doing so puts us at a disadvantage in trying to understand what the gnostics were all about. At the same time, we can't always be certain that a ritual act mentioned in a text was actually performed. Some gnostic documents, for instance, hint that gnostic baptism rituals may not have been celebrated in some groups. Although the language and imagery of baptism was retained, the act itself was more than likely done away with.

Some rituals seem to have gone by more than one name. For example, baptism and the bridal chamber are sometimes equated with one another. And sometimes we simply don't know what a certain rite or ritual consisted of (remember the rite of "redemption" from the Gospel of Philip, for example, in Chapter 8). Although we're on pretty safe ground by assuming that gnostics performed rituals, we have to be cautious about how much we read into the texts.

Running from Office

How gnostic groups conducted themselves drew at least as much fire from orthodox Christians as gnostic teachings did. One of the fundamental differences between gnostic and orthodox groups seems to have been the very loose level of discipline in gnostic organization. Since salvation, in gnostic terms, was a function of personal intimacy with the Divine, no one believer could really have authority over another.

From the Source

In a very famous passage, Tertullian attacked this lack of discipline in the gnostic groups:

"All are puffed up, all offer you knowledge. Their catechumens are perfect before they are full-taught. The very women of these heretics, how wanton they are! For they are bold enough to teach, to dispute, to enact exorcisms, to undertake cures—it may be even to baptize. Their ordinations, are carelessly administered, capricious, changeable. At one time they put *novices* in office; at another time, men who are bound to some secular employment; at another, persons who have apostatized from us, to bind them by vainglory, since they cannot by the truth. Nowhere is promotion easier than in the camp of rebels, where the mere fact of being there is a foremost service. And so it comes to pass that to-day one man is their bishop, to-morrow another; to-day he is a deacon who to-morrow is a reader; to-day he is a presbyter who tomorrow is a layman. For even on laymen do they impose the functions of priesthood."

—Tertullian, The Prescription against Heresies (41)

It's important not to overstate the case, since we know that certain gnostic groups did have a hierarchical structure of some kind, but by and large, they don't seem to have taken seriously the clergy/laity distinction that held sway in orthodox churches. In such an environment, anyone could administer baptism, teach, or preside over the eucharist. At the same time, when institutional authority is lacking, communities are usually held together by charismatic leadership. It comes as no surprise to find exactly that taking place among the gnostics.

The Rite Is Wrong

Always keep in mind the gnostic rejection of the material world. It was to them without value, a mistake in need of correction. Given that mindset, it's difficult to understand why the gnostics used physical rituals like baptism, the eucharist, and chrismation (we mentioned all of these in Chapter 10). Since, according to gnostic teachings, nothing good can come from the material world, these rituals could not have been vehicles for God's grace the way that they were regarded among orthodox churches. At best, they might be regarded as meaningless. At worst, they could be distractions from a deeper spirituality.

From the evidence that we have, it looks like many gnostics began to think the same way. By the time that Irenaeus wrote *Against Heresies* around A.D. 185, there were already groups of gnostics who had repudiated the use of water in baptism and the eating of the eucharist. Later orthodox Christian writers made note of similar groups in Egypt.

From the Source

Others, however, reject all these practices, and maintain that the mystery of the unspeakable and invisible power ought not to be performed by visible and corruptible creatures … These hold that the knowledge of the unspeakable Greatness is itself perfect redemption … The redemption must therefore be of a spiritual nature; for they affirm that the inner and spiritual man is redeemed by means of knowledge, and that they, having acquired the knowledge of all things, stand thenceforth in need of nothing else. This, then, is the true redemption.

Irenaeus, *Against Heresies* (1.21.4)

Often, these groups retained the language of rituals and sacraments, but used them symbolically rather than literally. We've already seen, for example, that The Revelation of Adam referred to gnosis as baptism. Zostrianos, in his ascent into the heavenlies, endured scores of baptisms that prepared him for each new level. In this instance, the benefits of baptism could be gained without the physical act. And there is this revealing line from The Exegesis of the Soul: "And so the cleansing of the soul is to regain the newness of her former nature and to turn herself back again. That is her baptism."

It needs to be pointed out here that some scholars see the gnostic use of Christian rituals as an indication that gnostic Christianity emerged out of orthodox Christianity, not prior to it or parallel to it. Although attempts have been made to show that the nonritualistic form of gnostic Christianity came first, that seems highly unlikely. It seems to makes more sense to imagine gnostics emerging from the larger Christian community, and eventually abandoning the rituals and sacraments, than it does to think of large groups of gnostics adopting these forms of worship where they previously had not used them.

The Prayer of the Apostle Paul (Codex I,1)

On the front flyleaf of Codex I, written down almost as an afterthought, is a very short prayer attributed to the Apostle Paul. Despite its brief length, it was important enough to the editor of Codex I to squeeze it in after that volume was already full. The prayer can't be dated accurately, though it would fit pretty comfortably in a Valentinian worship service. Since the other documents in the codex are Valentinian in nature (with the exception of the Secret Book of James), it seems safe to make the assumption that the prayer is Valentinian. That would mean that it could be no earlier than the middle of the second century.

The document has been damaged, and the first couple of lines of the poem are missing. The rest of the prayer bears some resemblance to similar prayers in the Corpus Hermeticum, and uses some of the language of invocation often found in magical texts. At the same time, the author was also familiar with the language of the Psalms, and used a direct quotation from the Apostle Paul, though with a couple of important changes.

From the Source

Compare this passage from the first letter of the Apostle Paul to the church at Corinth …

However, as it is written:
No eye has seen,
no ear has heard,
no mind has conceived
what God has prepared for those who love him
I Corinthians 2:9

… with the same passage from the Prayer of the Apostle Paul:

Grant what no angel eye has seen and no archon ear has heard and what has not entered into the human heart which came to be angelic and modeled after the image of the psychic God when it was formed in the beginning …"

The changes—that angels and archons have not seen these things and that unenlightened human hearts can't grasp what the author seeks from God—obviously conveys a deep gnostic sensitivity.

The prayer uses several names for Jesus, including some common Christian titles like "Redeemer," "the Lord of lords," "King of the ages," and "Son of Man." Other titles are used, however, that are more gnostic in their direction, such as calling Jesus "the Spirit" and "the *Paraclete* of truth." He is also called the "Firstborn of the Pleroma of grace" and the "Firstbegotten."

The author calls on God as "my mind," "my treasure house," "my fullness," and "my repose," all words that carried special meaning for Christian gnostics. The prayer invokes the aid of God and asks for several things, including "authority" and healing for the body. It also calls on God to redeem "my eternal light soul and my spirit." The gnostic character of the prayer becomes fully evident when it talks about the human heart as modeled "after the image of the psychic God," a reference to the Demiurge in Valentinian thought.

The Dialogue of the Savior (Codex III,5)

The Dialogue of the Savior is one of the more fragmented texts found in the Nag Hammadi library. It has suffered quite a bit of damage, and that sometimes makes it difficult to follow. The title was apparently added sometime after the work was written. Some scholars date the Dialogue to the early second century due to the large amount of "sayings" material. It's similar to The Secret Book of James in that way, as well as by the fact that the Dialogue doesn't seem to have been quoted in any other early Christian literature. Scholars argue that these kinds of independent sayings traditions flourished at the end of the first century and disappeared soon afterward, as they were incorporated into larger stories like the gospels.

The Dialogue appears to have been cobbled together from several different sources, the largest chunk being the sayings material we were just talking about. That portion takes the shape of a discussion between Jesus, who is never mentioned by name but is only called "Lord" or "Savior," and his disciples Mary, Matthew, and Judas. At one point, "the twelve" also speak. The additional pieces that make up the Dialogue appear to include a creation myth, some wisdom literature, and an apocalyptic revelation. These four elements were then spliced together to create the illusion of a complete text. Whoever compiled this document then added an invitation from the Savior to come and enter into rest.

Prepare for Initiation

The most plausible purpose for The Dialogue was to prepare initiates for baptism. Some scholars have suggested that the Dialogue seems to be organized around the pattern of redemption that we first saw in the Gospel of Thomas (way back in Chapter 6): seeking, finding, marveling, ruling, and resting. The disciples had already passed through the first three of these steps, but now they were stuck. When Matthew asked Jesus how to reach "that place of life" where evil is gone and everything is pure, Jesus told him he will not see it "as long as you are carrying flesh around." They were still carrying around bodies of flesh. How would they attain to the levels of ruling and resting?

That's where baptism comes into the picture. "Already the time has come, brothers," Jesus told them, "for us to abandon our labor and stand at rest." In the act of baptism, the candidate for baptism passes through death and comes to his or her new life. The baptized gnostic no longer needs to wait for death to release her. She could "die" right now, through baptism. The ruling and resting that gnostics longed for, then, was guaranteed to them. Having their future secured by their baptism, these disciples were free to engage in the same work that Jesus had been doing. They remained in their bodies for the time being as revealers of "the revealer."

The Works of Womanhood

Jesus tells the disciples that their task while in the body is to "destroy the works of womanhood," a statement that at least implies a strong asceticism and perhaps even sexual renunciation. It falls in line with other examples from gnostic "sayings" traditions, such as those we've seen from the Gospel of Thomas, which either anticipate or (more likely) are the result of the gnostic worldview. Remember, they saw the physical world and its powers (the "archons") as the creation of a "wild woman" with no participation from a man (see Chapter 13 again).

This apparently negative view of womanhood or the feminine should not be read simplistically as a denigration of women, however. The Dialogue is at pains to point out how insightful Mary was. In response to a salient observation that Mary made, it referred to her as a "woman who had understood completely." Mary's role in the dialogue is important, and of the three disciples, she seemed to be the only one who contributed something significant to the dialogue.

A Valentinian Exposition (Codex XI,2)

No movement, especially not one as organic and complex as the development of Christian gnosticism, is without differences and disagreements. The emphasis on philosophical speculation and personal revelation virtually guaranteed that differences would multiply not only between the various gnostic groups but also within them. Several of the early orthodox Christian writers made mention of divisions and disagreements among members of the Valentinian school, but prior to the Nag Hammadi find there was no way to confirm that accusation. The Valentinian Exposition gave us a first-hand view of an unnamed Valentinian gnostic teacher expressing viewpoints that were, at times, at odds with the teachings of Valentinus and at least some of his followers.

It also provides us with an important example of the link between doctrine and practice. The theological treatise that forms the first part of the work seems intended to serve as a kind of catechism. Prayers for three sacraments or initiation rites—anointing, baptism, and eucharist—follow it. Thus it serves as a partial glimpse into the initiation rites of at least one gnostic group.

Because it offers a Valentinian preparation for the sacraments, the Exposition must date to sometime after Valentinus ended his teaching career around A.D. 160. The author doesn't sound embattled by or embittered with orthodox Christians. In fact, there are hints that Valentinians still worshipped as part of the larger Christian community. That means it was definitely written prior to Constantine's Edict in A.D. 326 (see Chapter 5). So we're probably looking at a date sometime very late in the second century (after Irenaeus' *Against Heresies* is written in A.D. 180) or early in the third.

> **Word Knowledge**
>
> **Monad** derives ultimately from the Greek word monos, which means "one" or "unique." In philosophical or religious terms, the Monad is the first being in the universe, who exists alone.
>
> The **dyad**, in contrast to the monad, is a paired being, usually meaning a masculine-feminine pair.

Family Squabbles

One of the principal disagreements within the Valentinian school was whether the perfect Divine being was a *monad* or a *dyad*. In other words, was the Divine being a single being or a masculine/feminine pair? As we've seen (Chapter 9), Valentinus taught that initially the Divine existed as a pair of beings, a dyad, made up of the masculine Father and his feminine partner Silence, also called the Mother.

Valentinus' student Ptolemy, who was active in Rome at the same time that Irenaeus was writing his *Against Heresies*, also held that viewpoint.

The author of the Exposition, on the other hand, prefers the position that the Divine is a monad, a single, undifferentiated being. He further argues that Silence is not the Father's partner and equal, but is the state of rest in which the Father dwells. We'll see a similar view expressed in the Tripartate Tractate (in Chapter 18).

A second area of debate in the Valentinian school was over the role of an aeon named Limit or Boundary. Our author seems to attribute a greater role to Limit than the standard Valentinian myth does (take a look back at Chapter 9 for the details on Valentinus's version of things). He asserts that Limit was responsible not only for keeping the fallen Sophia out of the Pleroma but also for removing Sophia's passion from her.

Third, there was disagreement over the source of Sophia's fall. Some Valentinians asserted that it was a perfectly understandable longing to know the Father, a longing she shared with the rest of the Pleroma, that inadvertently led to Sophia's suffering. Others, including the author of the Exposition, felt that Sophia was motivated more by an overweening desire to be like the Father, who created out of himself alone. According to this latter view, she acted in a presumptuous fashion, trying to bring forth some kind of creation without the participation of her male consort, and this led to her fall.

Finding Yourself

The rest of the myth follows the basic lines of the Valentinian school. Sophia repented of her willfulness and received Christ when he came to rescue her. This was intended to confirm the Father's intention that nothing in creation could take place without the masculine-feminine pairing. "For this is the will of the Father," the author wrote, "not to allow anything to happen in the Pleroma apart from a *syzygy*." No being other than the Father himself can be entirely independent and autonomous.

> **Word Knowledge**
>
> A **syzygy** is a really fancy way of describing the union of a pair of things.

Salvation comes because the gnostic, who possesses a seed of Sophia, is united with his or her angelic consort. The angel is the male counterpart to the feminine spirit in the gnostic. With that union, the gnostic contributes to the eventual reunification of all the seeds of Sophia back into the Pleroma.

Oil, Water, and Food

This focus on the need to be reunited with our spiritual selves, to be made complete and whole again, is what sets apart the gnostic use of the ritual sacraments of the church. Having laid out a theology of restoration and spiritual reunification, the Exposition concludes with a set of prayers and declarations to be used with the three most important sacraments: anointing with oil, baptism, and eucharist. These are precisely the same kinds of sacraments that would have taken place in any Christian community. The difference is in the meaning attributed to them. Here we get a first-hand look at what was considered important to convey to new initiates.

Word Knowledge

An **exorcism** is both the act of driving out evil spirits from a person or place and the ritual used to do so.

The prayer for anointing would have been used prior to baptism, when the initiate was marked with oil. If the gnostic use was similar to the larger Christian community, this anointing was a sign of *exorcism*, empowering the initiate to "trample on the snakes and the heads of the scorpions and all the power of the Devil." Liberated from any evil spirits that might still cling to their lives, the initiates were now prepared for the act of baptism.

A declaration and a prayer are included for baptism. We've already seen some aspects of baptism as it was performed among Valentinians (see Chapters 8 and 9). Here it is clear that the Valentinians distinguished between two different kinds of baptism. One kind was available to the "psychic" Christians—the average, run-of-the-mill churchgoers. This baptism originated with John the Baptist and was effective for the forgiveness of sins. The second kind of baptism was available to the Valentinian gnostics. This second baptism corresponded to Jesus' baptism in the Jordan when, Valentinians asserted, the Christ came on him. In the wake of this second baptism, the prayer states, "from now on the souls will become perfect spirits."

After initiation came the eucharist. For regular Christians this would have been the first time that they had been allowed to eat the bread and wine representing the body and blood of Christ. Since Valentinians were already part of the larger Christian community, it is likely that they already participated in this ritual regularly. That may explain why the eucharist is often downplayed in gnostic texts. In this instance, the eucharist celebrates that fact that the initiates "are doing [the Father's] will" and that "they are complete in every spiritual gift and every purity." Both of these are the results of the baptism, so the focus of the eucharist seems to be on the baptism.

This would differ a great deal from the orthodox Christians, who put much greater emphasis on the eucharist.

It makes sense if you think about it. Gnostics saw redemption in spiritual enlightenment, so it's natural that they would be drawn to Jesus' baptism and the reenactment of that moment in their own baptisms. Orthodox Christians, by contrast, believed that redemption was anchored in the death of Christ on the cross, so the eucharist quickly became the central act of worship in their churches. Nothing else so explicitly demonstrates the way that a difference of teaching translated into a difference in worship.

The Prayer of Thanksgiving (Codex VI,7)

The gnostics were an eclectic bunch, drawing on many sources of spiritual inspiration and wisdom in their quest to know God. The Prayer of Thanksgiving, and the Discourse on the Eighth and Ninth that follow, are evidence of that questing mentality. Both are Hermetic in origin and have no distinctly Jewish or Christian qualities at all. How they came to be part of a collection of literature in a gnostic Christian library remains a mystery, as does the extent to which the owners of the library would have relied on either the Prayer or the Discourse for guidance in either wisdom or worship. Their very presence, however, is intriguing.

We know the Prayer of Thanksgiving from two other sources: it appears in the Papyrus Mimaut, where it forms part of a magical incantation, and in the Latin Asclepius.

Thanks and Joy

The Prayer opens with a thanksgiving to God, also called the Father. Affirmation is made of three God-given attributes:

- ◆ Mind, which enables us to understand God

- ◆ Speech, which enables us to expound God

- ◆ Knowledge, by which we know God intimately

These are followed by three reasons for rejoicing:

- We have been "illuminated" by knowledge

- God has shown us Godself

- We have been made divine through knowledge even while still in our bodies

The second half of the Prayer boils the thanksgiving down to one simple purpose: knowing God. Five times the Prayer extols God in the highest language for granting knowledge to the members of the praying community. One petition is offered in the wake of this focused worship language. The prayers ask that they will be "preserved" in their intimate acquaintance with God, and they will not "stumble" in their pursuit of a life lived according to knowledge.

The Human Element

The Prayer begins with the phrase, "This is the prayer that they spoke," making it clear that a communal setting was intended. That understanding is reinforced by the closing text, which tells us that in the wake of the prayer, the members of the community embrace one another and gather together for a meal of "holy food." It's an understated reminder that participation in the life of a community was a welcome and even necessary part of Hermetic, and presumably gnostic, spirituality. Despite the inherently individualistic quality of the experience of divine revelation, groups still gathered together for teaching and ritual worship.

Appended to the end of the text of the Prayer is a humorous note written by the scribe who assembled the codex. He seems to have thought it a good idea to add the prayer, but then it seems that he felt it necessary to justify his decision. It may be that adding the Prayer took up a little too much room in the codex. In any event, the scribe defended himself by assuring his readers that he actually restrained himself; he has all sorts of similar prayers in his library that he could have added along with this one. He hesitated, he wrote, because he thought that they might already have those prayers in their own libraries. You can almost hear him talking as fast as he can. It's a deliciously human moment captured purely by happenstance, and reminds us that those who compiled the Nag Hammadi library were real human beings.

Discourse on the Eighth and Ninth (Codex VI,6)

We've already noted that the Discourse on the Eighth and Ninth is a Hermetic text with no direct relationship to Christians, gnostic or otherwise. The text is damaged slightly, and the title is missing. The title that has been given to it comes directly out the text itself and describes its subject matter. In Codex VI, the Discourse actually precedes the Prayer of Thanksgiving.

Well Done, Grasshopper

The Discourse is an example of a common type of Hermetic text, with a student being initiated into new spiritual realities by an older, more experienced teacher, or *mystagogue*.

> **Word Knowledge**
>
> The **mystagogue**, literally "the one who guides the student," is a term usually reserved for those who lead others into new religious or spiritual experiences of a mystical nature.

Before we look at the text itself, a word or two about the title. Common wisdom held that the first seven heavens were those physical realms where the objects of the sky—the sun, the moon, the stars, and the planets—were visible. These realms influenced the earth and its inhabitants, something that astrologers today still claim. Beyond these visible realms, however, were the eighth and ninth heavens, where true spiritual freedom could be found. The eighth and ninth heavens are the subject of the Discourse.

The text of the Discourse begins with the student asking his teacher about the nature of spiritual growth. He asks the teacher to help him ascend to the eighth and ninth heavens. They have previously ascended as high as the seventh heaven together and now he feels prepared to go further. The teacher agrees, and leads his pupil in a prayer for a heavenly revelation or vision.

Silence Is Golden

The revelation that they both experience is not narrated by a neutral observer but is described in real time by the teacher and his student. At moments the text reads like a transcript of their session together, and this makes for an interesting effect. The student, for example, seems intent on describing each and every aspect of his experience. The teacher, on the other hand, keeps encouraging the student to pray or to praise out of "silence." At moments, it seems almost like he's telling the young man to shut up. For his part, the student is so exuberant at his experience that he can't stop talking about it.

It is the teacher who precedes and leads the student into the experience of revelation. It is the power of the presence of Mind through the teacher's conversation with his student that will elevate the young man into the next realm. The eighth heaven is filled with angels who are singing hymns to Mind, the ultimate God. The teacher encourages his student to join them as they sing.

In a sense, the teacher comes to embody the reality of Mind, and the student begins to address him accordingly. The teacher actually refers to himself as "Mind" at one point, and the student calls him "master of the universe." This then becomes the catalyst for the student's own experience of unity with Mind, the ninth heaven. As he enters into an experience of the ninth heaven, he sees the angelic choir of the eighth heaven singing its praises to him as if he were God. And, in fact, the point of the experience is to teach him precisely that he and the Divine are one.

In the wake of their experience, the teacher instructs his student to write up a copy of the revelation they have received, and to have it inscribed in hieroglyphics on stone steles. Those steles are then to be displayed in a local temple where they can be read by anyone. What had been a personal moment between two men becomes a public monument.

The Least You Need to Know

- The logic of gnostic belief eventually moved many gnostics to reject common Christian rituals and practices or at least to see them or use them as merely symbolic.

- The gnostics seemed to have been comfortable blending biblical language with philosophical terminology in their prayers.

- The "sayings" traditions could be reformatted in a number of ways to provide for teaching initiates to gnostic belief.

- Valentinian Christians continued to use the rites of anointing, baptism, and eucharist, though with their own twist on the meanings of the rituals.

- Gnostics drew from many different sources, including Hermetic texts that combined a Greek god with an Egyptian god and taught extreme self-denial.

Chapter 18

Speaking to the Church

In This Chapter

◆ The gnostics "borrow" some material from other early Christians

◆ The Testimony of Truth takes on Valentinians and orthodox Christians alike

◆ How the gnostics tried to find common ground between themselves and orthodox Christians

◆ The Interpretation of Knowledge preaches to a mixed audience

Gnostic Christians, initially at least, did not live separate from other Christians but mingled with them freely. Valentinians especially lived and worshipped alongside their orthodox brothers and sisters. This situation created all sorts of opportunities for sharing, and arguing, various ideas. The orthodox weren't the only ones persuading, cajoling, and condemning those whom they disagreed with. The texts in this chapter illustrate the many ways that gnostic Christians tried to champion their teachings, both inside and outside the church.

The Wisdom of Jesus Christ (Multiple Versions)

When the Nag Hammadi library was unearthed, scholars discovered something surprising. The library contained a pair of documents, Eugnostos the Blessed and the Wisdom of Jesus Christ, that appeared to be closely related. In fact, one seems to be based on the other.

Two copies of Eugnostos the Blessed appear in the Nag Hammadi library. There are significant differences between them, suggesting that Eugnostos was a popular text appearing in different versions. It's a short religious tract written perhaps very early in the first century A.D., which means it was probably written during the lifetime of Jesus. In it, Eugnostos took on the philosophers of his day—the way he described them makes it pretty clear he was talking about the Stoics, Epicureans, magicians, and astrologers—by describing a spiritual reality that was, he contended, beyond their grasp. According to Eugnostos, they couldn't know it because their methods were all wrong.

What he ended up describing is an elaborate universe emanated from one original, unique, and ineffable Father. The Father emanated a series of paired aeons—male and female—who proceed to populate the various levels of the heavens with angels, attendants, and assorted spiritual beings. The final part of the text focuses specifically on the realm in which human beings dwell, the realm of the "Immortal Man." With the exception of one line about the "defect of the female," Eugnostos the Blessed doesn't appear to be gnostic.

First-Century Copyrights

The Wisdom of Jesus Christ appears in the Nag Hammadi library only in Codex III (where it is the fourth text), but it is also one of the four texts preserved in the Berlin Codex. The two versions have differences, though they are far more alike than the two copies of Eugnostos. For reasons that we're about to explore, it makes sense to date the Wisdom after Eugnostos and certainly after the arrival of Christianity into Egypt in the mid- to late-first century. That puts the writing of the Wisdom in the very early part of the second century, but probably not any later than that.

If you were to read the Wisdom without having read Eugnostos the Blessed, you might come to the conclusion that you were reading a spiritual dialogue between Jesus and his disciples. The disciples asked leading questions about the nature of the universe or the origin of sin, and Jesus responded with a lengthy monologue. That was a common style of literature, and we've seen several examples already in this book. When read side by side with Eugnostos the Blessed, however, something more disturbing appears. Nearly all of Eugnostos appears in the Wisdom, where it comes from Jesus as his own teaching. We have ourselves a case of second-century plagiarism!

Making Changes

In the Wisdom of Jesus Christ, the material from Eugnostos has been rearranged to fit into a standard dialogue format. The disciples—Philip, Thomas, Mary, Matthew, and Bartholomew are mentioned by name—ask a series of questions. Jesus responds with blocks of text taken from Eugnostos. That's not to say that there is no original material in the Wisdom. Almost all of the first part of the Wisdom is drawn from Eugnostos, but the beginning and final sections are new.

The text begins with the 12 apostles and seven women gathering together after Christ's resurrection. Jesus, called the Savior, appears to them "not in his previous form" but spiritually. He looked like "a great angel of light." He laughs at their confusion, and begins to answer their questions.

In addition to what comes from Eugnostos about the structure of the universe, the author of the Wisdom added material that would be quite at home in any gnostic text. There is a god, called "Almighty" and "Ialtabaoth," who is in charge of the physical world. It's a place of bondage for those who are like "a drop from the Light." These "drops" rained down from Sophia when she tried to bring beings into existence without her male counterpart. Sex, "the unclean rubbing," is the primary means by which human beings are held in chains of forgetfulness.

The Savior himself has descended from the realms of Light to find and save those who belong with the Father. Not everyone can enter into the Divine realms, though. Some folks know the Father "in pure knowledge" and will enter in the rest of the presence of God. Some, on the other hand, only know the Father "defectively." They will be saved, but they may only ascend to "the Eighth," a reference to the eighth heaven.

The Wisdom ends with some words of encouragement from Jesus. I have come to heal people of their blindness, he tells them, and to "tell everyone about the God who is above the universe." It is possible to walk all over Ialtabaoth and his fellow rulers, Jesus continues, for every work of chaos and every destructive force is now subject to the "Sons of Light."

Riding His Coattails

Given the possible widespread popularity of Eugnostos the Blessed, it's hard to imagine that the author of the Wisdom of Jesus Christ thought he could get away with cribbing from the original work. Didn't he think that people would notice? Perhaps not, or perhaps they wouldn't care. Modern readers tend to be far more concerned with the historical accuracy of these kinds of texts than ancient audiences were. It's unlikely that the first concern most second-century readers had was whether or not the Wisdom was actually relating a real discussion between Jesus and his disciples. Putting widely accepted views on the lips of Jesus might have been an acceptable vehicle for communicating other, more Christian, religious ideas.

The Wisdom of Jesus Christ raises a larger question about the accuracy of other texts that include conversations with Christ. As we've seen, scholars have argued that collections of Jesus-sayings were eventually integrated into more free-flowing dialogue formats as part of the shift to full-fledged gospels. The Wisdom of Jesus Christ shows us, however, that Jesus may have been credited with someone else's material on occasion. We are left wondering if this is the only dialogue that attributes to Jesus sayings drawn from other sources.

The Testimony of Truth (Codex IX,3)

If anyone tells you that gnostic Christians were all peace loving and never tried to push their own views on anyone else, don't you believe it. The Testimony of Truth demonstrates quite convincingly that the gnostics could duke it out with the best of them. What we have here, ladies and gentlemen, is the gnostic equivalent of Tertullian and Irenaeus.

The text is badly damaged, especially the latter half of it. Thankfully we're still able to make out most of what the author had to say. The original title is missing, so the current title was drawn from the text itself. More than likely, the Testimony of Truth was written in Alexandria sometime early in the third century.

Preaching to the Choir

The audience is probably a gathering of gnostic Christians. The author spoke "to those who know to hear … with the ears of the mind." This is an argumentative work, intended to buck up the faithful and strengthen their resolve as they face conflict over their claim to be the true Christians, as opposed not only to orthodox Christians but to other gnostics as well.

Words to the Wise

Orthodox writers described the church in concrete terms because they accepted the status quo; that is, they affirmed that the actual community of those gathered for worship was 'the church.' Gnostic Christians dissented. Confronted with those in the churches whom they considered ignorant, arrogant, or self-interested, they refused to agree that the whole community of believers, without further qualification, constituted "the church."

—Elaine Pagels, The Gnostic Gospels

Some people have one issue to ride and they ride it for all it's worth. For the author of the Testimony, renunciation of the world is the goal of Christian life, and the world can be summed up in one word: sex. He began his sermon with an attack on the Law, a reference to the Old Testament. The Hebrew Scriptures commanded men and women to "be fruitful and multiply," a blatant invitation, in the author's mind, to defilement by helping to maintain the existence of this physical world.

Did You Know?

For modern folks, conditioned to think of population growth as detrimental to the continued health of the planet, the Testimony's assertion that procreation is what maintains the world's existence may seem to be upside-down thinking. The ancient world, however, had a different relationship with the environment than we do. War, disease, famine, drought, and natural disasters could strike at a moment's notice, depopulating towns and cities with ease. Civic leaders encouraged people to marry and have children in order to maintain a stable population; having a large family could be, for lack of a better way to put it, a patriotic duty. So when the author of the Testimony strikes out against maintaining the present world, that's what he's talking about. By having children, he is saying, we buy into this present life and its illusionary cares and concerns, to the detriment of our souls.

Friendly Fire

Don't think that other gnostic groups got away unscathed. The author's polemic extended to Valentinians, followers of Basilides, and the Simonians (second-century gnostics who claimed to follow the teachings of Simon the Magician). These groups continued to permit sexual unions, railed the author. They continued to submit to baptism in water, not realizing that the "baptism of truth" is "renunciation of the world." The Testimony gives evidence to Irenaeus' claim (we saw it in Chapter 17) that certain gnostic groups had done away with baptism and similar rituals. Since matter is a mistake, the author of the Testimony contended, how can it possibly be a source of spiritual enlightenment.

The Second Treatise of the Great Seth (Codex VII,2)

Of all the Nag Hammadi texts, the Second Treatise of the Great Seth is the only one that was perfectly preserved. Unfortunately, it was not translated well from the original Greek into Coptic, and some passages are difficult to understand. Although the text was named for Seth, he doesn't actually make an appearance in this text. It's possible that the author wanted to imply that Jesus was Seth, or the title may have been mistakenly added by someone who read just the first few pages.

There is no way of knowing who the author was. It seems unlikely that the Treatise was written prior to the third century, and may have been written even later.

The Jesus Puppet

The first part of the text describes Jesus coming to Earth and taking on the powers that rule the world. The mythology that forms the structure of The Second Treatise is the same Sethite myth that we have seen previously in The Secret Book of John and The Nature of the Rulers (see Chapter 13). Jesus (we discover who he is only at the end) was speaking in the first person throughout most of the text. He announced that he was coming "to reveal the glory to my kindred and my fellow spirits." He mentioned "our sister Sophia—she who is a whore" as he descended to communicate "the life-giving word" to those who Sophia has failed to adequately prepare.

True to the Sethite literature, the one who spoke told of finding "a bodily dwelling," meaning the human Jesus. He "cast out the one who was in it first, and I went in." This possession of the man Jesus by the Great Seth resembles the way that the Valentinians interpreted the coming of the Holy Spirit on Jesus at his baptism in the Jordan, which demonstrates how gnostics found different ways of integrating their mythological story in the story of Jesus. This act of possession deeply troubled the powers that ruled the world, most of whom aligned themselves against Jesus. The text describes a frenetic conflict, which ended with the attempt to crucify Jesus. He, however, refused to die. "For my death which they think happened, happened to them in their error and blindness, since they nailed their man unto their death … Yes, they saw me; they punished me. It was another, their father, who drank the gall and the vinegar; it was not I. They struck me with the reed; it was another, Simon, who bore the cross on his shoulder … And I was laughing at their ignorance."

From the Source

Irenaeus and Epiphanius both described this same view, that Simon of Cyrene was crucified in Jesus place, attributing its origin to Basilides. As Irenaeus reports in his *Against Heresies,* Basilides taught that:

[Jesus] did not himself suffer death, but Simon, a certain man of Cyrene, being compelled, bore the cross in his stead; so that this latter being transfigured by him, that he might be thought to be Jesus, was crucified, through ignorance and error, while Jesus himself received the form of Simon, and, standing by, laughed at them.

Spiritual Warfare with Live Targets

The second part of the text is an attack on the orthodox Christians and their view on nearly everything. The author of the Treatise was at war. Conflict with the orthodox Christians is described as being open and frequent. It is evident that the author and the group to which he was speaking were under a great deal of stress.

Jesus described the orthodox Christians as the enemy. He told his audience that they hated and persecuted the gnostics out of ignorance. At the same time they "think that they are advancing the name of Christ." They didn't realize that they were "empty," "like dumb animals" who should "shut their mouth." They have "proclaimed the doctrine of a dead man" that led to "fear and slavery." He laughed off the entire Old Testament, calling Adam, Abraham, Moses, David, and more "laughingstocks."

The final part of the text is an exhortation to live well and in unity with one another. "Do not become female," Christ enjoins his hearers, or you will "give birth to evil." Instead, they should look forward to the "wedding of truth" and the "rest of incorruption."

The Treatise is interesting first because it was obviously written to a group who was excluded or in the process of being excluded from the larger Christian community, yet they seemed defiant nevertheless. Related to that is the fact that the text is jumpy and broken at times. Elements of the text are repeated, and sections are told twice in different ways. The text changes person abruptly, which can be disconcerting. It appears to have been cobbled together from a whole bunch of sources, without much discrimination. Evidently, the group to which the Second Treatise is addressed had access to a large body of literature from which to cobble together this text.

Tripartate Tractate (Codex I,5)

One of the longest of all the Nag Hammadi texts, and one of the least damaged, the Tripartite Tractate was named for its three basic divisions. Written sometime in the mid- to late-second century, before the conflict between the gnostic and orthodox views was widely recognized as irreconcilable, the Tractate is a very involved attempt to explain a form of Western Valentinian mythology to an orthodox audience.

Perfect Bliss

Like the Valentinian Exposition (introduced in Chapter 17), the Tripartate Tractate differs from the original teachings of Valentinus by assuming that the Divine Parent is monadic, a single being rather than a male-female pair.

> **Did You Know?**
>
> It is significant that the two fullest descriptions of the Valentinian myth found in the Nag Hammadi library (the Tripartate Tractate and the Valentinian Exposition) both have developed beyond Valentinus on this point. Either both texts come from the same small subgroup of Valentinians or this view was more widespread than previously thought.

The Father is described in terms that will be familiar to readers of the Valentinian Exposition: ineffable, indescribable, entirely unique, and self-existent. From the Father, we are told, emanated two aeons, Christ and the church. This is clearly another change from the typical Valentinian myth, where the initial male-female produced a total of 30 aeons. Here, the godhead consisted of just the Father, Christ, and the church. The complexity of the Valentinian myth was retained by having church produce a vast number of aeons, all of whom had "a love and a longing for the perfect, complete discovery of the Father."

Gender Bender

Sophia isn't mentioned at all in the Tripartate Tractate, so who screwed things up? Instead of blaming it on female Wisdom, the Tractate lay the blame on a male aeon called the Logos, a term that orthodox Christians would certainly associate with Jesus because of the opening lines of the Gospel of John ("In the beginning was the Word [Logos] ...).

What's going on here? Some have suggested that this book demonstrates a real doctrinal development in the gnostic approach to the Jesus story and another step away from the classical gnostic myth. Those who favor looking at gnosticism as an independent religion that was infiltrating Christianity have pointed to the continuing presence of wisdom language in the Tractate as evidence that Sophia is not really all that far away. They have argued that the Logos was just a smokescreen, used here to allay orthodox suspicions long enough for the gnostic author to communicate his essential point that the creation of our world is the result of a falling away in the heavens. In this instance, the Logos was just a form of propaganda.

The Logos, filled with the desire to know the Father and thwarted in that attempt, began to create on his own. There is a strong hint that the Father was secretly pleased with what the Logos was doing. The Logos was setting in motion events by which the Father would be able to make himself known to all the aeons, and this ultimate aim was viewed by the author as a source of delight. Unlike the typical Sophia myth, where the fall is viewed as a rescue and repair operation, the Tractate sees the actions of the Logos as positive all along.

There is yet another distinction between the normal presentation of gnostic ideas and what is presented in the Tractate. Critics of the gnostics argued that the gnostic explanation for things tended to squash the possibility for free will. Everything in the gnostic myth seems to act according to a pattern set by the Divine Parent, so that no truly free decisions are made. Since human beings are either born of the gnostic race or not, there is little to hope for, outside of a vague and unapproachable kind of *predestination*. Yet, the Tractate is at pains to describe how each movement of the aeons was the result of free will decisions, and that this capacity extended all the way down to human beings. It shows that someone on the other end of this debate was hearing the criticism and responding.

> **Word Knowledge**
>
> **Predestination** is a theological claim that certain persons or groups of people have been specially chosen by God in advance to receive salvation. Some theories of predestination limit the scope of God's choice, trying to preserve as much free will as possible. Other explanations put God in complete control of every detail and every event in human life.

It's Okay to Be Psychic

A good-size chunk of the Tractate is devoted to exploring and explaining the Valentinian view of the "psychics" or soul folks, the people in the middle who have a certain degree of choice about their ultimate destiny. In contrast to so many gnostic texts, a great deal of hope is extended to the average Christian in the Tractate. Rather than open contempt for those who just don't "get it," those who lack gnosis, the Tractate demonstrates that some gnostics had deep concern and compassion for those they felt were spiritually inferior. Gone is the absolute kind of elitism that so often characterizes gnostic views of the human race. In its place is a lengthy and lavish attempt to describe the various types of psychics that exist.

From the Source

The Tripartate Tractate makes it clear that the existence of the church is grounded in the Pleroma itself. Rather than a later creation, the church is emanated directly from the Father just like the Son is. "Not only did the Son exist from the beginning," explains the Tractate, "but the Church, too, existed from the beginning." Consequently, only those spirits who were created as part of the church right from the start would find reunion with the Pleroma. This explanation corresponds closely to the typical Valentinian view that "spiritual" Christians were so because they had been part of the eternal church in the Pleroma.

The ultimate end of the three classes of people makes up the last section. The fleshly folks just end up being destroyed. They have nothing to hope for. These are the people who simply reject Christ out of hand. The spiritual people, to the contrary, immediately embrace Christ and his teaching. As for the psychics, they have the opportunity to come to rest with the Demiurge, who is described in milder and more respectful language than in any other gnostic text. There are even hints that some psychics might have the opportunity to enter the bridal chamber and join the spirituals in their enjoyment of the Divine presence. They do so, however, like members of the wedding party rather than the ones getting married. The poor psychics are always bridesmaids, never brides.

The Tripartite Tractate is remarkable for both its complexity and attention to detail, and for the willingness it demonstrates to go the extra mile in striving to communicate gnostic ideas. Whether that willingness comes from a genuine humility and desire to find a middle ground, or whether the Tractate is designed as a cleverly written piece of stealth gnosticism, is up to you to decide.

The Interpretation of Knowledge (Codex XI,1)

There is a definite pastoral concern in the Interpretation of Knowledge, which had as its audience both sides of the conflict between gnostic and orthodox Christians. If other texts in this chapter were written with the intention of propagandizing orthodox Christians or arguing with them, this short sermon seems determined to bring gnostics and orthodox Christians together.

The author was speaking to a congregation of Christians, some of whom were gnostic and some of whom were not. Whether he was addressing the entire group or just a small group of spiritual elites in the congregation is unknown. What is clear is that there was tension in the group over the issue of spiritual gifts. Some were jealous that certain persons had the right to speak or teach, while others were offended at prophecies or the gift of knowledge (gnosis) being given to certain members of the church.

The speaker reminded his hearers about how the Son came from the Father, taking on himself the humiliation of his "small brothers." He used Christ's example to prod the gathered believers toward a more humble attitude of service toward one another. Believers, he told them, have been freed from the "old bond of debt" that was their due because of their descent from Adam. In its place, they have forgiveness of sins and have been secured from the threat of death.

The church members are part of a body, the speaker reminded them. Drawing from the writings of the Apostle Paul, he told them that they all belong to the "same body." They are all unified by their "head," which is Jesus. From him, each member has an equal status in the body, no matter what their particular function or gift might be. Like the roots of a tree, they "have a connection with one another" and they all join together to produce a unified result. The speakers offered a final reminder that Christians, particularly "adepts at the Word" such as the gnostics, faced the possibility of persecution and should steel themselves to face it. And along with the danger of external threats, there is the insidious nature of sin. All are capable of sinning, but for those who "surmount every sin" there is a "crown of victory" to be won.

The Interpretation of Knowledge is a wonderful example of how gnostic and orthodox believers could continue to live and work in the same church together despite fundamental differences in their approach to and interpretation of Scripture. The speaker, while holding a Valentinian view, spoke to all equally. Valentinian theology created a space for "regular" Christians in its system, and this text demonstrated how that theology was applied in the real day-to-day life of a Christian community.

The Least You Need to Know

♦ Many of the Nag Hammadi texts appear to be attempts to communicate gnostic teaching to orthodox Christians, which suggests a continuing relationship between the two streams of thought.

♦ Gnostics were not above plagiarizing material from well-known spiritual texts in order to get their message across.

♦ Whether for propaganda or peace-making, some gnostics were eager to find common ground for theological discussion and teaching, while other were happy to fight back.

♦ Gnostics and orthodox Christians continued to worship and pray side by side in early Christian communities.

19

Gnu Gnostics

In This Chapter

- ◆ Popularizing the Gnostic Gospels
- ◆ The gnostics are loose in America
- ◆ Keanu Reeves: Sci-Fi Kung Fu Gnostic Redeemer

In the next couple of chapters we'll wind up our whirlwind tour through the Nag Hammadi library by taking a step back for a brief look at the impact that the discovery of the Gnostic Gospels have had on modern society, pop culture, and religion.

Academic Gnostics

The Nag Hammadi find was one of several major discoveries in the twentieth century that promised to redefine our understanding of the roots and development of the Christian faith. In terms of popular interest, the library discovered at Nag Hammadi was overshadowed by the recovery of the Dead Sea Scrolls, despite the fact that the Dead Sea Scrolls have a more limited application to Christian history. That situation began to change in the 1960's as a new generation of scholars began to concentrate on publishing their explorations of the Nag Hammadi texts and the implications that these new gnostic texts had for Christianity.

Elaine Pagels

It's possible that the Gnostic Gospels would have eventually resonated with the popular consciousness no matter what happened. Possible, but not likely, since John Q. Public rarely reads professional journals in the fields of New Testament studies and early church history. And most academics have a difficult time communicating with the general public in a way that informs them without putting them to sleep. To emerge from academic obscurity into the light of full public awareness, the Gnostic Gospels would need someone who was equal parts academic and advocate, with a journalist's eloquent simplicity and a novelist's love of story.

Enter Elaine Pagels, who as a graduate student at Harvard University in the late 1960s got involved in the effort to transcribe and translate the Nag Hammadi manuscripts. Her 1979 award-winning book *The Gnostic Gospels* introduced the public at large to the Nag Hammadi find and to an alternative form of Christian faith described as "Gnosticism." What Irenaeus did to undermine the gnostics, Pagels did to popularize them.

The Gnostic Gospels demonstrated that, contrary to the typical story of Christian origins at the time, the earliest Christians were a far more diverse lot than most people had ever suspected. Pagels depicted the gnostics as a legitimate form of Christianity, not an aberrant splinter group or an infectious form of Christianized paganism. Her point wasn't just academic. *The Gnostic Gospels* was published just as a resurgent Religious Right was becoming more politically and culturally influential. Pagels' story of tolerant, pluralistic gnostics squeezed out of existence by a militant orthodoxy resonated uncomfortably with some of her readers as they noticed the beginning of the "culture wars" in the early 1980s.

Apart from her obviously sympathetic portrayal of the gnostics, one of Pagels' unique contributions was to suggest that the triumph of what today we call "orthodox Christianity" had as much to do with political and social issues as it did with religious doctrine and practice. Mainstream churches, with their emphasis on centralized authority, were better able to withstand persecution and were better situated to take advantage of the legalization of Christianity under the emperor Constantine. They developed a religious hierarchy and a way of worshipping that was flexible yet still accessible to the average person. The gnostics, on the other hand, lacked such a strong structure. That, plus the fact that only a relative handful of Christians were attracted to their teachings, made the various gnostic groups less able to survive.

Did You Know? _____

Pagels has continued to write, though none of her more recent works has matched the monumental influence of her first book. *Adam, Eve and the Serpent,* written in 1988, explored differing interpretations of the Genesis creation accounts and their impact on Western attitudes toward sexuality. *The Origin of Satan,* written in 1995, explored ways that belief in supernatural conflict translates into groups demonizing those whom they fear or hate. Her most recent book, *Beyond Belief: The Secret Gospel of Thomas,* described Pagels' explanation for how Christianity, a faith predicated on a personal experience of God, became narrowly defined in terms of doctrinal beliefs.

The success of *The Gnostic Gospels* has ensured Pagels' place as the principal inter-preter of the Gnostic Gospels to the average reader. One can't help but get the feel-ing, though, that Pagels' descriptions of both gnostics and orthodox Christians has as much to do with wishful thinking and her own spiritual longings as it does with the historical data. In *The Gnostic Gospels* and her other writings on the subject, the gnostics are all creative, artistic, open-minded, and egalitarian. The orthodox are almost always bureaucratic, dogmatic, often malicious, and usually thick in the head. Pass out black and white 10-gallon hats and you'll have yourself a classic Western, with Valentinus played by '60s hippie icon Abbie Hoffman and Irenaeus portrayed by a suitably self-righteous and conservative Richard Nixon. The truth, as they say, is much more complex.

Words to the Wise

The reaction to Pagels' works in the orthodox Christian community has been mixed. While many disagree with her, the reaction to much of her writing has been more bemused than angry. After reading Pagels' recent book *Beyond Belief: The Secret Gospel of Thomas,* Frederica Mathewes-Green commented, "I can't be the only Christian reading *Beyond Belief* … and thinking, 'What's so heretical about this?'" Mathewes-Green, a writer and convert to Eastern Orthodox Christianity, puts her finger on precisely the point at which Pagels has been so vulnerable to criticism, "Early Christians rejected Gnosticism, all right. But what Pagels presents is not the part they rejected. What they rejected, Pagels does not present …. The problem wasn't the insis-tence that we can directly experience God. It was that the Gnostics' schemes of how to do this were so wacky."

It's the less palatable side of the gnostics—their complex mythology, their elitism, their contradictory images of the feminine, and their negation of bodily existence—that boosters for gnostic Christianity frequently overlook or excuse away. At the same time, those parts of gnostic spirituality that seem so attractive—the intimate experience of God, tolerance, creative reading of Scripture, and an appreciation for the intellect—have parallels in orthodox Christianity. As Mathewes-Green points out with regard to the supposedly unique gnostic teaching that "the Kingdom of God is within you," "Today's NeoGnostics would find a crowd around them, from seventeenth-century Spanish nuns to polyester-clad Pentecostals, saying, 'That sounds like what I'm talking about.'"

Despite these criticisms, Elaine Pagels deserves a tremendous amount of credit for championing a more realistic vision of the development of the Christian faith in its earliest centuries. Her books and articles have made the Gnostic Gospels accessible to a broader audience and have compelled orthodox Christians to reexamine the way that they tell both the Jesus story and the story of the Christian faith.

There Is No Gnosticism

If Michael Allen Williams has his way, we won't use the word "gnosticism" anymore. Williams, a professor at the University of Washington, stirred up quite a debate with his 1996 book *Rethinking Gnosticism: An Argument for Dismantling a Problematic Category*. For Williams, the words "gnostic" and "gnosticism" carry with them far too much baggage and tend to obscure more than they illuminate. The terms assume that the people who authored and used the Nag Hammadi documents all subscribed to a universal set of beliefs that you could generalize about with terms like "gnostic." Instead, Williams argues that the Nag Hammadi library demonstrates a great deal of diversity. On top of that, words like "gnostic" are integrally tied into the language of "heresy" and "orthodoxy," and therefore carry a kind of stigma.

Williams isn't alone in questioning the value of terms like "gnosticism." Karen King follows the same line of thinking in her book, *What is Gnosticism?* King, however, focuses more on twentieth-century studies of gnosticism, arguing that modern scholars have continued to distort and stereotype early Christian origins by following the "master narrative" put forward by the Irenaeus and the other orthodox writers; namely, that gnostics were outsiders who were corrupting a once-pure apostolic heritage in the church. Like Williams, King has a low opinion of the terms now in use.

A certain amount of demolition work has to be done from time to time in academic circles. Old ideas and perceptions need to be cleared to make way for (hopefully) better scholarship to take their place. Williams and King have made a good case for the inadequacy of using terms like "gnosticism." For the average reader, however, such arguments are of little help. We need to be able to talk about the different ways of telling the Jesus story that emerged in Christian communities in the first, second, and third centuries. Even King and Williams recognize that there are certain similarities in the story told by the Nag Hammadi documents that distinguishes them from other Christian interpretations of Jesus. Otherwise, where did the conflict come from inthe first place? And if those similarities exist, why not call them something? Williams' suggested alternative, "biblical demiurgical traditions," has all the poetry of a legal brief, however accurate and neutral it might be. King agrees that Williams' alternative won't fly, but has no suggestions of her own. In the end, we are forced to continue using "gnosticism," while hopefully being more conscious of the complexities involved.

Not Your Father's Gnosticism

With the discovery of the Nag Hammadi library, gnostic ideas are suddenly in vogue again in a way that they haven't been since perhaps the second century. As the Gnostic Gospels become better known to the general public, we will continue to see more people reading and studying gnosticism as a form of religion or spirituality, as well as greater sensitivity to gnosticism as a category for analyzing religion and society. Already, several authors have addressed the larger implications of a revival of gnosticism, or at least the awareness of gnosticism. We'll look at three of them here.

Philip J. Lee

There's something rotten in the state of American Protestantism, and Philip J. Lee thinks he knows what it is. A Presbyterian minister active in Canada, Lee's 1987 book titled *Against the Protestant Gnostics* was a shot across the bow of the American Protestant Church. Taking his cues from Irenaeus, to whom the title of Lee's book alludes, Lee charges that certain gnostic tendencies latent in Western Christianity have emerged to dominate the theology, worship, and ethics of American Protestants.

What is this gnosticism that Lee finds infecting modern America? Any tendencies that deny the goodness of the world and bodily existence, or that elevate private spiritual experiences above the public revelation of the Bible and the various creeds devised by the church. Anything that exalts the individual above the believing community, that leads Christians to retreat from public life and concerns, or that rejects the "ordinariness" of God's grace in human life in favor of an unrealistic mysticism. These are the characteristics of modern gnosticism that Lee senses infiltrating Protestant churches.

That's quite a definition, and Lee finds traces of it throughout Christian history. More to the point, he argues that the individualistic nature of American culture is a failure of New England Puritanism and its preoccupation with the spiritual state of the soul. The resulting Protestant despair in the nineteenth century, Lee claims, opened the floodgates for a gnostic response. Lee criticizes both liberal and conservative Christians for falling into the trap.

> ### Words to the Wise
>
> Is it possible that by identifying a gnostic thought pattern with those outside the Christian community, we have failed to locate it in its natural habitat?
>
> —Philip J. Lee, *Against the Protestant Gnostics*

Not everyone has taken Lee seriously. Critics accuse him of finding gnostics under every church pew. Plus, they argue, other influences for the problems Lee identifies can be found in the history of the church. Both Neoplatonism and the ascetic lives of the encratites could account for certain world-denying tendencies in Christian thought as easily as gnosticism could, and the desire for knowledge of God was as much the promise of the Old Testament prophets (Habakkuk, for example, promised that "the earth shall be filled with the knowledge of the glory of the Lord, as the waters cover the sea." Hab. 2:14) as it was the goal of the gnostics. Lee's historical argument has been attacked as well. For example, the nineteenth century, far from being a time of despair in American Protestantism, was a period of energy and confidence best demonstrated by the growing belief in Manifest Destiny.

Despite the criticism, Lee's book is still widely read. And although his historical arguments are not always embraced, his diagnosis of the current situation in the Protestant world is highly regarded. One person who expressed admiration for Lee's diagnosis, if not his polemical intent, was Harold Bloom.

Harold Bloom

After more than 50 years as a literary iconoclast and professor at Yale and New York University, Harold Bloom achieved a new notoriety in recent years by turning his attention to what he called the work of "religious criticism." In his books *The American Religion* and *Omens of Millennium*, Bloom began to outline his understanding of the uniquely American religious impulse.

In *The American Religion*, published in 1992, Bloom challenged the notion that America is a distinctly Christian nation. In fact, Bloom argued, at its heart, America is decidedly Ggnostic. Essentially ignoring those branches of Christianity that were transplanted here with colonization, Bloom focused on those indigenous forms of religious faith that have sprung up out of the soil of American culture: Mormonism, Christian Science, Pentecostalism, Seventh Day Adventism, and the Southern Baptists. He also looked at the New Age movement and ended with a lyrical look at African American religious experience.

The American experiment in religion began, for Bloom, with the Cane Ridge revival, which he referred to as America's first Woodstock. Cane Ridge, Kentucky, was the site of a week-long, emotionally charged revival meeting in 1801. Drawing more than 25,000 people, Cane Ridge altered the American religious landscape, softening people's denominational affiliation, and opening them to charismatic leaders with little or no religious credentials. More important, Bloom argued, it confirmed in American religion a tendency toward what Bloom called "creedlessness" or "the doctrine of experience." Americans are drawn to me-and-Jesus-alone kind of spiritual experience that relegates most doctrine and practice to a secondary concern, even if only subconsciously. These qualities, for Bloom, define the heart of the gnostic experience.

> ### Words to the Wise
>
> The American finds God in herself or himself only after finding the freedom to know God by experiencing a total inward solitude. In this solitary freedom, the American is liberated both from other selves and from the created world. He comes to recognize that his spirit is itself uncreated. Knowing that he is the equal of God, the American Religionist can then achieve his true desideratum, mystical communion with his friend, the godhead.
>
> —Harold Bloom, *The American Religion*

Bloom's assessment of these home-grown American religions is principally an aesthetic one. He wants to imbibe the experience of those religions rather than examine the nuts and bolts of their creeds and confessions. Bloom listened to people talk about their encounter with God more like you would listen to a poet than to a college lecturer. That means that at times he makes statements that seem wildly inaccurate, conjuring up seemingly bizarre explanations when a simpler one was at hand. At the same time, there are moments when his insights are penetrating, precisely because he is not listening for the explanation that these groups give for their experiences. Focusing on religious experience itself rather than the way that different groups labeled and explained it, Bloom argues that these different faiths were pointing toward a common experience.

Whether Bloom is right in defining the American impulse toward individualistic spiritual experience as a kind of gnosis is another matter. By raising the question, however, he has offered a complementary view to that of Philip Lee. In contrast to Lee's commitment to Presbyterian Christianity, Bloom describes himself as a Gnostic Jew. The same diagnosis that "fascinates" Bloom moves Lee to "dread and wrath."

Stephan A. Hoeller

In the afterward he wrote for Marvin Meyer's *The Gospel of Thomas*, Harold Bloom wrote, "No one is going to establish a gnostic church in America, by which I mean a professedly gnostic church, to which tax exemption would never be granted anyway." Stephan Hoeller would disagree. He is the Director of Studies for the Gnostic Society, an organization based in Los Angeles, and an ordained bishop in the Ecclesia Gnostica, a Gnostic church. Ecclesia Gnostica is the American branch of an English Gnostic church founded in 1952. In addition to Los Angeles, they have groups in Portland, Seattle, Salt Lake City, and Oslo, Norway. Ecclesia Gnostica is only one of several organizations attempting to revive gnosticism not simply as a personal form of spirituality, but as a living faith comparable to any church.

> **Did You Know?** _____
>
> The Ecclesia Gnostica is the modern incarnation of an organization started in England and has been active in the United States since 1959. You can find them on the web at www.gnosis.org along with The Gnostic Society, another organization committed to educating people about gnosticism as a contemporary spiritual path.
>
> Ecclesia Gnostica isn't the only "gnostic church" active in the United States. Interested readers can also check out l'Eglise Gnostique Catholique Apostolique at geocities.com/ega_church.

Hoeller first made a name for himself with a work on psychologist Carl Gustav Jung's *Seven Sermons to the Dead*, in which he examined the relationship between Jung's depth psychology and the writings of the second-century gnostics. His most recent book, *Gnosticism: New Light on the Ancient Tradition of Inner Knowing,* lays out the general gnostic myth that we have come to know so well in this book. What makes Hoeller's contribution unique is his insistence that the gnostic experience cannot be fruitfully explored without reference to the gnostic tradition. Right at a time when scholars are beginning to argue that no such thing as gnosticism ever really existed, Hoeller and his group (and others like them around the world) are insisting that they are the contemporary equivalent of those early gnostic communities.

Words to the Wise

What is the good of having unusual experiences without an appropriate context in which to understand them? The tradition of Gnosticism developed on the basis of such experiences in the first place and is uniquely suited to facilitate further Gnostic experiences. Clearly, gnosis and Gnosticism are intimately and usefully linked and, in fact, cannot safely be separated.

—Stephan A. Hoeller, *Gnosticism: New Light on the Ancient Tradition of Inner Knowing*

Gnostic Fiction

If you've been reading any of the gnostic texts that we've introduced in this book, you've probably had a few difficult moments. The mythology that the gnostics constructed can be hard to wrap your mind around when Plato's philosophy isn't part of your cultural language. For most of us, aeons and pleromas and emanations are pretty tough to swallow.

The mythological nature of the gnostic story, however, makes it possible to retell the story in ways that make more sense to today's audiences. The symbols may change, but the ideas behind them remain the same. Science fiction has become the language for an entirely new way of describing the essential gnostic view of reality.

Counting Electric Sheep

Philip K. Dick was one of science fiction's most eccentric authors, and his writing was highly regarded by serious sci-fi fans in the 1960s and '70s. Even if you've never heard of Dick, you've probably seen one of the movies based on his stories: *Blade Runner, Total Recall,* and *Minority Report* are all major box-office hits drawn from Dick's writings. Largely as a result of these recent successes, a new audience is beginning to rediscover him.

Dick's life is a study in contradictions. A prolific writer widely regarded as a genius, he was a drug addict who suffered from debilitating psychological problems. Personable and friendly, he couldn't maintain any of his five marriages. At times paranoid and convinced that he was the subject of CIA surveillance, Dick later descended into a mania of mystical experiences and intense self-examination that he recorded and analyzed in a treatise he called the Exegesis, a document that eventually spanned thousands of pages.

Dick was convinced that he was receiving transmissions from an orbiting satellite, an alien intelligence that might even be God, called Vast Active Living Intelligence System, or VALIS for short. At the same time, Dick started having experiences that led him to believe he was connected somehow with a first-century gnostic Christian living in the Roman Empire. He even began to wonder if he was a twentieth-century man hallucinating about the first century or vice versa.

Dick collectively referred to these experiences as "2-3-74," a reference to February and March of 1974, the time frame during which he had them. Out of his attempts to grasp what had happened to him, Dick authored a series of novels remarkable for their spiritual questing. The first, *VALIS*, was published in 1980. It was intensely autobiographical, with a protagonist named obliquely after Dick himself. Dick transferred his "2-3-74" experience to the character Horselover Fat and attempted to explore the meaning of what happened to him. VALIS was followed by *The Divine Invasion*, in which God returned to Earth as a young boy with amnesia. Dick's final novel, *The Transmigration of Timothy Archer*, was a thinly veiled reference to his friend Bishop James Pike, who had died tragically while wandering in the area around the Dead Sea in Israel. Pike, a highly controversial bishop in the Episcopal Church, became famous in the late 1960s for engaging in séances to try and contact his deceased son. The book had not yet been published when Dick died in 1982 from complications following a series of strokes.

Philip Dick's influence on pop culture and literature is incalculable. Beyond just those stories that emerged from his own pen, Dick's unique stylistic approach, slanted outlook, and gnostic views have left their mark on movies like *The Truman Show*, *Dark City*, *Vanilla Sky*, and *Pleasantville*, and television shows like *The X-Files*. It's certain that Dick blazed the trail for the cyberpunk genre, and consequently created an aesthetic space for a movie called *The Matrix*.

Cyberpunk Gnosticism

Computer programmer Thomas Anderson, a computer hacker who goes by the alias Neo, lies asleep in front of his computer. The screen rhythmically blinks the word "Searching." Suddenly, it goes blank, replaced by the phrase, "Wake up, Neo." It's a moment that captures the entire tantalizing message of Andy and Larry Wachowski's 1999 hit movie *The Matrix*, starring Keanu Reeves as Neo.

One of the most popular science fiction franchises in recent years, *The Matrix* trilogy broke all sorts of boundaries in terms of its special effects and the number of different genres that the Wachowski brothers drew on to make their films. At least as astonishing as the brilliantly choreographed fight scenes and the eye-popping "bullet time" was the audacity of the storytelling. *The Matrix* movies dared to explore some of the most daunting metaphysical questions ever proposed by philosophers and theologians, and they did it with a lot of flash.

Numerous critics have recognized hints of the Christian story in *The Matrix* and its sequels. Neo discovers that he is The One, a long-prophesied savior who will deliver the human race from enslavement to a deceptive world crafted by evil forces. But it's the brand of Christianity that gets presented that stirs up interest. It would be foolish to try and sum up all three *Matrix* movies as simply a gnostic myth retold. There are just too many different influences at work, and elements of the plot do run counter to what you would expect from gnostic myth. But broadly speaking, gnostic ideas are at the core of the trilogy's view of reality.

Follow the White Rabbit

The gnostic elements underlying all three movies are fairly clear. The physical world is a lie, a deception designed to keep human beings ignorant of their true state. In charge of this prison of the mind are malicious powers that were themselves created by higher beings, in this case the very human race that they now hold hostage. Deliverance comes through forces from outside of the "world." These agents of redemption slip in stealthily past the guardians, called Agents, to deliver their message. And that message? That we are more than we seem to be, and the world is less than it seems to be.

Only a few people are capable of receiving and acting on this knowledge. The character Morpheus points out that most people are not yet ready to be "unplugged" from the system. Those who are must still be approached carefully. To simply be informed of the truth is not enough. The knowledge must be experienced, and the experience has to be accepted before it is received. Neo doesn't know what will happen to him when he takes the red pill, but that act initiates his liberation from the Matrix.

Like any good gnostic myth, names are significant. Take Neo, whose real name in the movie is Thomas Anderson. Neo means "new," of course, and is an anagram for the word "One." The name Thomas has obvious gnostic overtones, with its connection to Judas Thomas the Twin. Anderson has a revealing meaning. Ander means "man" or "human being," so Anderson is, literally, "son of man," a common title for Jesus.

The two characters who help awaken Neo to his true self are Trinity and Morpheus. Trinity seems like an obvious reference to the three persons of the Christian godhead—Father, Son, and Holy Spirit. From a gnostic perspective, however, Trinity could also represent the Father/Mother/Son of the Barbelo, who so often appears as feminine in gnostic texts. "I thought you were a guy." Neo remarks when he meets her. "Most guys do," Trinity responds.

Morpheus is named for the Greek god of sleep. In the movie, Morpheus is the one who awakens Neo to reality. His attempt to explain the Matrix to Neo is still chilling for anyone aware of the movie's gnostic subtext. "It is the world that has been pulled over your eyes to blind you to the truth." "What truth?" Neo asks. "That you are a slave, Neo," Morpheus tells him. "Like everyone else, you were born into bondage, born into a prison that you cannot smell or taste or touch. A prison for your mind." In the dramatic scene where Neo is disconnected from the Matrix, Morpheus engages him with a question that seems drawn almost directly from the Valentinian Gospel of Truth. How do you tell the difference between dreaming and being awake? It is a question that is decidedly gnostic.

While the two sequels to *The Matrix* were not as successful at the box office, the Wachowski brothers had already made their mark. The sheer audacity of the attempt to present such complex philosophical and religious issues in a series of popular films is remarkable. They reaffirm the potential of science fiction to provide a new mythical story to communicate ancient gnostic ideas, and to do so in a popular medium like film. Let's face it, Valentinus could not have been as much fun to watch as Keanu.

Science fiction movies aren't the only place we've been seeing the gnostics lately. In the next chapter, we'll look at ways that the rediscovery of gnosticism by the public has been generating new and controversial takes on history and what we think really happened 2,000 years ago. That means we're finally going to take a look at today's hottest selling conspiracy theory, *The Da Vinci Code*. So here we go.

The Least You Need to Know

♦ Elaine Pagels was largely responsible for introducing the Gnostic Gospels to the general public.

♦ Academics are increasingly uncomfortable with using words like "gnosticism" and "gnostic" to talk about the Nag Hammadi texts and the people who wrote them, but they have yet to introduce a helpful alternative.

♦ Public awareness of gnosticism continues to grow, resulting in the emergence of new "gnostic churches."

♦ Science fiction has emerged as a new kind of mythology capable of telling the gnostic story.

Chapter 20

New Stories, Old Stories

In This Chapter

- ◆ British journalists unravel a hidden mystery ... and find a hoax
- ◆ Christians fiction through the ages
- ◆ A publisher's dream
- ◆ What's with this Da Vinci guy?

The recovery of the Nag Hammadi library has sparked a resurgence of retellings of the Christian story. Some of these are fictionalized entertainment, while others are serious attempts to reconstruct history. In no case do they rely entirely on the gnostic texts, but these new documents have provided the impetus for a new generation of conspiracy theories and alternative histories.

Holy Blood, Holy Grail

In 1982, Michael Baigent, Richard Leigh, and Henry Lincoln scored a best-seller with their book *Holy Blood, Holy Grail*. Lincoln, with the assistance of Baigent and Leigh, had produced a series of BBC documentaries in the 1970s that explored the story we're about to relate. Encouraged by the documentaries' popularity, the three published their book, which quickly became the subject of heated debate.

The basic outline of the story is as follows: In 1885, Berenger Saunière became the parish priest at the church of St. Mary Magdalene in Rennes-le-Chateau, a small town in the southwestern region of France. This, you may remember from Chapter 5, was once the home of the Cathar movement. While renovating part of the church building, Fr. Saunière allegedly discovered several pieces of parchment hidden in a hollow pillar. In the wake of the discovery, the priest seemed to have come into a significant amount of money. He began living a lavish lifestyle, one far above his means as a simple, parish priest. Locals speculated that he had discovered hidden treasure during the church renovation, but no evidence for such a treasure was ever uncovered.

Baigent, Leigh, and Lincoln used Saunière's story as a springboard into a bewildering exploration of European history and myth. Guided by their sources, particularly one Gerard de Sede (who had written two popular books on Rennes-le-Chateau and Saunière's discovery), they quickly drew connections between the existence of a seemingly secret society called the Priory of Sion, the Cathar movement in twelfth-century France, a Catholic order known as the Knights Templar, and the various legends of the Holy Grail.

From these disparate elements, Baigent, Leigh, and Lincoln constructed a story of deepening mystery revolving around the Merovingian dynasty that ruled what is now France from the fifth through the eighth centuries. The Merovingian line was eventually supplanted by Charlemagne's Holy Roman Empire but, the authors contended, the line continued to exist hidden from view. The Priory of Sion, whose leadership supposedly included a virtual who's who of great names in European history, had secretly protected the Merovingian line for centuries.

The continuing existence of a royal French dynasty hardly seems earth shattering, even if it involves a shadowy organization. What made the story so fascinating, and boosted the book's sales, was the connection that the authors drew between the Merovingian line and the founder of the Christian faith, Jesus of Nazareth. Jesus, they alleged, had been married to Mary Magdalene, and the pair had at least one child. After the Crucifixion, Mary had fled to southern France, where the descendants of Jesus eventually married into the Merovingian line. Baigent, Leigh, and Lincoln asserted that Saunière had discovered documents that proved this story, and the source of his sudden wealth was a pay-off from the Catholic Church seeking to keep the truth hidden.

It's at this point in the story that the gnostic documents came into play. The authors used the existence of the Nag Hammadi documents as part of their attempt to demonstrate that the official Christian accounts of what happened to Jesus were inaccurate, even deceptive. They claimed that church authorities had suppressed the truth about Jesus in order to maintain their own monopoly on power and control. Alternative stories, such as those provided by gnostic books like the Gospel of Philip, threatened the all-male celibate hierarchy of the Roman Catholic Church, and, so the authors alleged, were eliminated. For Baigent, Leigh, and Lincoln, the discovery of the Gnostic Gospels was a recovery of evidence about Jesus untainted by the hands of the Catholic censors.

Words to the Wise

On the basis of the Nag Hammadi scrolls alone, the possibility of a bloodline descended directly from Jesus gained considerable plausibility for us. Certain of the so-called Gnostic Gospels enjoyed as great a claim to veracity as the books of the New Testament. As a result, the things to which they explicitly or implicitly bore witness—a substitute on the cross, a continuing dispute between Peter and the Magdalen, a marriage between the Magdalen and Jesus, the birth of a "son of the Son of man"—could not be dismissed out of hand, however controversial they might be.

—Michael Baigent, Richard Leigh, and Henry Lincoln, *Holy Blood, Holy Grail*

Unfortunately for Baigent, Leigh, and Lincoln, the whole thing turned out to be a hoax. A flood of books written by French researchers in the 1970s and '80s revealed the details that had eluded the BBC documentarians. Berenger Saunière's fortune, for example, derived not from a frightened Catholic hierarchy but from the parish priest's secret side-business: selling mass indulgences by mail, for which he was removed from his position.

Researchers also found an explanation for the supposed link between the Priory of Sion and the Merovingians. Nearly 40 years after Saunière's death, an article about him appeared in a French newspaper, where it was noticed by Pierre Plantard, the leader of a recently established group calling itself the Priory of Sion. Plantard, a con man with a long history of fraud, had led the group into all sorts of right-wing political causes. He had become interested in trying to associate the Priory and himself with the Merovingians, and seized on Saunière's story as a convenient way to do so.

Words to the Wise

Holy Blood, Holy Grail is a masterpiece of insinuation and supposition, employing all the techniques of pseudo-history to symphonic effect, justifying this sleight of hand as an innovative scholarly technique called "synthesis," previously considered too "speculative" by those whose thinking has been unduly shaped by the "so-called Enlightenment of the eighteenth century."

—Laura Miller, "The Da Vinci Con," *The New York Times*

With the help of some friends, Plantard planted documents in the Bibliotheque Nationale, a kind of French Library of Congress. These documents, later cited in *Holy Blood, Holy Grail,* made the Priory look like it had been around for nearly 1,000 years. The group then recruited de Sede to write his books about Rennes-le-Chateau and the "mystery" of Fr. Saunière's documents, but when disagreements erupted over royalties, Plantard and others began leaking the truth. Eventually, several books were published detailing the hoax, including one by de Sede himself. A 1997 BBC documentary finally admitted that the story was a fraud.

The Novel Christian Faith

Christians have produced some very creative stories and literature. From the beginning of the Christian era, believers in Jesus have been filling in the blanks, so to speak, about his life, death, and resurrection. Additionally, the various members of Jesus' entourage became fodder for clever and entertaining tales (remember in Chapter 4 the stories about Simon Peter and Simon the Magician magically duking it out in Rome?).

In a moment we're going to talk about how the Nag Hammadi finds have found their way into modern fiction, but first let's take a look at the many kinds of Christian fiction writing that have appeared in the past.

The Divine Brat

Some of the most amusing stories to emerge out of the early Christian imagination are the so-called "infancy gospels." These were fanciful and often downright incredible stories written to fill in the gaps in the New Testament record, specifically those regarding Jesus' childhood.

The biblical gospels tell us almost nothing about Jesus' earliest years. In fact, the Gospels of Mark and John fail to deal with the subject at all. What little we know came from Matthew and Luke, and they offered up only fragments. Outside of Jesus' infancy, which included the frantic flight to Egypt and eventual return, we have only Luke's account of Jesus in Jerusalem at age 12. Apart from these tantalizing hints, there is nothing more.

Ancient Christians were no less curious about the formative years of Jesus' life than we are today. The infancy gospels were pious "additions" to the New Testament, relating tabloid-style snippets from the childhood of Christ. They were very popular, a fact attested to by the large number of manuscripts that remain and the number of languages in which they appear.

Did You Know?

The earliest of the Infancy Gospels appears to be the Infancy Gospel of James, also known as the Protoevangelium. Origen was familiar with it under the title The Book of James, and there are hints that earlier writers like Clement of Alexandria and even Justin Martyr had heard of it as well. That suggests that at least parts of the Infancy Gospels were circulating as early as the beginning of the second century.

Could that mean that there is something to these stories? It's very unlikely. The Infancy Gospels are clearly expanding on the birth stories from the Gospels of Matthew and Luke. They lack the kind of simplicity in storytelling style characteristic of the gospel accounts. They also show a passionate, even obsessive, interest in miracle stories involving Jesus and his family members. While the miracle stories in the gospels are intended to convey some aspect of Jesus' purpose and mission, the stories in the Infancy Gospels are pure eye-candy, with no connection to anything else.

Finally, the Infancy Gospels resemble childhood accounts of other famous figures from ancient history, many of whom were said to have exhibited strange and miraculous powers at a young age. The Infancy Gospels look exactly like what they are; fictional stories made up by creative authors to fill in the gaps in our knowledge about Jesus. When taken that way, they are actually quite entertaining.

The two best known of the infancy gospels are the Infancy Gospel of James and the Infancy Gospel of Thomas. James focused principally on the Virgin Mary—her birth and childhood, her life in the Temple in Jerusalem and sudden pregnancy at an early age, and her marriage to the elderly Joseph. The story carried Mary and Joseph through their travels to Bethlehem and the birth of Jesus. The gospel's importance has to do with its early impact on Christian views of the Virgin Mary.

In the Infancy Gospel of Thomas, Jesus was hardly the meek and mild Savior so many people imagine. Nor did he resemble the passionately self-giving Christ of the Bible. Instead, as New Testament scholars like to say, he was a "divine brat." On one occasion, when another boy happened to run into him, Jesus immediately pronounced judgment on the clumsy lad and the boy fell down dead on the spot. In another story, less violent though no less precocious, Jesus made 12 sparrows out of clay and, with a divine word, brought them to life and watched them fly away.

The Infancy Gospel of Thomas may have originated in eastern Syria along with so many of the other texts that were ascribed to the Apostle Thomas (several of which we've looked at in this book). It's significance lies with the evolution that we see in Jesus as he learns to use his powers for good rather than selfishly.

From the Source

And after a few days passed, Jesus was up on a roof of a house. And one of the children playing with him died after falling off the roof. And when the other children saw, they fled and Jesus was left standing alone. When the parents of the one who had died came, they accused Jesus, "Troublemaker, you threw him down." But Jesus replied, "I did not throw him down; rather he threw himself down. When he was not acting carefully, he leaped off the roof and died."

Jesus leaped off the roof and stood by the corpse of the boy and cried out with a loud voice and said, "Zeno,"—for that was his name—"rise up, talk to me: Did I throw you down?" And rising up immediately, he said, "No, Lord, you did not throw me down, but you did raise me up." And when they saw this, they were overwhelmed. The parents of the child glorified God on account of the sign which had happened and they worshipped Jesus.

—The Infancy Gospel of Thomas

Other infancy gospels exist that tell us more about the flight of the Holy Family into Egypt. The Arabic Infancy Gospel relates stories of idols falling down before Jesus and of healing powers attributed to Jesus' swaddling clothes. Our personal favorite is the opening story, in which Jesus started talking to his mother while he was still in the crib. Any mother would know right then and there that she was in deep trouble.

Saint Romeo

Romance novels are not a recent phenomenon. The Greeks were writing them right about the time that Jesus and his followers were traipsing around the Mediterranean. They sold just as well back then as they do today, though without the cheesy, half-naked lovers on the cover. The Greek romances were stories of lovers who were torn apart by circumstances and reunited only after many adventures. It's not the kind of literary genre that you would think early Christians would be drawn to, but they were, and they found a way to make the genre their own.

We've already been introduced to the Acts of Thomas in Chapter 6. This work was one of several Christian romances that flourished beginning in the second century. In these novelized stories, we saw Christians reworking the ideal of love as a celibate devotion to Christ. The separation between lovers was no longer a matter of circumstance, but now became part of the struggle to follow Jesus as a disciple, even in the face of opposition from family and society.

The Gospel According to Monty Python

Fans of Monty Python will readily agree that looking for the Holy Grail isn't all that it's cracked up to be. In fact, it can be downright painful. In their ever-popular movie *Monty Python and the Holy Grail*, the British comedy group pit King Arthur and his companions against annoying Frenchmen, Knights Who Say 'Ni', and a very bad-tempered rabbit, all while searching fruitlessly for one of the most illusive objects in Christian lore.

Okay, okay, Monty Python may not have much to do with the development of Christian fiction (of course, there is *Life of Brian* … hmm), but the Holy Grail certainly does. Medieval Europeans invented all sorts of stories and legends starring characters from the Bible, but few that have been as enduring, and as subject to reinterpretation, as the legends of the Holy Grail. We've already seen how the authors of *Holy Blood, Holy Grail* reread these stories, but you don't have to accept their interpretation to see that the Grail legends were another attempt to retell popular stories through a Christian framework.

The earliest references to the Grail are pagan in nature, things like horns of plenty and magical cauldrons. Only beginning in the twelfth century do we start to see Christians reimagining these emblems and putting their own spin on them. Modern conspiracy theorists have alleged that the Grail legends were created to protect Mary Magdalene and the child or children that she bore to Jesus. The rather late date for the development of the Grail stories, however, suggests that what we're getting is really just another example of Christians reinterpreting pagan stories through the lens of Jesus Christ. Christians have long been masters at adapting local cultures and symbols to the Jesus story. The Grail legends appear to be nothing more, and nothing less, than another creative rereading of pre-Christian mythology.

From the Source

ARTHUR: Go and tell your master that we have been charged by God with a sacred quest. If he will give us food and shelter for the night, he can join us in our quest for the Holy Grail.

GUARD: Well, I'll ask him, but I don't think he'll be very keen ... Uh, he's already got one, you see?

ARTHUR: What?

GALAHAD: He says they've already got one!

ARTHUR: Are you sure he's got one?

GUARD: Oh, yes, it's very nice-a

—*Monty Python and the Holy Grail*

Da Vinci, da Gnostics, and da Church

Okay, it's pretty obvious that stories about Jesus and the idiosyncrasies of the Christian faith have been fair game for writers down through the ages. To the degree that they have been regarded as entertainment, they have certainly never threatened the viability of the essential Christian story embodied in the New Testament. But for one thing, modern Christians would probably regard Dan Brown's runaway best-seller *The Da Vinci Code* as just another here-today, gone-tomorrow product of pop culture. Except for one thing. You see, people are actually taking the book seriously.

For the host of detractors and debunkers who have assailed *The Da Vinci Code* during its rocket ride into the publishing stratosphere, nothing has been more frustrating than the vast numbers of people who seem to find the book's underlying plot entirely plausible. Blurring the lines between fiction and fact, the popularity of Brown's novel has translated into an equally passionate interest in the larger conspiracy theory that his characters uncovered.

A Brief Summary

In case you're one of the three people in the world who hasn't read *The Da Vinci Code* or had it described to you by countless friends, family members, or coworkers, here's a short summary: Harvard professor Robert Langdon was summoned in the middle of the night to solve a mystery in the Louvre, the famous art museum in Paris. The museum's curator, Jacques Saunière, mortally wounded by an assassin's bullet, has left a mysterious message in his own blood. Joined by Sophie Neveu, a cryptologist, Langdon follows a path of riddles that leads him to some startling conclusions.

The curator, Saunière, is actually the head of the Priory of Sion. He and the other leaders of the Priory have all been murdered by an order of the Catholic Church. Langdon and Neveu, running frantically from one clue to another, attempt to locate the Priory's treasure before the church does. Accompanied by Leigh Teabing, an independent expert and Grail seeker whose own passion to discover the Priory's secret is all-consuming, they learn that what they are really looking for is the lost history of Christianity and the restoration of the Divine feminine embodied in the remains of Mary Magdalene herself.

Conspicuous Sources

I hope you noticed that the underlying plot is essentially the same as the one described in *Holy Blood, Holy Grail*. This is no coincidence. Brown makes mention of Baigent, Leigh, and Lincoln in the novel, citing their book by name. When Leigh Teabing explained the essentials of the conspiracy to Sophie Neveu, he pointed her to several books by "historians" who have detailed the relationship between Jesus and Mary Magdalene. One of those books, the one that Teabing pulled off the shelf to show Sophie, was *Holy Blood, Holy Grail*.

The connections are even deeper. The most obvious is that the head of the Priory of Sion, Saunière, was named after the priest whose discovery of secret documents was so significant to Baigent, Leigh, and Lincoln's speculations. Less obvious is that Leigh Teabing was named for two of the authors; Leigh is pretty clear, but also notice that Teabing is an anagram of Baigent. Brown took pains to integrate them deeply into the story.

Here They Come Again

During this same conversation, the longest of several sometimes-tedious expositions in the book, Teabing introduced the gnostic texts from Nag Hammadi. The same, familiar passages from the Gospel of Philip and the Gospel of Mary were cited to demonstrate that Jesus and Mary had an intimate relationship that threatened the other disciples led by Peter. Beyond the simple citing of a few passages, however, it's not clear how much the Gnostic Gospels have impacted the plot. The idea that the Gospel of Philip demonstrated a sexual union between Mary and Jesus is, as we discussed in Chapter 10, a complete misunderstanding. The Gospel of Philip clearly disdains sexual union. So, like many other writers, Brown seemed to be using the gnostic texts to further his own plot, one where Jesus and Mary did have sex. The importance of the gnostic writings, then, lies not in what they assert but in the simple fact that they assert something different than the typical, orthodox version of events. Beyond that, their actual content is relatively unimportant.

For many folks, reading *The Da Vinci Code* is their first introduction to the gnostic writings. Journalist Sandra Miesel, no fan of *The Da Vinci Code*, has written that "[*The Da Vinci Code*] may well do for gnosticism what *The Mists of Avalon* did for paganism—gain it popular acceptance." That might not be a bad thing, if it leads to real exploration. The gnostic texts won't bite you if you read them. The real danger that Brown's book poses is that folks who read it will think that they now know what the gnostics actually taught. Whether they are drawn to or repelled from that view is secondary to the recognition that, in either case, it is built on ignorance. If you want to know what the gnostics thought and taught, you have to read what they wrote. And that's why we're glad that you picked up this book.

Monster Hit

The intense popularity of *The Da Vinci Code* shows no signs of letting up. As we write this, the book remains on *The New York Times* best-seller list in hardback, a status it has maintained now for nearly two years. For anyone in the world of publishing, that alone would be proof of the existence of God. Previous books by Brown have been reissued and are doing very well. The success of *The Da Vinci Code* has carved out space on bookstore shelves for a flood of new books detailing or debunking every aspect of the plot. Work continues, as well, on the movie version, which will likely be as successful at the box office as it has been at the bookstore. All in all, Dan Brown must be a pretty happy fellow.

At the same time, thoughtful people are wrestling with the obvious question: why has this book struck such a chord with the public? It is not, after all, Dostoevsky. It does, however, present a very American form of spirituality, a romantic mysticism on the run. At the same time, a tremendous suspicion about authority and institution, especially with regard to the Roman Catholic Church, has prepared people for a greater interest in different forms of spirituality. Brown's story seems to have touched on a hunger in the American psyche.

The End ...?

From dusty research libraries to bookstores and living rooms, the Gnostic Gospels are continuing to reshape our perceptions of Christian faith and history, and to demonstrate the world's enduring fascination with Jesus of Nazareth. Who would have imagined 60 years ago, when Muhammed Ali unearthed that clay jar in Nag Hammadi, that these obscure Coptic documents would generate such controversy and speculation?

Like ripples on a pond, the voices of Nag Hammadi have spread to every corner of cultural life. What was once the province of a handful of experts in historical and biblical studies can now be found reported on in popular magazines, projected in box-office blockbusters and glitzy television documentaries, and integrated into the plots of best-selling novels. The Gospels of Thomas and of Mary, once only mentioned in obscure conferences and journal articles, are now topics of conversation in knitting clubs and book discussion groups.

Where the fascination with these ancient texts will go next is impossible to predict. Whether the worldview that they embody will survive and possibly flourish is even less certain. Whether it should flourish will undoubtedly be a matter of intense debate. What is certain is the utter unpredictability of discovery. Who could have guessed that the random turn of a shovel would so drastically challenge our picture of the origins of the world's largest religion? Who can say what we might find tomorrow. The unlikely discovery of the Gnostic Gospels ended one centuries-long journey from the past to the present. A much longer journey, into the future, still remains.

The Least You Need to Know

◆ *Holy Blood, Holy Grail* turned out to be based on an attempted fraud.

◆ Christians have always written fictionalized stories that drew on biblical characters as subject matter.

◆ Dan Brown's *The Da Vinci Code* is based largely on *Holy Blood, Holy Grail*.

◆ The immense popularity of *The Da Vinci Code* may indicate that Americans are eager for a new kind of spirituality.

Glossary

Achamoth   The "lower Wisdom" who results from the division that takes place in Sophia when she is separated from her passions. This separation and the fall of Achamoth is what creates the material world in the Valentinian form of the gnostic myth.

aeon   In gnostic thought, aeons were emanations of the Divine. As such, they were both creations of and expressions of the Divine. Although they were presented as individual beings, they also seemed to represent impersonal cosmic or psychological forces.

androgynous   Literally means "male female." In the gnostic myth, androgyny is the state of being where the division of humanity into male and female does not exist.

apocalyptic   From the word "apocalypse," which literally means "revelation." Often used to describe literature that is highly symbolic in character, that describes spiritual experiences and encounters with angelic and demonic beings.

apocryphal   A story or document that is of questionable authenticity is considered to be apocryphal. In talking about Christianity, apocryphal works would not be considered a legitimate part of the Bible. What's considered apocryphal depends on whom you're talking to. Roman Catholics and Eastern Orthodox Christians say that several Old Testament documents, such as 1 and 2 Maccabees, are inspired by God and part of the

Bible. Protestants consider them "Apocrypha," saying that they are not inspired and are not part of their canon of Scripture. Catholics, as well as Protestants, call the gnostic works discussed in this book "apocryphal." No one includes them in the Bible, and few believe that they were written by the people whose name appears as their author.

apologists   From the word apologia, which means "defense." The apologists were Christian writers primarily in the second and third centuries who wrote with the intention of presenting the Christian message to nonbelievers and of defending the Christian faith against rumors and misunderstandings. After Christianity became a legal religion in the fourth century, the role of the apologists became less significant.

archon   Greek for "ruler," the term was used by the gnostics to refer to those spiritual beings—usually demonic in nature—who hold sway over the material world and consequently prevent human spirits from returning to the Pleroma.

ascetic   A lifestyle characterized by self-denial, especially in regards to sex, and self-control, especially in regard to food and money. Ascetics also sometimes inflict pain on themselves.

Autogenes   Literally "self-begotten." The name given to the Christ aeon who emanates from the Barbelo.

baptism   The act of immersing or sprinkling a person with water as a sign of purification and initiation. Among Christians, baptism took on the additional significance of imitating Jesus Christ, who was baptized in the Jordan River by John the Baptist.

Barbelo   Barbelo, which means "Forethought," was the name given to the first being emanated from the original Divine being.

Basilides (active A.D. 120–140)   The first known Christian gnostic teacher. Basilides was active in Alexandria, where he created a school of gnosticism supposedly based on a secret tradition handed down to him from a disciple of the Apostle Peter. His son Isidore succeeded him, but the Basilidian form of gnosticism was overshadowed in the church by the success of Valentinus.

catechesis   Oral instruction given to new Christians as preparation for baptism. The earliest Christians, all of them Jews or converts to Judaism before they became Christians, required little in-depth instruction on such issues as the authority of Scripture and biblically-based ethics. As the numbers of non-Jews entering the church increased, it became clear that these new believers would require a deliberate reorientation. Early in the history of the church, catechesis (from the Greek "katecheo," meaning "to echo the sound") came about through a one-on-one relationship with a teacher. Later, schools for catechesis like the one in Alexandria were founded to work in cooperation with the church in preparing new believers to take their place in the Christian community. As infant baptism became more and more the norm in the church, the process of adult catechesis gradually faded away.

Clement of Alexandria (A.D. 150–215)   The second head of the catechetical school in Alexandria, Clement is important for his attempt to find a middle way between the rigid orthodoxy of most Egyptian Christians and the speculations of the gnostics.

codex   The first form of the modern book, which superceded the scroll. Essentially an assembly of pages stacked and bound at one end, the codex (the plural is codices) was the preferred form for documents used by Christians, since you can get a whole lot more into a codex than you can on one roll of a scroll, and they are easier to manage.

Coptic   The language spoken in Egypt during the first and second centuries. It survives today only as the liturgical language of the Coptic or Egyptian Church. All of the Nag Hammadi texts exist in Coptic.

cosmogony   A mythical story that describes the creation of the cosmos, including the physical world.

creed   A formal statement of belief. The Christian creeds developed in part as a means to combat groups like the gnostics, who were using the same story as orthodox Christians but interpreting it differently. The creeds were the refined form of the "Rule of Faith," free form summaries of the meaning of the Jesus story from an orthodox point of view.

deficiency   The characteristic quality of the material world. Separated as it is from the Pleroma, the world lacks completeness. The gnostic ambition was to overcome that deficiency through gnosis or knowledge, reuniting with the Divine.

Demiurge   Craftsman or maker. The Demiurge first appeared in Platonic philosophy as a kind of middleman between the unknowable God and the physical world. For gnostics, the Demiurge tended to be a much more sinister character.

docetism   From a Greek word that means "to appear or to seem." The belief that Jesus of Nazareth had no physical body and therefore could neither suffer nor die.

dualism   Any body of belief alleging that existence is divided between two, usually equally, opposite forces or substances.

dyad   A paired being, usually meaning a masculine-feminine pair.

elect   To be chosen. While in orthodox Christian thought, election is a matter of God choosing who and how to save, for gnostics, the word applies more to a person's state of being. Those who are spiritual (see Pneumatic) are part of that immortal race who are the elect.

emanations   The various aeons that emerge out of the unknown God or original Divine being.

Encratite   Members of a deeply ascetic second-century Christian sect, located primarily in Syria. This group disavowed marriage and sex, and engaged in severe fasting and dietary restrictions. Although the word refers to a specific group of Christians, it is also used more generally to speak of Christians who exhibited this kind of rigorous ascetic practice.

Ennoia   Meaning "thought," in Greek suggests a hinting thought, a suggestive one. In gnosticism, the word refers to the female being who is brought forth by the Great Power. Her name implies that she/it is a pregnant, suggestive, forward-looking "thought." The Ennoia becomes responsible, then, for the creation of the physical world.

Epicureanism   A branch of Greek philosophy founded on the teachings of Epicurus, who argued for a materialistic view of the universe. Epicurus rejected spirituality in favor of living a modest life of moderate pleasures.

Epinoia   Literally "thinking." In the gnostic myth, Epinoia is the aeon who comes to the earthly Adam to give him knowledge of his origin.

Epiphanius of Salamis (A.D. 310–402)   Bishop of Salamis from A.D. 367 until his death. Epiphanius was a traveling heresiologist, attacking aberrant teachings wherever he found them. He is best known for a book that he wrote called Panarion or "Medicine Chest," a description of 80 different heresies, many of which are otherwise unknown.

eschatology   The teaching or belief in final or last things, usually dealing with death, the afterlife, divine judgment, and the Second Coming.

eucharist   One way of referring to the ritual act of eating and drinking bread and wine as part of Christian worship. The practice was initiated by Jesus at his Last Supper, and from the beginning seems to have been one of the defining characteristics of Christians no matter where they were or what theological camp they belonged to. The word eucharist comes from the Greek "eucharisteo," which means "to give thanks" or "to bless."

excommunication   A formal act of excluding someone from participation in the life of the Christian community. The exclusion is an extreme act intended as discipline rather than punishment.

exorcism   Both the act of driving out evil spirits from a person or place and the ritual used to do so.

gnosis   Means "knowledge" in Greek, but it's not simply head knowledge. Instead, gnosis refers to intimate knowledge, being in relationship or having acquaintance with something or someone else. For gnostics, gnosis is an experience of divine self-knowledge that catapults the "knower" into a new and higher realm of being.

Heracleon (active A.D. 170–180)   A gnostic teacher in the Western or Roman Valentinian school, Heracleon is most famous for his Commentary on John, the first known commentary on New Testament writing. Origen quotes from it extensively in his own commentary on John.

heresiologist   A writer who spends at least some of her time refuting the teachings of groups considered to be heretical.

heresy   (From the word *haeresis*, which means "choosing") originally referred to the act of choosing between several opinions. As such, it was a fairly neutral term. It was the Apostle Paul in Galatians 5:20 who gives "heresy" a negative meaning, calling it one of the "works of the flesh" and listing it in between "seditions" and "envy." Following Paul, the mainstream church used the word to indicate a person or group that was deviating from the publicly received Christian story in order to pursue an alternative private belief or practice. The key distinction between a heresy and a schism is that schismatics break away from the church in order to pursue their own views, while heretics follow their own visions while remaining within the church.

hermetic   Writings that stem from the practice of an occult form of magic and philosophy associated with Hermes Trismegistus, a legendary deity in Egypt formed by a combination of the Egyptian god Thoth and the Greek god Hermes. The Codex Hermetica preserves a number of Hermetic works.

hylic   Material or fleshly human beings, without any connection to the Divine. They form the lowest of the three classes of human beings in the gnostic system, behind the pneumatic gnostics and the psychic average Christians.

Ialtabaoth   Ialtabaoth is one of the names used to describe the being brought forth by Sophia in her separation from the Pleroma. This being, also called Samael and Saklas, is the creator of the physical world and of the bodies of human beings. Ialtabaoth is essentially synonymous with the Demiurge.

Ignatius of Antioch (A.D. 50?–110?)   Bishop of Antioch in Syria. Ignatius is famous for seven letters that he wrote to various churches while on his way from Antioch to Rome to be executed. Ignatius' letters strongly emphasize the role of the bishop as the central hub of the Christian community and the source of its authentic tradition and message. He also attacked the docetic view of Christ, which had begun to appear in his own congregation.

Incarnation   The belief that Jesus Christ was God "in the flesh." The Incarnation asserts the full humanity of Christ as well as his full divinity.

ineffable   Something that cannot be described in words.

Irenaeus of Lyons (A.D. 130–202)   Bishop of Lyons in Gaul (France), Irenaeus was the most significant opponent of the gnostic movement in the second century. His five-volume *Against Heresies* laid the foundations for modern Christianity, with its emphasis on a sound canon of Scripture, creeds, and the authority of the church hierarchy.

Johannine writings   Five New Testament works—the Gospel of John, 1, 2, and 3 John and the Revelation—have all been attributed to the apostle John Zebedee. Only one of the five, the Revelation, names its author, and even then only as "your brother John." The others are anonymous, and their link with the apostle John comes from early church tradition. According to modern biblical scholars, the five texts were not all written by the same person, and many experts argue that the apostle John could not have authored any of the works now attributed to him.

Justin Martyr (A.D. ?–165)   One of the earliest Christian apologists. Justin presented Christianity as the perfect philosophy and the fulfillment of what the Greek philosophers were seeking. As such, he prepared the way for later Christian engagement with philosophy.

liturgy   Literally, "the work of the people." In religious terms, it refers to the prescribed rituals and forms of public worship.

Marcion (A.D. 85–160?)   Founder of the first major split in the second century Christian community. Marcion's teaching centered on his belief that the God of the Old Testament and the Father of Jesus Christ could not be the same being. Consequently, the church that formed around him rejected the Hebrew Scriptures and all of the New Testament writings except the Gospel of Luke and the letters of Paul. Because of Marcion's rival church, the orthodox Christian community became more explicit in its embrace of the Hebrew Scriptures and the story of Israel.

Marcosian   A member of the gnostic group associated with Mark, one of the disciples of Valentinus.

Mark (active A.D. 170–190)   One of the many gnostic teachers who carried on the teachings of Valentinus. Mark melded Valentinian teaching with mystical numerology and, according to Irenaeus, induced many of his female followers to exercise the gift of prophecy. Mark was part of the Eastern or Oriental school.

Menander (active A.D. 60–100)   Allegedly a disciple of Simon the Magician. Tradition says that Menander taught Basilides, but that is unlikely. According to orthodox critics like Irenaeus, Menander believed himself to be the gnostic Savior. He was based in Antioch.

Mithraism   One of several mystery religions that started to flourish in the Roman Empire around the time that Christianity appeared on the scene. Mithraism was the worship of the Iranian god of the sun, and became popular with Roman soldiers during the second and third centuries. It swiftly died away after the rise of Constantine and the Roman Empire's turn toward christianity.

monad   Derives ultimately from the Greek word monos, which means "one" or "unique." In philosophical or religious terms, the Monad is the first being in the universe, who exists alone.

Montanism   A second-century prophetic movement that began in modern-day Turkey. The leader, Montanus, claimed that the Holy Spirit promised in the Gospel of John was now beginning to speak through him. The group was morally legalistic and expected an imminent Second Coming of Jesus Christ. After a period of tolerance, the orthodox Christian community felt compelled to identify the movement as a heresy. The Montanists continued to exist until the sixth century, and vestiges of the movement survived into the ninth century.

mystagogue   Literally "the one who guides the student." A term usually reserved for those who lead others into new religious or spiritual experiences.

myth   A story, usually involving supernatural beings and extraordinary events, which forms the foundation for a particular worldview. Myths are used by particular groups to embody and explain why they see the world the way that they do.

Naasene   A gnostic group that revered the serpent as the source of all wisdom. They attributed the creation of the cosmos to three powers, but believed that the physical world was fashioned by a fourth being, the Demiurge.

Nag Hammadi   A location along the Upper Nile not far from the ruins of the Pachomian monastery Chenoboskion. In 1945, Egyptian farmers accidentally discovered a cache of 13 codices containing numerous gnostic books, most of which had never been of before.

Neoplatonism   A branch of Greek philosophy founded in the third century A.D. Neoplatonism based itself on the thoughts of Plato, but developed them in unique and unexpected ways principally through the works of Plotinus. Neoplatonism was the final form of non-Christian Greek philosophy to develop, and had profound impact on many early Christian thinkers.

Origen (A.D. 185–254)   The most important Christian theologian in the early church. A native of Alexandria, Origen was the third head of the catechetical school there. He authored numerous commentaries, textual studies, and theological works. In addition, Origen made a career of debating gnostics and other opponents of orthodox Christianity. Origen had a profound impact on the development of early Christian theology. Just a few centuries after his death, however, Origen's writings were condemned.

orthodoxy   Literally means "right worship." In historical terms, orthodoxy refers to those Christians who accepted (a) the New Testament canon as Scripture, (b) the "rule of faith" or the creeds, and (c) the authority of the bishops as authorized representatives of the Christian tradition.

Pachomius (A.D. 290–346)   An Egyptian soldier who retired from military life and retreated into the deserts of Egypt to live out a monastic existence. His military background enabled him to organize other monks, who were used to living pretty much on their own, into a kind of loose, communal structure. Although another famous Egyptian monk, Antony, is credited for making monastic life popular, it was Pachomius who created the first forms of what we today call monasteries. By the time he died, he had established 11 such monasteries, with more than 7,000 monks and nuns.

papal bull   A church pronouncement signed by the Pope himself. The name comes from a ball of lead, called a "bulla," which hung from document by a cord and bore the papal seal. The seal was a sign that the Pope was taking personal responsibility for the contents. Papal bulls were solemn and weighty documents reserved for serious matters.

paraclete   In Greek, the word "parakletus" is an advocate or companion, literally "one called alongside." Jesus used "paraclete" four times in the Gospel of John to refer to the Holy Spirit. The word appeared again in 1 John 2:1, where it referred to Jesus as our "paraclete."

Pharisee The Pharisees were one of two powerful Jewish religious parties that existed during Jesus' lifetime. They are often regarded as the principal opponents of Jesus and his disciples despite the fact that the New Testament often portrays them in a positive light. The Pharisees, despite their debates with Jesus, seem to have had no hand in his execution. Two of their number, Nicodemus and Joseph of Arimathea, buried Jesus' body at great personal risk. Another Pharisee, the highly regarded rabbi Gamaliel, is portrayed as speaking in favor of leniency when the apostles were later arrested for preaching in Jesus' name. The Apostle Paul was a Pharisee prior to his conversion to the Christian faith, and the Acts of the Apostles makes it clear that he wasn't the only Pharisee to make the switch.

pleroma In Greek, "that which fills." It is usually translated as "fullness," and in gnostic teaching refers to the real, spiritual world as opposed to this corrupt physical world.

pneumatic From the Greek word "pneuma" meaning "spirit." Pneumatics or "the spiritual" are the highest of the three classes of human beings in most gnostic systems. The gnostics saw themselves as spiritual, as opposed to the psychic or "soul" oriented regular Christians and the hylic or "fleshly" nonreligious folks.

predestination A theological claim that certain persons or groups of people have been specially chosen by God in advance to receive salvation. Some theories of predestination limit the scope of God's choice, trying to preserve as much free will as possible. Other explanations put God in complete control of every detail and every event in human life.

Pronoia Literally "forethought." Another name for the Protennaoia or Barbelo. It was usually used in reference to the Pronoia's responsibility for planning out the means of redeeming the fallen Sophia and gnostic human beings.

Protennaoia Literally "first thought." A name for the first being emanated by the Divine Parent. Synonymous with the Barbelo.

pseudepigrapha A literary work written under the assumed name of a famous person. Almost all gnostic works are regarded as pseudepigraphical.

psychic From the Greek work "psyche," which means soul. The psychics are, in certain gnostic schemes, those persons who have some sensitivity to the Divine but lack genuine gnosis. Their fates differ from one system to another. Typically, the average orthodox Christian was considered a psychic by their gnostic neighbors.

Ptolemy (active late second century A.D.)   Probably Valentinus' most successful student, Ptolemy was the principal gnostic teacher in the Western or Roman school. Around A.D. 170, Ptolemy wrote his Letter to Flora, an attempt to persuade a young Christian matron of the gnostic way of reading the Old Testament. Irenaeus, in his *Against Heresies*, attacked Ptolemy and his teachings specifically and at length.

Q   From "quelle", which is German for "source." Q is a hypothetical document or source that many biblical scholars believe underlies much of the New Testament gospels Matthew and Luke. In theory, Q was mostly a series of sayings attributed to Jesus. No actual copy of Q has been discovered, though some scholars point to the Gospel of Thomas as proof that such a document could have existed.

sacraments   Rites believed to be a means of or visible form of grace. The two generally accepted sacraments are the Eucharist and baptism.

Saturninus (active A.D. 100–120)   A disciple of Menander, Saturninus may have been the one of the first gnostic teachers to adapt the Jesus story to gnostic thought. Saturninus taught that the world was the creation of seven angels, one of whom was the God of the Jews, and that Christ had come to free humankind from their clutches. He may have been the source for the docetic teaching that Ignatius of Antioch mentions in his letters.

sesterce   One fourth of a denarius, which was a typical day's pay for a laborer in the Roman Empire.

Sethian   Scholars use this term to refer to gnostic texts which have in common a focus on Seth, the son of Adam, as the progenitor of an enlightened "immortal race." Whether there were specific Sethian groups or not is unknown.

Simon the Magician (active A.D. 40–60)   A figure who appears in the Acts of the Apostles as an opponent of Peter. Some gnostic groups later looked to Simon as their founder, and orthodox writers roundly condemned him as the father of all heresies.

Sophia   Means "wisdom," the last aeon to be created in the Pleroma. Whether through some kind of illicit act or purely by accident, Sophia ended up creating or bringing forth the Demiurge and making possible the material universe. While she was ultimately rescued, some part of Sophia remained in the physical world where it has taken up residence in certain human beings.

stele   A large upright stone tablet or pillar, usually inscribed with a text of some kind. Often, steles were used as memorial stones to some royal achievement or as a means to publish a code of law or rules regarding worship in a temple. Stele were meant to be permanent records, lasting through the ages.

Stoicism   A school of thought in Greek philosophy that advocates independence from all desire, pain, or pleasure. Stoics attempted to rely entirely on reason and logic (think of Spock from *Star Trek*). Stoicism had a strong ascetic streak, which made it an attractive philosophy to Christians.

Synoptic Gospels   Includes the Gospels of Matthew, Mark, and Luke, so named because they can be viewed side-by-side (from the Greek words syn, "together" and opsis, "view"). These three gospel accounts give are very similar, and thus offer parallel views of Jesus' ministry, literally giving a synopsis of his life.

Syriac   The language of Syria during the early Christian period and a close cousin of Aramaic, the language that Jesus and his followers spoke on a daily basis.

syzygy   A really fancy way of describing the union of a pair of things.

Tertullian (A.D. 160–240)   A brilliant but temperamental orthodox apologist from Carthage. Tertullian was the first Christian theologian to write in Latin, helping to shape the vocabulary and doctrinal structure of Western Christianity. Late in his life, Tertullian broke with the mainstream church and joined the Montanist movement.

Theodotus (active A.D. 160–170)   A follower of Valentinus and a gnostic teacher in the Eastern school. Theodotus was active in Asia Minor during the late second century. A collection of his quotations from his works was compiled by Clement of Alexandria that gives us some insight into what Theodotus and others were teaching.

Two-Source Hypothesis   The theory that the Gospels of Matthew and Luke depend for most of their content on two sources, the Gospel of Mark and another, unknown source that is usually referred to as Q.

Valentinian   Followers of Valentinus or, more likely, one of several teachers who succeeded Valentinus and built on his teachings.

Valentinus (A.D. 100?–160)   The most important gnostic teacher of the second century. A native of Alexandria, Valentinus creatively adapted gnostic thought to orthodox doctrine and practice. His followers remained in the church longer than any of the many gnostic groups. The teachings and followers of Valentinus were one of the most significant internal threats facing the church during the second and third centuries.

Further Reading

***The Nag Hammadi Library: Revised Edition,* edited by James M. Robinson** (HarperCollins, 1990)

The definitive English translation of the Nag Hammadi library, recently updated. Although better translations exist for individual texts, this volume is the sole source for some of the more obscure documents.

***The Gnostic Scriptures,* translated by Bentley Layton** (Doubleday, 1987)

If the translations in *The Nag Hammadi Library* give you a headache, give Layton a try. While not exhaustive, this collection contains all of the major gnostic texts. Layton's introductions and commentary are very helpful, particularly with reference to Valentinus, whom Layton obviously holds in high regard.

***The Gnostic Gospels,* by Elaine Pagels** (Random House, 1979)

The book that started it all. When it was first published, Pagel's book introduced the gnostics to a popular audience eager for a form of Christianity that was creative, egalitarian, and spiritual without being religious. The book has flaws, and more recent introductions have surpassed Pagel's in scope, but few have matched her for passion and accessibility. Other very readable books by Pagel's include *Adam, Eve and the Serpent, The Origin of Satan,* and *Beyond Belief.*

***Gnosis: The Nature and History of Gnosticism,* by Kurt Rudolph** (HarperCollins, 1986)

An in-depth and well-balanced examination of gnostic beliefs. Rudolph delves into the entire range of gnostic literature, including Mandaean and Manichian literature, to create a dense but thorough picture of gnostic teachings.

***Gnosis: An Introduction,* by Christoph Markschies** (T&T Clark, 2003)

Translated from German, this is a helpful overview of gnosticism and modern gnostic scholarship. A good, relatively brief orientation.

***The Rise of Christianity,* by W.H.C. Frend** (Fortress Press, 1984)

At over 1000 pages, this is not a book for the weak of heart (or back!), but if you want a thorough introduction to the early development of the Christian faith, this is the book. Frend is judicious in his conclusions, thoughtful in his approach, and completely thorough.

***Irenaeus of Lyons (Early Church Fathers),* by Robert M. Grant** (Routledge, 1997)

Grant offers an introduction to the life, thoughts, and writings of one of the most significant Christian writers in the history of the church.

***The Gospel of Thomas,* by Marvin W. Meyer** (HarperCollins, 1992)

Meyer's translation of Thomas is very readable, and this volume has the Coptic original running parallel to the English text. Additional works by Meyer worth looking at include *The Secret Teachings of Jesus* (contains translations of The Gospel of Thomas, Thomas the Contender, and the Secret Books of James and John), *Ancient Christian Magic* (with Richard Smith; surveys magical incantations and amulets used by Egyptian Christians), *The Gnostic Bible* (a huge collection of texts, many in English for the first time) and *The Gospels of Mary* (collecting in one place all of the Gnostic texts that mention Mary of Magdala).

***The Fifth Gospel: The Gospel of Thomas Comes of Age,* by Stephen J. Patterson and James M. Robinson** (Trinity Press International, 1998)

Contains a translation of the Gospel of Thomas and essays by both Patterson and Robinson that attempt to locate Thomas in the historical process that created the Gospels, and describe the twists and turns by which the Nag Hammadi library finally became available to us.

***Mary Magdalen: Myth and Metaphor,* by Susan Haskins** (Kenocky, William S. Associates, 2004)

Susan Haskins has written the must-read book on Mary of Magdala. She traces the popular conception of Mary through 2,000 years of Western history, in church tradition, art, literature, and popular legend. Haskins' tour-de-force is so jam-packed that it is almost too intimidating to pick up, but readers who dare will find a hoard of information and analysis.

***The Gospel of Mary of Magdala,* by Karen L. King** (Polebridge Press, 2003)

Including a new translation of the Gospel of Mary along with extensive commentary and analysis, King's book on Mary is must reading on this topic. Other books by Karen King worth looking at include *A Revelation of the Unknowable God* (with a fresh translation and examination of Allogenes), *Images of the Feminine in Gnosticism* (which King edited), and *What is Gnosticism?*

***The Fall of Sophia: A Gnostic Text on the Redemption of Universal Consciousness,* by Violet MacDermot** (SteinerBooks, Inc., 2002)

For those interested in learning more about gnostic literature prior to the Nag Hammadi discovery, Violet MacDermot provides a good translation of the Pistis Sophia.

***Gnosticism and the New Testament,* by Pheme Perkins** (Fortress Press, 1993)

Though it's not always smooth reading for the novice, Perkins book explores the complex relationships between the Nag Hammadi writings and the New Testament.

***The Gnostic Religion: The Message of the Alien God,* by Hans Jonas** (Beacon, 1963)

While it is certainly dated now, Jonas' book was at one time the critical introduction to gnosticism, and it still bears reading.

A Separate God: The Origin and Teachings of Gnosticism, by Simone Pétrement (HarperCollins, 1990)

Petrement argues that gnosticism is a development within Christianity, not something imported from without.

A History of Gnosticism, **by Giovanni Filoramo** (Basil Blackwell, 1990)

This is more an exploration of themes associated with gnostic thinking. Filoramo also assesses modern parallels to gnosticism.

***The Gnostics*, by Tobias Churton** (Weidenfeld and Nicolson, 1987)

Churton's book was written to accompany a British documentary series by the same name. It begins with the early gnostics, but attempts to identify gnostic thinking throughout European history (they make it all the way to John Lennon!). Readers looking for more information on the Cathars would do well to start here. Churton writes well without bogging down.

***Rethinking 'Gnosticism': An Argument for Dismantling a Dubious Category*, by Michael Allen Williams** (Princeton University Press, 1996)

Williams stirred up quite a conversation with this book, arguing that the discussions about "gnosticism" carry so many assumptions and false images as to make the word itself useless as way of categorizing early Christian beliefs. It's not easy going for the novice, but well worth reading.

Selected Web-Based Resources

Christian Classics Ethereal Library
www.ccel.org

This site, maintained by Calvin College, is a treasure trove of Christian literature from all eras. Although the library doesn't contain copies of the Nag Hammadi documents, it does host an electronic version of the multi-volume Early Church Fathers series, where readers can find translations of the works of orthodox Christian writers such as Irenaeus, Tertullian, and Clement of Alexandria.

Early Christian Writers
www.earlychristianwritings.com

Peter Kirby's very helpful site lists translations of texts from the first two centuries of the Christian era along with brief commentaries on them. The documents, which include several from the Nag Hammadi library, are arranged in chronological order (as best as possible), which makes it much easier to see how the gnostic documents fit into the larger body of Christian writings. The site also includes links to a long list of important works on Christian history and biblical studies.

Diotima: Women and Gender in the Ancient World
www.stoa.org/diotima

For anyone wanting to explore the way that women lived and were viewed in the Mediterranean world during the first and second centuries, this site is the place to go. Original essays are sparse, but the site contains a veritable forest of links to primary sources and other websites. The bibliography alone is worth a visit, as is the list of links to art and architecture.

Ecole Initiative
www2.evansville.edu/ecoleweb

A self-described effort to create a hypertext encyclopedia of Christianity, the Ecole Initiative's glossary is worth the time to explore for anyone interested in the expansion of Christianity from its origins to about A.D. 1500. While not all subjects are treated in depth, for readers wanting find information quickly it is quite helpful. Also contains links to artwork in the Christian tradition.

The Gnosis Archive
www.gnosis.org

This site is associated with Ecclesia Gnostica, an association of gnostic churches. The Archive's Library is a goldmine of gnostic literature. In addition to hosting translations of the entire Nag Hammadi library, the Archive includes access to Manichaean, Mandaean, and Cathar texts as well as major documents from the Corpus Hermeticum. A section on the Dead Sea Scrolls, Jewish and Christian apocryphal writings, and a wealth of material from Plato (including Timaeus) and Platonic writers (including Plotinus) rounds out what is a must-see resource.

The Gospel of Thomas Homepage
home.epix.net/~miser17/Thomas.html

While it is a little disorganized, this site contains all sorts of resources, translations, book reviews, and essays regarding the Gospel of Thomas. Among other resources, you'll find links to all of the documents in the Thomas tradition (outlined in Chapter 6) as well as translations of the Gospel of Thomas into Spanish, Dutch, French, German, and several other languages.

Magdalene.org
www.magdalene.org

Lesa Bellevie's website is dedicated to exploring the significance of Mary Magdalene in popular culture. The site contains not only book reviews and links to translations of the Gospel of Mary Magdalene, but also poetry, fiction, and devotional materials centered on Mary. One very enjoyable feature is a substantial collection of links to works of art featuring Mary. The list is organized by subject matter and is annotated well enough so that you know what you're looking at.

Index

F–G

H

I

W–X–Y–Z